SCIENCE AND HEALTH
Detecting and Correcting
Special Needs

Joyce S. Choate/Series Consulting Editor
Northeast Louisiana University

THOMAS A. RAKES
Memphis State University

JOYCE S. CHOATE
Northeast Louisiana University

ALLYN AND BACON
Boston / London / Sydney / Toronto

THE ALLYN AND BACON
DETECTING AND CORRECTING SERIES

Joyce S. Choate, *Series Consulting Editor*

Q
181
,R35
1990

Copyright © 1990 by Allyn and Bacon
A Division of Simon & Schuster, Inc.
160 Gould Street
Needham Heights, Massachusetts 02194-2310

Editorial Production Service: Karen G. Mason
Copyeditor: Susan Freese
Cover Administrator: Linda K. Dickinson
Cover Designer: Susan Slovinsky

Library of Congress Cataloging-in-Publication Data

Rakes, Thomas A.
    Science and health
    (The Allyn and Bacon detecting and correcting series)
    1. Science—Study and Teaching   2. Special education
3. Learning disabled children—Education 4. Educational tests and measurement
I. Choate, Joyce S.   II. Title.   III. Series
Q181.R35 1989   371.9'0445   LC 89-18265

ISBN 0-205-12150-0

Printed in the United States of America

10 9 8 7 6 5 4 3 2 1   94 93 92 91 90 89

Contents

FOREWORD vi

PREFACE vii

PART ONE   SCIENCE AND THE SPECIAL LEARNER x

CHAPTER 1   SCIENCE: CONTENT AND SKILLS 2

The Content of Science 2
The Science Skills 4
    Information Acquisition Skills 4
    Information Processing Skills 6
    Integration Skills 8
Summary 10

CHAPTER 2   SPECIAL SCIENCE NEEDS OF SPECIAL LEARNERS 11

Regular/Remedial Students 11
    Culturally Different Students 11
    Slow-Learning Students 13
    Teacher-Disabled Students 13
    Underachieving Students 14
Special Education Students 15
    Cross-Categorial Handicapped Students 15
    Behavior-Disordered Students 16
    Hearing-Impaired Students 17
    Language-Disabled Students 18
    Learning-Disabled Students 18
    Mentally Retarded Students 19
    Physically and Medically Handicapped Students 10
    Speech-Disordered Students 21
    Visually Impaired Students 21
Academically Gifted: A Special Case 22
Summary 23

CHAPTER 3   DETECTING AND CORRECTING SPECIAL SCIENCE NEEDS 24

Detection 24
Correction 31
Summary 46

REFLECTIONS 48

PART TWO   LIFE SCIENCE 50

CHAPTER 4   LIVING THINGS 52
Topical Needs

      1. Plants 52
      2. Animals 56
      3. The Human Body 60

CHAPTER 5   ECOLOGICAL CONCERNS 64
Topical Needs

      4. Land 64
      5. Water 68
      6. Air 72
      7. Interdependence of Living Things 76

CHAPTER 6   HEALTH AND NUTRITION 80
Topical Needs

      8. Personal Hygiene 80
      9. Diet 84
    10. Exercise 88
    11. Psychoactive Drugs 92
    12. Recreation and Safety 96

CHAPTER 7   UNDERSTANDING ILLNESS 100
Topical Needs

    13. Causes of Illness 100
    14. Treatment of Illness 104
    15. Prevention of Illness 108

REFLECTIONS 112

PART THREE   EARTH SCIENCE 114

CHAPTER 8   THE EARTH 116
Topical Needs

    16. Land Formations 116
    17. Rocks 118
    18. Oceans, Lakes, and Rivers 120
    19. Forest Resources 122

CHAPTER 9 WEATHER 124
Topical Needs

    20. Temperature 124
    21. Precipitation 126
    22. Storms 128
    23. Seasons 130
    24. Weather Prediction 132

CHAPTER 10 ASTRONOMY 134
Topical Needs

    25. Planets 134
    26. Stars 136
    27. Space Exploration 138

    REFLECTIONS 140

PART FOUR PHYSICAL SCIENCE 142

CHAPTER 11 ENERGY ALTERNATIVES 144
Topical Needs

    28. Nonrenewable Fuels 144
    29. Water Power 146
    30. Solar and Wind Power 148
    31. Nuclear Power 150
    32. Magnetism and Electricity 152
    33. Conservation of Energy 154

CHAPTER 12 USING MACHINES 156
Topical Needs

    34. Force and Work 156
    35. Simple Machines 158
    36. Complex Machines 160

CHAPTER 13 TECHNOLOGICAL LITERACY 162
Topical Needs

    37. Information Processing 162
    38. Physical Technology 164
    39. Biotechnology 166
    40. Problems and Rewards of Technology 168

    REFLECTIONS 170

INDEX 172
About the Authors 179
Reader's Reaction 180

FOREWORD

Science and Health: Detecting and Correcting Special Needs is one of several books in an affordable series that focuses on the classroom needs of special students, both exceptional and nonexceptional, who often require adjusted methods and curricula. The purpose of this book, as well as the others in the series, is to supplement more comprehensive and theoretical treatments of major instructional issues—in this case, teaching science—with practical classroom practices.

The underlying theme of each book in the *Detecting and Correcting* series is targeted instruction to maximize students' progress in school. Designed for informed teachers and teachers-in-training who are responsible for instructing special students in a variety of settings, these books emphasize the application of theory to everyday classroom concerns. While this approach may not be unique, the format in which both theme and purpose are presented is in that it enables the reader to quickly translate theory into practical classroom strategies for reaching hard-to-teach students.

Each book begins with an overview of instruction in the given subject, addressing in particular the needs of special students. The groundwork is laid here for both Detection and Correction: observing students' difficulties and then designing individualized prescriptive programs. Remaining chapters are organized into sequentially numbered units, addressing specific skill and topical needs of special students. Each unit follows a consistent two-part format. Detection is addressed first, beginning with a citation of a few significant behaviors and continuing with a discussion of factors such as descriptions and implications. The second part of each unit is Correction, which offers a number of strategies for modification according to individual students' learning needs.

This simple, consistent format makes the *Detecting and Correcting* books accessible and easy to read. Other useful features include: a) the Contents organization, designed for quick location of appropriate topics and problem skills and behaviors; b) a concise explanation of skills, special needs, and guiding principles for implementing instruction; c) a "Reflections" section ending each part, providing discussion and application activities; and d) an index of general topics and cross-references to related subjects.

Science, much like social studies (the topic of the most closely related book in the series), represents an area in which special students often can be accommodated with minor but important instructional adjustments. Together, these and the related books on basic mathematics, classroom behavior, instructional management, language arts, reading, and speech and language, comprise an expanding series that simplifies teachers' tasks by offering sound and practical classroom procedures for detecting and correcting special needs.

Joyce S. Choate
Series Consulting Editor

PREFACE

Science and Health: Detecting and Correcting Special Needs is designed to address the science needs of special students who are functioning on an elementary skill level. It is intended for use as a field resource and supplementary text by teachers and prospective teachers who are concerned with increasing the science achievement of special learners in both regular and special education classroom settings. A practical complement to theoretical texts and teaching wisdom, this book is deliberately brief and concise. The intent is to enable the reader to quickly translate the theories of science and special education into practical classroom strategies to improve the science knowledge and skills of special students.

ASSUMPTIONS

In this book, special students include both formally identified exceptional learners and nonexceptional learners who demonstrate particular learning needs. The text specifically addresses the needs of those special students in learning the skills and content of science. It is designed for use as a modestly priced supplementary text in several settings: as the special education module in science methods courses; as the science module for special education methods courses; as a resource text for field-based experiences in both regular and special education settings; and as a resource for inservice teachers. The basic assumptions underlying the structure and content are these:

- By definition, special students have special needs that may necessitate adjusted instruction in science.
- Varying the instructional emphasis renders much of the content of the regular science curriculum appropriate for many special students.
- When dealing with special students, some of the science skills can be directly taught and then substituted for other science skills to circumvent learning differences.
- An activity-based format can compensate for many knowledge and skill weaknesses.
- Certain instructional principles facilitate the selection of topics and adjustment of instruction to meet the individual learning needs of special students.

These assumptions are incorporated into the Detection and Correction model for identifying the special needs of individual students and then meeting those needs with targeted instruction in science and health.

ORGANIZATION

The Contents is designed to provide a specific, at-a-glance guide, facilitating quick location of the science topics and needs of special students. For ease of reference and discussion, categories of special students and specific science skills are often treated as intact units. Although labeled as discrete segments, it is important to remember that, in the real world, neither student behaviors nor skills operate according to such tidy classifications. Enumerated science topics are selected from the ones traditionally included in the science classroom but with an eye toward emphasizing knowledge essential to the everyday welfare of special learners: safety, health, social adjustment, and informed consumerism. This emphasis on survival information reflects the authors' conviction that, to some special learners, certain content is equally as important as the science skills and that the science skills should be taught in the context of meaningful and relevant content.

The text is divided into four major parts. Each begins with an overview and concludes with suggestions for reflecting on the content. The introductory material serves as both a preview and a review of the section. "Reflections" are intended for clarification, discussion, extension, and application. In each part, the final "Reflections" item refers to additional resources for further information.

Part I lays the foundation for understanding and implementing the corrective strategies for the science topics detailed in remaining sections. The three chapters in this part focus on the science curriculum and special students. Chapter 1 briefly explains the content and skills of science. Chapter 2 outlines categories of special students, both exceptional and nonexceptional, and suggests a few implications for instruction of each group. Chapter 3 reviews the teaching practices that form the foundation for what we consider to be special instruction in science. These teaching practices provide the framework of the corrective strategies for each of the science topics in later chapters.

Parts II, III, and IV contain discussions of detecting and correcting special needs in each of 40 topics. Part II, Life Science, emphasizes not only living things but also ecology, health and nutrition, and illness. Because of the basic nature and relevance of these issues to special students in particular, discussions here are more detailed than in the next parts. Part III focuses on earth science and includes discussions of earth formations, weather and its effects, and astronomy. Selected physical science topics are considered in Part IV, beginning with various types of as well as conservation of energy. Other topics include machines and their use, a highly practical subject, and technology, focusing on the application of science that is constantly changing lifestyles.

Although we strongly recommend activity-based experiences for each of these topics, due to space constraints, the lengthy details of experiments available elsewhere are not described here. Instead, throughout these sections, we encourage the use of such experiments, briefly sketch a few, and then focus on topical emphasis, building conceptual foundations, teaching and adjusting for skill needs, and providing direct teacher and peer interactions.

FEATURES

These detecting and correcting strategies are grounded in theory but shaped by practitioners. Their uniqueness resides in their practicality and versatility. Most can be implemented with relative ease in both regular and special education classrooms with individuals or both small and large groups of students. Because the strategies must be adapted to fit individual students and teachers, only the most salient features are described. To keep the text clear, succinct, and practical, theories of science and special education are built into the strategies.

As a study and reference aid, a consistent format is used throughout. The skills described in Chapter 1 are incorporated in each discussion that follows. In Chapters 4 through 13, the discussion of the Detection and Correction of each topic is contained on either two or four pages. Each treatment begins with a list of a few behaviors that may signal potential problems or indicate a special need for instruction in the particular topic. Next is a description of the topic and associated skills and the special problems that may be related. At least five corrective strategies are then described for each topic. Many of these are also appropriate for most students, but it is the special student who must have the special accommodations to maximize achievement in science.

ACKNOWLEDGMENTS

This book reflects assistance and support from varied fronts, ranging from the trenches to the hearth. To the many teachers and students who field tested and shaped the strategies, we are grateful. We appreciate the skillful guidance provided by our field reviewers: Paula Arya (West Virginia University), Tom Barner (Newton, Massachusetts Public Schools), and Judith DiMeo (Rhode Island College).

For accommodating our own special needs, a particular thank you is due our editorial team at Allyn and Bacon: Mylan Jaixen, Ray Short, and Karen Mason. And for their continuing encouragement and support, we are indebted to our colleagues and our families, especially Sandy and Jerry, our resident consultants.

PART I

SCIENCE AND THE SPECIAL LEARNER

Science, unlike the basic skills of reading, writing, and arithmetic, is sometimes considered a content subject; this would suggest that the objective of study is the mastery of content. While this is one of the objectives, science also has process skills that must be learned and utilized to master the content of a planned program and applied to learning concepts outside of school. Part I focuses on the content and skills of science and the needs of certain groups of special learners, and then offers some general suggestions for detecting and correcting some of the science needs of special students.

Several of the compilations listed in the last "Reflections" activity for Part I summarize the references and research base for the first three chapters. Noted in Chapter 1 is the wide scope of scientific content from which to select topics and skills. This discussion is followed by an explanation of three groupings of science skills: information acquisition; information processing; and integration. The next two chapters apply this skill model to the needs of special learners and principles of science instruction.

In Chapter 2, we briefly describe two sets of special learners: students who are designated as regular and remedial learners but who often experience some difficulty achieving, and students who by virtue of their learning differences are eligible for special education services. The first set contains the groups of students informally categorized by teachers according to assumed causes of learning interference; in the second set are students classified according to diagnosed handicaps. Gifted students are treated as a separate group because of their unique exceptionality. Derived by logical inference from each group's frequently cited learning characteristics, implications for instruction in science are sketched for each category of special learners. Although never applicable to every student in any group, each discussion presents a brief description of some likely instructional needs of the different types of special learners.

Even though instruction in science is considered a vital component of the regular education curriculum, some argue that science is relatively unimportant to students who have yet to master the basic skills: Why, they question, steal time from reading or math instruction? The answer rests on one's basic philosophy of education. If the primary purpose of education is to enable students to perform better in school, then perhaps the question and implied answer are valid. But if the purpose of education is to prepare students for life during and after school, then the answer is clear. Why teach science to special students? Because scientific knowledge and process skills can enhance the quality of their lives.

Chapter 3 begins with ways to detect special science needs, including the use of available data, formal and informal tests, interviews, and observations of students at work in the science classroom. Classroom observations are recommended because they offer the most realistic picture of a student's performance. We suggest using a checklist to structure the observations and interviews. The interpretation of diagnostic data should provide direction for both specific skill instruction and topic selection.

Special learners probably require fewer and less dramatic accommodations in science than in any other academic subject. In fact, carefully structured and supervised activity-based science classes are tailormade for mainstreaming special students. Fourteen basic principles, applicable to most students but vital for meeting the needs of special learners, are recommended for adjusting and individualizing science instruction. Of particular importance are using an activity-based instructional format, selecting real-life topics, and teaching and adjusting for special skill needs. These principles are intended for use as guidelines for implementing the special strategies for the topics described in Chapters 4 through 13.

CHAPTER 1 /
SCIENCE: CONTENT AND SKILLS

The content and skills of science are the substance of a science program. Both can and should be manipulated to meet the needs of the particular learners. This chapter focuses on the nature of scientific content and skills as an introduction to understanding the classroom needs of special groups of learners and ways in which to detect and correct those needs in the science classroom.

Scientific content and skills are interrelated. The content of a science program is the knowledge to be acquired; the skills of science provide the means to master the particular content knowledge, utilize that knowledge meaningfully, and then continue to acquire and apply scientific knowledge beyond the content presented. Meaningful content expedites skill mastery; skill mastery facilitates content acquisition. While portions of the content itself are basic, static, and vital, scientific advances are occurring at such an exploding pace that the skills and strategies for learning that content are equally if not more important than the some of the actual content. Thus, the dual emphasis of this and later chapters is the careful selection of content to insure personal relevance and the accommodations for special needs to enable the students to master both the skills and content.

THE CONTENT OF SCIENCE

Scientific content represents one of if not the most diverse and encompassing bodies of knowledge available for study. The rapidity of change and broad topical coverage within science make it unusually difficult to learn without sound instruction. Thousands of different specialty areas exist, ranging from the study of sound and how it is perceived and transmitted, to artificial intelligence, and even to such narrow interests as fish earbones. Each specialty often involves more than one area of science. Ecology, for example, involves biology, chemistry, physics, and several earth sciences.

To further complicate the knowledge base in science is the burden created by the complexity of the technical and nontechnical vocabulary. Some experts believe that the vocabulary load in science textbooks is the highest of all modern textbooks. In lesson after lesson, teachers are faced with selecting and then carefully teaching the most important words, which by themselves often require knowledge of other difficult words and concepts. Both the volume and the diversity of content associated with the study of science render the subject exciting to explore but sometimes difficult to teach, particularly to special learners. In addition to instruction in the pertinent skills, judicious selection of topics simplifies the teaching process.

There is an almost limitless array of topics from which to choose the content for a science program, and within each topic are possible innumerable levels and degrees of specificity. Therefore, criteria for systematic topic selection should be utilized. We suggest that topics be chosen with particular students in mind, considering a number of factors. First of all, topics should be appropriate for not only the abilities of the target students but also the ages of the students; both these factors influence students' interests and the relevance of the science content to the students' lives. The potential for practical application to students' everyday lives, both in and out of school, should be another major determinant in choosing topics. Familiarity with topics that are apt to appear often in the news and occur in general discussions contributes to the overall literacy of students; such topics should be emphasized because of their contribution to literacy. Topics that hold promise for enhancing the quality of students' lives should receive priority treatment as should those that are likely to increase students' interest in science. Whether guided by this set or another set of factors, topic selection and utilization should be systematic and purposeful.

In this book, the content of science is divided into three major categories: life science, earth science, and physical science. Each category alone is worthy of several volumes of discussion. However, for practicality and to encourage the implementation of the teaching practices espoused throughout this book, only the most general concepts for each subtopic of these three major areas are included. Subtopics that are the most vital to understanding of self and surroundings—living things, health and nutrition, understanding illness, ecology—are allotted broader coverage than the subtopics less important to everyday functioning. The focus on relevant content makes teaching easier, helps students understand and remember the content, and presents students with real-life knowledge.

Although topics such as astronomy are certainly worthy of study, they are not viewed here as vital to everyday existence and safety. Topics such as these are included in later sections, but are given surface treatment. They may be difficult for special students to understand because of their abstractness, complexity, and removal from students' daily experiences and needs.

Students' abilities to master scientific concepts are affected by not only the content emphasized but also the manner in which the scientific information is presented. The type and purpose of presentation determine the skills that must be used to understand scientific information and principles.

THE SCIENCE SKILLS

A variety of schemes can be used to depict the skills and strategies involved in understanding scientific information. The common ingredient in each depiction is the inclusion of higher-order thinking skills. Regardless of how the thinking skills are labeled, the overall theme is generally the same: beginning with the acquisition of information; moving to the manipulation or processing of information; and ending with the integration of the information. The skill groups and labels that are used throughout this book are outlined in Figure 1.1. Although the three groupings of skills are somewhat sequential, in actual practice, neither the sequence of the groupings nor the order of the skills within each group are static. Instead each skill is selected for use, irrespective of skill sequence, according to the needs of the learner, the nature of the concepts, and the demands of the teacher. In order to achieve full understanding of a scientific principle, some skills may be used concurrently and/or recursively while others may never be needed.

FIGURE 1.1 Science Skills

INFORMATION ACQUISITION	INFORMATION PROCESSING	INTEGRATION
•Observation	•Organization	•Synthesis
•Listening	•Analysis	•Hypothesis
•Reading	•Measurement	•Independent Experimentation
•Study	•Classification	•Generalization
•Directed Experimentation	•Prediction	•Evaluation
	•Communication	

Information Acquisition Skills

The process of acquiring scientific information can be categorized on two general levels, obtaining and expanding. Obtaining involves having students observe, listen, and/or read to accumulate scientific information. On a second level, students must be able to expand and enrich information through study, research, and experimentation. Students who have not mastered the basic academic skills often find acquiring information a difficult task, even with teacher guidance and special accommodations; and independent acquisition of information can be even more difficult unless most of the basic skills either have been mastered or can be circumvented. Proficient observation supplements and often can substitute for the other acquisition skills.

Observation

Observation skills are essential tools for gaining the maximum learning benefits from real or vicarious experiences. Whether students are watching events, reactions, people, a single cell dividing, or an experiment in progress, careful attention to detail can provide invaluable information not available through different means. Skilled observation involves utilization of all the senses to perceive the properties or actions of an object or event. It also requires discriminating the relevant from the irrelevant so that attention is focused on the most salient features. Observation is an important precursor to information-processing skills, particularly analysis, classification, and prediction.

Listening

The need for preciseness is a routine part of the scientific world and listening activities are no exception. Listening to obtain scientific information requires students not only to listen carefully but also to listen in a critical manner. The types of listening experiences that students confront when studying science are often complicated by the use of difficult terminology and unusual concepts. Although listening is an integral part of instruction in most subject areas, scientific listening may be particularly difficult for students because much of the content is unique to science and is not repeated or reinforced in other classes or out-of-school activities.

Reading

Reading science material requires careful attention to details and almost paradoxically involves students in making inferences, drawing conclusions, predicting outcomes, and other information-processing skills. Proficient reading skills are frequently required to read and understand scientific materials. Due to the complexity of scientific vocabulary, when traditional readability formulae are applied to science textbooks, the readability level is often found to be several grade levels above the grade for which the text is intended. Both technical and nontechnical terms carry a heavy concept load. To be comprehensible, many of the terms require more than skillful use of contextual analysis; often, explanations involving the same terminology do not clarify concepts. The abstractness of many scientific terms makes reading more than a recognition task. Scientific information must be read and understood beyond a literal level of meaning for students to use and build upon ideas. Reading is one of the most frequently used methods for independently acquiring scientific information both in and out of the classroom.

Study

Reading is a major vehicle for studying a topic. Studying can mean several things, ranging from developing good learning habits to the actual development of positive attitudes and procedures that are helpful in learning science material. Study involves discipline and practice and is also dependent upon listening and reading skills. Because studying is often a solitary activity, students must develop a routine that includes organizing the information to be learned, understanding it, and then reviewing the ideas and concepts in a fashion that will store them in memory. Studying scientific information often involves both memorizing and making inferences as well as recognizing the need for additional study through research. Research, an extension of study, involves additional reading and experimenting to confirm and extend concepts.

Directed Experimentation

Research and experimentation are considered to be the substance of science. Directed experimentation is a type of research but with parameters defined by a teacher or textbook. Activity-based science that actively involves students in manipulating variables to observe the consequences is classroom science at its best. The opportunity to actively participate in the process by which concepts are verified, clarified, expanded, or even refuted is probably the most exciting of the scientific activities. To extract maximum meaning from experimentation, students must rely heavily first upon their observation skills and then their listening, reading, and/or study skills. Directed experiments can be used to introduce topics, present discrepant events, confirm theories, and formulate questions for additional study and independent experimentation.

Information Processing Skills

Information processing involves six related functions: organizing ideas; analyzing the information; measuring the properties and data; classifying information; predicting outcomes; and communicating effectively by speaking, writing, demonstrating, or performing in such a manner as to provide objective information. To process scientific information, students must internalize and then make decisions about ideas.

Organization

As a discipline, science seeks to explain phenomena and to bring order and organization to them. Organizing ideas involves structuring the information on hand so that it makes sense and can be used. This often includes all of the information processing skills and may involve arranging data sequentially or in any number and type of groupings. Organizing requires developing a general plan for sorting information and a basic understanding of the topic at hand. Learning to organize ideas is difficult for many students, not only because of the problems associated with managing data but also because some students are not very organized in their daily lives.

Analysis

Analysis is a process that recurs throughout the cycle of understanding scientific concepts and principles as learners assess what they know and what they need to know and then decide how to go about obtaining the missing data. Analysis includes a number of the previously mentioned skills as well as more than a superficial knowledge of the scientific information under consideration. As a part of organization, data must be scrutinized to identify unique features, relationships, patterns, and the like. This may involve such procedures as comparing and contrasting, breaking elements into their smallest units, identifying changes across time or space, and taking stock of what is known about an object or event at the present time. Effective analysis often requires spoken or written communication as well as reciprocal sharing of information.

Measurement

Measuring information is an area of information processing that can be dealt with directly. Students can be taught specifically to use measurement instruments and techniques. The necessary content includes scientific information plus tools and procedures appropriate for use in, for example, determining a payload, elapsed time, the degree of change, the differences among variables, or the width of a leaf. Effective use of measurement involves identifying both the best unit and the best method of measurement for accomplishing the particular goal, actually using that unit and method to measure, selecting and following the proper procedures for organizing and recording the data, and then interpreting the measurements. Quantification of scientific data relies heavily on competence in basic mathematics as well.

Classification

Classifying information is a key component of both understanding concepts and organization. Grouping ideas by commonalities or categorizing by sets of properties are not unique to science. However, in the study of science, classification is often carried to a high degree of specificity. Items or groups of information are sometimes classified according to more than one criterion. In cases involving different species or elements, students must analyze or arrange information using hierarchical, metamorphical, or some combination of characteristics. This requires students to focus on multiple criteria for identifying group membership.

Prediction

Similar to making inferences and drawing conclusions after reading or listening, predicting outcomes involves anticipating events and relation-ships. When given a set of data, students attempt to foretell an event or identify possible interrelationships. Understanding of and previous experiences with at least a portion of the elements involved are necessary for students to make educated guesses. Hands-on practice with concrete examples can assist students to make logical predictions. Skilled prediction is an important precursor to formulating appropriate hypotheses to test through experimentation.

Communication

The final processing skill, effective communication, includes basic skills such as speaking, writing, demonstrating, and performing specific tasks. Whether students report or discuss their understandings, write about them, or perform an experiment to demonstrate their accuracy, communication is a vital science skill. As previously noted, mastery of the basic academic skills facilitates the mastering of scientific concepts. The basic skills are also vehicles for students to organize their data for several purposes: enhancing their own understanding; clarifying interrelationships; identifying additional information they must seek; sharing knowledge with their peers; and demonstrating their understandings for teachers to evaluate. When communication is used for these purposes, effective integration is more likely to occur.

Integration Skills

Integrating and applying scientific information and principles are necessary if the knowledge is to be useful. Included in the skills of integration are synthesizing, hypothesizing, planning and implementing experiments, as well as generalizing and evaluating, the two most meaningful skills. It is only when a topic is understood well enough to generalize and evaluate that particular scientific principles can be transferred beyond the topic of study.

Synthesis

Synthesizing ideas based on observations and experiences requires students to participage in critical thinking. Pulling together ideas and facts involves a number of skills of information acquisition as well as information-processing skills. Particularly important to synthesis are classification and organization. Another vital element of synthesis is critical reflection, which enables students to weigh and interweave data and relationships to form new ones. To synthesize ideas is to connect and combine information into an integrated whole.

Hypothesis

The development of hypotheses is similar to formalized prediction, an extension of the prediction earlier described as a processing skill. Relying heavily upon most of the previously mentioned acquisition and processing skills, formal statements of hypothesis specify an informed guess about future events. Required are specificity, preciseness, and an overall ability to see cause and effect relationships as well as utilization of a rich experiential background. Hypotheses serve as advance organizers for directed experimentation and represent the initiation of the planning stage for designing original experiments.

Independent Experimentation

Unlike directed experiments which are devised by a teacher or textbook, independent experiments are designed by students themselves. The teacher's role is to guide and approve students' plans and to insure that safety and ethical precautions are observed. The guided planning of experiments, beginning with statements of hypotheses, is equally as important as the actual conduct of experimentation. Students must not only consider the logic of their designs but also their practicality and safety. Possible outcomes must be anticipated as well. As students conduct their experiments, they must utilize information acquisition and processing skills to gain maximum understanding. The hands-on objective exploration and investigative activities involved in the testing of hypotheses are rich opportunities for expanding students' experiential knowledge, increasing excitement about science, and perhaps most importantly stimulating the need to know more.

Generalization

To generalize is to transfer ideas and concepts from one event to another and ultimately to understand scientific principles. Both inductive and deductive thinking are involved as students observe, verify, quantify, synthesize, and interpret the information to make applications to other phenomena. Using inductive logic, students draw conclusions from discrete facts, or reason from specific to general principles. Using deductive logic, students apply conclusions or general principles to individual instances, or reason from general to specific. Thus, inductive reasoning leads to generalizations while deductive reasoning leads to "particularizations." Regardless of semantics, both inductive and deductive reasoning are basic components for applying scientific information. Along with evaluation, generalization is the heart of usable scientific knowledge.

Evaluation

Evaluation involves critiquing the worth as well as the logic of scientific information and principles. It is here that conceptual change occurs through the modification of pre-existing concepts. It also may include verification by seeking additional information, reprocessing information, reanalyzing data, or even repeating experiments to insure that conclusions are accurate. Aside from identifying inaccurate conclusions, the most important outcome of evaluation is the establishment of personal and societal relevance. Relevance is what renders scientific knowledge useful. When students recognize the relationship of either isolated bits of information or generalizations to their lives, that piece of science takes on personal meaning. Science content that is personally meaningful is typically more interesting, easier and better understood, remembered longer, and more likely to be generalized by students and applied to understanding and improving both self and society.

SUMMARY

Because the content of science is limitless, it must be chosen purposefully and with particular students in mind. Factors to consider when selecting topics from the broad and general categories of science include the abilities and ages of the target students; practical application to the students' everyday lives; enhancing students' lives; improving students' general literacy; and increasing students' interest in science.

In this chapter, the skills of science are grouped into three categories: 1) information acquisition skills—observation, listening, reading, study, and directed experimentation; 2) information processing skills—organization, analysis, measurement, classification, prediction, and communication; and 3) integration skills—synthesis, hypothesis, independent experimentation, generalization, and evaluation. As students attempt to master scientific content, some of the skills may be used concurrently and recursively as needed to understand the particular topic of study. Generalizing and evaluating both validity and worth, especially worth for personal and societal application, are two of the most important tasks that students confront in science. Establishing relevance is particularly significant when teaching the special students described in the next chapter.

All learners differ in the ways in which they approach learning. When the learning differences depart from the regular classroom norm to such a degree that the students are at risk for academic failure or are eligible for special education services, then the students have special learning needs. These special learners and the manifestation of their special needs in the area of science are the focus of this chapter.

Certain groups of students are classified by the schools according to the similarity of their learning and performance characteristics. In some instances, the classification process is an informal one that represents an opinion of school personnel; students who are so categorized are typically taught in regular and/or remedial classes. Students who are labeled *exceptional* go through formal classification procedures and must meet rigid criteria to be eligible for special education services. Although discussed here as special education students, many exceptional students are taught in regular classes in collaboration with special educators. Because gifted students are handled differently in various regions, we will consider them as a special case, grouped neither with regular education nor special education.

Many special students share particular science needs and also have a number of science needs similar to those of nonclassified students. Regardless of classification, however, the goal of instruction is the same: to maximize each student's opportunity to learn the content and the skills of science. Thus, the instructional goal as well as many of the instructional strategies that facilitate the learning of special students also apply to most students.

REGULAR/REMEDIAL STUDENTS

Although there are numerous special groups of students within the regular and remedial classroom population, this discussion is limited to four groups: the culturally different, slow learners, the teacher disabled, and underachievers. Mastery of a science program need not pose a problem for these students if proper measures are taken in planning and then delivering instruction.

Culturally Different Students

Teachers usually label students *culturally different* on the basis of poor academic achievement and a spoken accent or speech patterns that vary from the norm. Nonetheless, low achievement is the key to the category. Cultural differences are seldom noted in an achieving student who also happens to speak with an accent. Regardless of achievement level, cultural differences are generally thought to complicate the task of the learner.

Description. Students may differ culturally in one of two ways: 1) Their cultural background differs from that of the majority of students attending their school, or 2) they share the culture of the majority of their schoolmates, but that culture differs from most of the students for whom the science curriculum and textbooks were developed. In either case, a language difference often accompanies a cultural difference and results in limited language fluency and a narrow vocabulary. Some culturally different students also are considered disadvantaged because they have not been exposed to many of the types of experiences that educators consider to provide the foundation for academic achievement.

Special Problems. The major problems that cultural diversity presents in the classroom result from the students' different experiential backgrounds, values, and language. These differences may interfere with students' understanding of the common reference points and examples typically used to illustrate scientific concepts in class. Having a narrow vocabulary may limit students' manipulation of ideas and understanding of concepts and interfere with information acquisition skills such as listening, reading, and studying. Where language is markedly different, the students often must think in their primary language and then translate to Standard American English. Observation and directed experimentation are not likely to be affected if the directions are understood. Once students acquire the necessary information, processing information may not be noticeably affected. However, weak vocabulary, speaking, and writing skills often interfere with students' abilities to communicate the true extent of their knowledge. Their lack of common experiences is most noticeable in the integration of information, particularly in generalizing.

Instructional Implications. Culturally different students need extended background concepts and experiences with emphasis on the common reference points familiar to them. Activities that stress relevance and use concrete objects are especially valuable. It may be necessary to present vocabulary in terms of the students' cultural definitions and experiences and then translate into scientific terms if full understanding is to be achieved. It is important to confirm students' understanding of both the vocabulary and the instructions. If speaking and writing skills are weak, have students perform or demonstrate their understandings. Walk and talk students through the generalization process. Begin with a multiple-choice format and model the thinking process for valid conclusions. Have students follow your model and later a similar model for expressing generalizations. To accommodate a slower learning rate, concentrate on the real-life topics and if necessary omit or postpone the topics of lesser practical value.

Slow-Learning Students

Students whose learning rate is noticeably slower than the rate of their peers are often termed *slow learners*. In this case, the learning rate of the particular group of peers and the curriculum they follow are the determining factors. It is interesting to note that students who might be termed *slow learners* may escape notice and even excel when they are taught within entire groups that progress slowly.

Description. Slow learners are students whose learning rate is slower than the rate of their peers, the pace of the teacher, and the pace of the curriculum. That is, these students learn at a rate that is faster than mildly retarded students but slower than average students. This means that they often struggle to keep up and without special provisions fall farther behind. The social skills of many slow learners are slightly below those expected for their chronological age.

Special Problems. Slow-learning students are likely to experience some difficulty in acquiring information via reading and study. Observation and listening skills may require direct training. Acquiring information through directed experimentation is not especially problematic, particularly if the teacher (or a peer) verbalizes the events and conclusions. A few focused lessons can often take care of organizing to process information and measurement. Many of these students display weak written expression skills but can orally communicate their understandings. Integration skills are likely to be difficult for slow learners to master unless students are guided carefully through the processes for each topic. A slow learning rate typically cuts across all areas of the curriculum, resulting in these students requiring extra guidance and accommodations in most subjects.

Instructional Implications. Slow learners need a slower pace of instruction that emphasizes practical scientific knowledge. They may require extra review and reinforcement for each concept, even to the extent of repeating key experiments. In order to provide in-depth treatment and devote the time required for mastery of the most vital topics, target a few units of study to skim lightly. Much like culturally different students, slow learners need to be walked and talked through the generalization and evaluation processes.

Teacher-Disabled Students

Often the term *teacher-disabled* is spoken in hushed tones and behind closed doors. Fortunately, most students are "teacher enabled." However, some students have suffered due to teacher-related problems. *Teacher-disabled* students are usually so labeled only when the offending teacher is *not* the one doing the labeling. It is always those *other* teachers who are judged to be either unperceptive or inept or both.

Description. Teacher-disabled students are those who experience academic difficulties that primarily result from incorrect or ineffective teaching. Many of these students have a history of trying diligently to follow the instruction of their teachers and attempting to comply with their requests. However, because the instruction fails to meet the students' learning needs, they seem to lose faith in themselves and in the schools. Many teacher-disabled students become underachievers as a defense mechanism.

Special Problems. The negative effects of inept or inappropriate teaching may be confined to science alone or may be reflected in students' performance in most subjects. When restricted to science, this disability may appear as a pronounced dislike and avoidance of the content, a condition resulting from exposure to teachers with limited knowledge and/or a dislike for science. Students whose science instruction has consisted primarily of rote memorization of facts rather than the application of facts to the scientific process may exhibit a negative attitude as well as limited understanding of the process and unsatisfactory mastery of information processing and integration skills. When problems extend to other school subjects, information acquisition is usually noticeably difficult, with reading and study skills being the most obvious deficits.

Instructional Implications. The task of the teacher is to compensate for inappropriate teaching of the past, impart enthusiasm for science, improve students' attitudes, and show students that they can trust teachers and succeed. Offering students a choice of subtopics may improve their interest in science. When information acquisition skills are problematic, increased emphasis must be placed upon key vocabulary, methods of collecting and organizing information, and strategies for compensating for reading difficulties. Taking special care to highlight personal relevance for as many topics as possible is also recommended.

Underachieving Students

Underachievement is often identified as such when teachers compare students' classroom work to achievement test scores and find their typical classroom performance falls far below their test scores. The term is also applied when students' performance in a subject vascillates between excellence and failure or if there is a wide disparity in performance when two subject areas are compared. In reality, some underachievers may be undetected learning-disabled students.

Description. *Underachieving students* are those who are capable of performing at a higher level than the one at which they typically perform. They often have a very negative attitude toward school in general. Underachievement is usually not confined to science alone but cuts across all areas of the curriculum.

Special Problems. Underachievement can result from a variety of factors, including inept or incorrect teaching and cultural differences. Underachievers may exhibit difficulties with any one of the science skills initially. However, if the pattern of underachievement continues, eventually the student will fall behind in the basic skills required for information acquisition and experience great difficulty achieving at higher levels.

Instructional Implications. Improved self-concept and motivation are major needs of underachieving students. Permitting underachievers to choose from an assortment of subtopics often increases their interest. The teacher's attitude and enthusiasm and such practices as specific skill instruction, constant monitoring, establishment of relevance, and purposeful instruction are all key elements for increasing these students' achievement in science (and in other subjects as well). When the cause of underachievement can be attributed to cultural differences or poor teaching alone, instruction should proceed accordingly.

SPECIAL EDUCATION STUDENTS

Students who are eligible for special education are those whose learning needs vary from the norm to the extent that they require individualized adjustments to their educational programs. The manifestation, nature, and degree of students' handicaps (or giftedness) determine the amount of regular classroom instruction that is appropriate. Even though substantial accommodations may be needed for some handicapped students to master other subjects, the science program may need only minor but important modifications.

This section begins by considering the needs of cross-categorical, or generic, handicapping conditions and proceeds to discussions of the traditional categories of handicapped learners. These categories are arranged alphabetically but include an incidence range from high (e.g., learning disabled and mentally retarded) to low (e.g., visually impaired). Academically gifted learners are described later as a separate group even though they are included in special education services in some regions.

Cross-Categorical Handicapped Students

Instead of grouping students for instruction on the basis of a particular type of handicap, some school systems classify students according to the degree of their handicap. Thus, for instructional purposes, students whose handicap is considered to be of a mild or moderate degree form one group, and those whose conditions range from severe to profound form another.

Description. Cross-categorical handicapped describes an instructional services model, not a type of learner. Although when evaluated to determine eligibility for special services these students must meet the criteria for a particular category of exceptionality, it is the degree of handicap that determines placement, not the categorical label. That is, students qualify for services on the basis of learning patterns that are characteristic of one of the specific categories of handicapped learners but thereafter are known and taught as a generic group. Many of the students share such characteristics as low academic achievement (particularly in basic skills), short attention span, distractibility, weak memory, and difficulty generalizing.

Special Problems. Many handicapped students exhibit weak skills for acquiring information, experience difficulty processing the information, and have particular problems integrating scientific concepts. A large percentage of these students display reading disabilities and ineffective study skills.

Instructional Implications. Students who are mildly to moderately handicapped are likely to be expected to master portions if not all of the regular science curriculum; rudimentary health, hygiene, and safety practices are the major thrust of the science program for the severely to profoundly handicapped. As a group, handicapped students tend to require very direct instruction, extra review and reinforcement, activities with concrete materials, and personalized accommodations to achieve. Reading materials must often be adjusted. Some handicapped students seem to benefit from multisensory instruction. Many of the students need a guided discovery instructional approach to structure their learning. It is important to vary instructional formats for each student's learning characteristics and to establish the personal and societal relevance of each topic. Topics should be selected for in-depth study according to each student's age, degree of disability, needs, and skills. Numerous more specific instructional implications also apply and are cited for each exceptional category in the pages that follow.

Behavior-Disordered Students

Teachers frequently complain about behavior-disordered students. Aggressive students who annoy their teachers and peers are often referred for evaluation with the hope that they will be eligible for services in someone else's class and if not that the offending behaviors will disappear. Those whose problems bother only themselves are less likely to be noticed and referred as quickly.

Description. Students who are classified as *behavior disordered* display inappropriate behaviors that interfere with their own progress and often the progress of others. These behaviors persist despite ordinary attempts to change them. Among the characteristics often cited are attention deficits, weak interpersonal skills, and low tolerance for frustration. The emotional problems of these students may lower their level of functioning in some or all academic areas.

Special Problems. Although science need not be problematic, many behavior-disordered students exhibit reading and study difficulties that limit their options for acquiring information. They may have problems observing and listening because of attention deficits. Without strict supervision and structure, any type of experimentation can present an opportunity to display negative behaviors. Many of these students have weak organization skills and some have difficulty classifying concepts; some students experience problems verbalizing their knowledge orally or in writing. Without guidance, these students may make faulty generalizations and have difficulty evaluating.

Instructional Implications. Whatever the subject area, structure and consistency are important elements in an instructional program for behavior-disordered students. In science, structure, including well-defined rules and supervision, is essential when any type of experimentation is conducted. Strategies to limit distractions and keep students on task are needed to facilitate learning. Contracting and permitting a choice of science subtopics and activities help students assume some responsibility for their own behavior and learning. Teacher and peer modeling of the processes by which information is gathered and interpreted may improve mastery of concepts and skills.

Hearing-Impaired Students

Hearing-impaired students are quite often closely attuned to visual stimuli as a compensatory learning strategy. Although a few students occasionally mumble or make distracting noises, their visual attention (once gained) tends to impress their teachers.

Description. Much like students with language disabilities or speech disorders, hearing-impaired students often exhibit general language weaknesses. Their language facility is often inversely proportional to the degree of hearing loss and directly related to the age at which their hearing loss occurred. Not only are these students less able to learn from the oral facts presented in class, they are less able to interpret those facts because of their language problems. Although hearing impairments do not imply difficulty mastering science content and skills, such mastery is not as easy for these students as it is for those with normal hearing.

Special Problems. Most hearing-impaired students must overcome at least two barriers: difficulty learning from information that is presented orally and limited language facility. Their hearing problems limit their options for acquiring information through oral teaching and discussions. Limited language presents a more serious impediment because it may interfere with reading skills and with the ability to manipulate concepts and ideas. Whereas hearing students can glean incidental learning and broaden their experiences from what they hear, hearing-impaired students are often denied such opportunities. Some hearing-impaired students also exhibit difficulties analyzing, predicting, synthesizing, and generalizing. Oral expression, typically a specific weakness, may limit their ability to communicate their knowledge.

Instructional Implications. Hearing-impaired students should be provided not only with advantageous seating but also with as many visual cues as possible. This means that the teacher must directly face them and present numerous visual cues and demonstrations. Each oral direction, concept, and step should be clearly named with written as well as oral labels. In some instances, extra trials and experiments may be necessary for understanding. Before attempting to generalize, ample demonstrations must be presented. The strain of trying to hear or compensate appears to tire some of these students, necessitating shortened assignments in many cases. Selection of topics depends upon the extent of reading and language problems. When these problems are minimal, no special selections may be required, but if reading and language are particular deficits, then the most practical topics should be given in-depth treatment.

Language-Disabled Students

Language-disabled students share many of the characteristics of learning-disabled students whose primary deficit is in the area of language and some of the characteristics of the language different. Such students are unduly penalized in the classroom because of the heavy reliance on language for instruction and for evaluating progress.

Description. Language disabilities are of three types: receptive, expressive, or both. Some students do not understand parts of what they receive as they listen or read. Others understand what they receive but cannot express that knowledge by verbalizing it orally or in writing. Still others experience difficulty both understanding what they receive and expressing their knowledge. Whatever the exact nature of the language problem, it can interfere with mastery of concepts and oral and written demonstration of the mastery of content as well.

Special Problems. Language is an intricate part of learning and learning science is no exception. However, certain science skills do not rely as heavily as others upon skillful manipulation of language. Observation, directed experimentation, measurement, and demonstration are among the information acquisition and processing skills that demand less language. Spoken and written communication tend to be particularly difficult for some language-disabled students. Except for experimentation, the integration skills place heavy demands upon expressive language; although difficult for some, other language-disabled students can generalize and evaluate the validity and worth of concepts, especially at the receptive level, when they are guided to do so.

Instructional Implications. The major tasks of the teacher are to provide numerous and concrete hands-on activities, emphasize vocabulary, and verbally label each step of each concept. As students perform directed experiments, the teacher should talk them through, labeling everything both orally and in writing. Both formative and summative evaluations of knowledge may need to follow a multiple-choice format that also requires the students to attempt to restate answers after they have been selected. Topic selection depends on the extent of the language disability. Adjustments for communicating but not for topic selection may be appropriate for a mild expressive disorder, while topics may have to be restricted to the most rudimentary (health and safety) when language problems are severe.

Learning-Disabled Students

Learning-disabled students probably present more diverse learning characteristics than any other special learner group. This handicap label usually carries the least social stigma.

Description. Learning-disabled students exhibit deficits in one or more of the psychological processes for understanding language. Among the skills that may be impaired are the language arts—including listening, speaking, reading, writing, and spelling—as well as mathematics and even thinking skills.

Academic weaknesses are usually counterbalanced by one or more strengths in these same skills areas. In addition to the specific academic deficits, other frequently cited characteristics are attention deficit disorders and impulsiveness. Perhaps the social acceptance of this particular label stems from the causes that are excluded in the definition, since the learning problems must not primarily stem from either physical, emotional, or retardation weaknesses or from environmental disadvantages.

Special Problems. As a very diverse group, learning-disabled students are notorious for their inconsistencies. Their individual abilities and performances seemingly fluctuate both within and across skill and content areas. The science skills with which these students are likely to succeed or experience difficulty are not static. With the exception of directed experimentation, all of the information acquisition skills may present problems to some of these students. A large percentage of learning-disabled students experience much difficulty reading and studying independently. Organization and written expression are also likely to trouble many of these students. While demonstrating their knowledge may not be a special problem, the other information-processing skills may be. The integration skills are apt to be difficult for some learning-disabled students to master.

Instructional Implications. Activity-based science instruction need not pose problems for learning-disabled students if they are assisted to compensate for their weak skills. When the stimulus/response format is adjusted to their learning and performance needs, most students are able to master and communicate their understandings of concepts. Some students may need multisensory instruction, while others need only to see the written labels for information that is presented orally. Carefully supervised and structured small-group activities present opportunities to increase learning and social interaction in controlled situations. It is important to avoid an overstimulating environment lest distractions interfere with learning.

Mentally Retarded Students

Along with learning disabilities, mental retardation is one of the most common exceptional categories. Unlike learning-disabled students, however, mentally retarded students typically present a relatively even profile of ability and performance. Their depressed level of functioning manifests itself both in and out of the classroom.

Description. Mentally retarded students function significantly below average, both intellectually and socially. Their adaptive behavior occurs at a level commensurate with their subaverage learning skills. Their learning rate is markedly slow and many have difficulty with short-term memory. Their language and thinking skills are usually noticeably weak for their chronological age.

Special Problems. Even students whose retardation is mild are likely to experience some problems mastering all of the science skills. Mentally retarded students tend to need extensive instruction to understand key vocabulary terms. To master concepts, they need constant review and reinforcement and regular practice. Many of these students exhibit specific difficulty reading, studying, writing, analyzing, classifying, and predicting in addition to problems with all integration skills. Generalization and evaluation skills are often particularly weak.

Instructional Implications. The problems of the mentally retarded are not confined to science but permeate their performance in all subject areas. Because of their very slow learning rate, these students cannot be expected to attempt a large number of topics. Their need to review, practice, and overlearn basic concepts limits the number that can be presented. Mentally retarded students require extensive readiness activities with concrete examples to prepare them to understand vocabulary and concepts. Key features and events as well as the application of information and principles to other examples and everyday life should be directly taught. Slow learning rates and low levels of achievement necessitate judicious selection of only topics that are most vital to everyday functioning, particularly for older students. Because the processing and integration skills place heavy demands on high levels of cognitive functioning, these skills may need to be circumvented and the content presented at least initially in a rote memory format. Retarded students do not necessarily have to understand what makes poison harmful to humans; they simply may need to know the effects of poisoning or that poisons are harmful to humans and animals and should be avoided. For such vital concepts, the most expedient instructional strategy may be a "trust-me" approach that is followed by familiar examples. The greater the degree of retardation, the more pressing the need to concentrate on topics about basic health and safety.

Physically and Medically Handicapped Students

As a group, physically and medically handicapped students are not noted for experiencing particular problems in the area of science. Because of their particular handicap, many of these students display particular interest in the scientific topics related to their disability.

Description. Students with physical and/or medical problems are only considered to be educationally handicapped when their academic progress is adversely affected. In such cases, their academic problems often reflect gaps in basic skills and sometimes concepts. Physical handicaps may interfere with the acquisition and demonstration of knowledge through usual means, while medical handicaps may reduce students' stamina and alertness.

Special Problems. Unlike most handicapped learners, the problems these students confront are mostly physical. They are often absent from school because of physical and medical complications; their performance tends to fluctuate with their physical condition and the medications they take. Some seem to tire easily from physical strain. Physical limitations may also decrease their opportunities for developing a wide range of experiences from which to understand and interpret science content. Some students may exhibit mild difficulties in reading, especially word meanings, and in written expression, while others exhibit gross- and fine-motor incoordination that interferes with mobility or preciseness in handwriting and handling objects. Some types of experiments cannot be performed because of physical limitations.

Instructional Implications. When teaching science as well as other school subjects, the three accommodations needed by most physically and medically handicapped students are adjustments to the physical environment, stimulus/response format, and lesson length. These students may also benefit from extra related experiences to prepare them for new topics and build the foundation for understanding vocabulary. Pairing each handicapped student with a nonhandicapped buddy for peer teaching after absences can help to fill in missed information and skill gaps. A buddy can also assist students whose motor coordination interferes with performance

Speech-Disordered Students

Speech disorders do not directly interfere with mastery of science. Speech-disordered students are briefly described here due to their large number and because a discussion of special education would be incomplete without them.

Description. Speech disorders are of three primary types: articulation, fluency, and voice. Articulation difficulties, or mispronunciations of certain sounds or words, are the most prevalent and what teachers often think of when speech problems are mentioned. Stuttering is the most common fluency problem. Voice disorders result in inappropriate pitch, intensity, or quality.

Special Problems. When auditory discrimination problems accompany speech disorders, information presented as a listening experience may not be acquired as readily as information presented through another channel. Some speech-disordered students prefer to communicate their knowledge in writing or by demonstrating instead of speaking. Others hesitate to participate in classroom discussions.

Instructional Implications. In the absence of other learning problems, only minimal adjustments are needed for teaching science to speech-disordered students. Be sure they understand oral information and offer alternative means of communicating knowledge when necessary.

Visually Impaired Students

When visual experiences are heavily emphasized in teaching science, visually impaired students are quite naturally penalized. However, both students and teachers can supplement visual stimuli.

Description. Visual impairments range from partial sight (despite maximum correction) to total blindness. The degree of visual impairment dictates the amount of adjustments students require for all types of classroom learning.

Special Problems. Vision is a major channel for acquiring information both in the classroom and in the real world. Visually impaired students must substitute or supplement with auditory information and what they can read. Whether they are straining to see print or translating Braille, these students often read slowly. Experiments may be difficult for them to perform and should be carefully supervised. Denied the visual stimulation and learnings of their sighted peers, these students often lack some important background experiences with which to interpret, generalize, and evaluate information and events.

Instructional Implications. Visually impaired students should be given preferential seating for all instruction. They may need extended preparatory experiences for each new science topic. Reading assignments should be shortened and the deadlines for completion lengthened, or assignments should be presented on audiotape or read aloud by a peer. Perhaps the most valuable adjustments a teacher can offer these students are to always accompany visual stimuli with an oral description and to encourage the use of touch as a learning strategy. Verbalization and touch assist students to acquire and interpret information and guide them through the stages of experimentation. Assignment of a buddy to also verbalize visual stimuli and provide reinforcement may be helpful.

ACADEMICALLY GIFTED: A SPECIAL CASE

Although there is agreement that gifted students are indeed exceptional, they are handled differently in various regions of the country. In some areas, gifted students are part of special education; in others, they are an extension of regular education.

Description. Academically gifted students learn and achieve at a level that is significantly above their chronological age. As a group, they are known for their intellectual superiority, creativity, high verbal and leadership abilities, task commitment, and numerous other superlative qualities. While many excel in the area of science, others achieve far below capacity levels.

Special Problems. Below grade-level achievement in science by academically gifted students is the exception, not the rule. However, underachievement is quite common. It is not the science skills that foil gifted students but the manner in which the skills and topics are presented. Two problems confront academically gifted students in science: confinement and boredom. All too many students are confined by the boundaries of the science textbook and curriculum and the limits of the teacher. When such confinement is accompanied by repetition and review (directed toward less able students), boredom is apt to result.

Instructional Implications. Gifted students need an enriched program that grants them considerable freedom to expand and explore beyond the topics that are typically included in the grade-level curriculum. Early and direct instruction in research skills may be helpful. The students should be encouraged to pursue original experimentation and prove their conclusions. This means emphasizing the integration skills to stretch the students' limits; evaluating present and future societal relevance should become an integral part of every lesson. Science can offer gifted students challenge, stimulation, and excitement when the boundaries are removed.

SUMMARY

Science should not be the most difficult subject that special students confront in school. In fact, when taught in the right manner, it can be among the easiest and most interesting and motivational subjects to master. Certain topics and subtopics are more relevant to functioning in real life than others. The greater the degree of handicap and the older the student, the more pressing the need to carefully select the most practical topics for study.

The learning characteristics of certain special learners render some of the science skills particularly difficult to achieve. Of the skills involved in acquiring information, reading is the one with which the greatest number of special learners are likely to experience problems; observation and directed experimentation may be considerably less difficult. The information processing skills may also be troublesome to these students, particularly the communication skills of speaking and writing. Generalizing and evaluating, perhaps the two most important complex integration skills, present great difficulty to a number of special learners. Although academically gifted students typically master the science skills with ease, in order to begin to realize their potential, they too need special consideration.

When instruction is adjusted to meet individual learning needs, the problem areas can often be bypassed. Some general suggestions for accommodating special needs in science are described in the next chapter.

CHAPTER 3
DETECTING AND CORRECTING SPECIAL SCIENCE NEEDS

In Chapter 1, the focus was on the content and processing skills associated with scientific and technological information. Chapter 2 described special groups of learners. This chapter is designed to synthesize and extend the content of the previous chapters by answering two questions: 1) How can special needs for certain scientific information and selected skills be detected? and 2) How can some of these special needs in science be corrected?

In science, as in most any subject, planning instruction for all learners but especially special learners involves first detecting the extent of content knowledge and mastery of the skills. Next, on the basis of the assessment data, an instructional plan must be designed that will both increase scientific knowledge and students' skills. Fourteen principles are suggested to help special learners master both the appropriate content information and the learning strategies and skills.

DETECTION

Assessment of achievement in science is often less precise than in the basic skill areas of reading or arithmetic. However, the general methods for detecting special needs in science are essentially the same as those used for most areas of school achievement: 1) synthesizing available data; 2) conducting direct formal and informal testing; 3) interviewing students; and 4) observing students in the classroom.

Synthesis of Available Data

The review of students' previous report cards, cumulative records, old science tests, standardized test results that include science content, and teacher comments can yield an indication of past achievements in science. The purpose of such a review is to identify performance patterns that may have instructional implications. In particular, the comparison of students' progress across subjects and across teachers can be revealing. Answers to questions such as these should be sought: What type of science program has the student experienced? How does the target student's performance in science compare with that of peers? How does a student's progress in science compare to his or her progress in other subjects? Does poor performance in science coincide with poor performance in other areas during the same grading period? Is excellent progress in science accompanied by excellence in other subjects during the same marking period? How do scores on the science portions of standardized tests compare? What do teacher comments suggest about the student's interest in science? Is it higher or lower than interest in other subjects? Have teachers cited any particular strengths or weaknesses in science?

Answers to these questions suggest both the nature and the possible cause of problems students might be having in learning science. If performance in all subjects is weak, then it is likely that inadequate basic skills, particularly reading, are preventing the student from acquiring the scientific information needed to understand the content. When both science and social studies are areas of poor performance, then the demand for independent acquisition of content information is probably high, forcing students to rely on their reading and study skills. If science is a specific weakness, then the particular instructional format or the topics studied may be the source of difficulty. When performance fluctuates according to the teacher, then the teacher in whose class the student performed best should be interviewed to identify the variables that increased progress. In instances where teachers have cited specific skill strengths or weaknesses, the implications are clear. In many cases, the synthesis of these answers will present a composite picture of a target student with some general implications for instruction and occasionally specific direction for instruction in science.

Direct Testing

Both formal and informal tests can be used to measure some degree of performance in science. Keep in mind that the major strength of test information is not the level of achievement that is measured but the type and specificity of performance information that is revealed. It is the individual breakdown of strengths and weaknesses based on skill competencies and content knowledge that are of use in developing intervention strategies.

Some textbook publishers provide tests that can be used as pretests before beginning a unit of study. If these are available and if the information tested is appropriate for particular students, the tests should be used. If these tests are not provided, consider the use of test information gained from other sources such as standardized test instruments.

Formal Testing. For some time, many experts have suggested that standardized test scores in specific subject areas are heavily influenced by reading ability. Poor readers do not generally score high on standardized science tests or the science subtests of general achievement test batteries. Although a lack of science knowledge may be part of the problem, poor reading skills may be a greater problem. If students already happen to have a strong schema base in science, they may do well on a standardized test because of their prior knowledge. Many handicapped students score poorly on formal tests because they have a limited background in science in general and in the scientific content covered by the tests in particular. Many are not as "testwise" as their age peers; their test scores may be falsely deflated in some areas. Other factors, such as time limits, difficult test formats, and an overall weakness in reading skills, further frustrate special students. Therefore, information gained from standardized test scores tends to provide overall or general indications of achievement and not specific information detailed enough to be of diagnostic value. This may be particularly true if students have been administered a group-standardized test for their age level. Thus, resulting scores may reflect guessing, frustration, and reading difficulties instead of science knowledge.

Standardized tests have been frequently criticized for testing for information, not process-related abilities. This means that the typical formal test assesses students' ability to read and comprehend science material. The content itself may or may not resemble what the students have encountered in their respective science classes. Regardless of the topical area, most formal tests present information in a written format and follow up with a group of questions designed to test the readers' knowledge of what was just read. Because the number and length of questions are limited on timed tests, questions involving the actual skills of science may not be included.

The traditional formal achievement test measures only one or two of the information acquisition skills. Almost all test batteries include subtests for reading. However, listening is tested by only a few, study skills are seldom included, and observation and directed experimentation skills are almost never mentioned. An occasional information-processing skill may be tapped by an inference question about what was read, but precious few if any of the integration skills are usually incorporated. Processing and integration questions are very difficult to construct using a multiple-choice, timed test format. The reluctance of most test makers to allow for more than one possible correct answer also limits the use of questions that would tap the skills of science. Convenience, tradition, and technical skills all tend to make standardized science test scores useful but not entirely appropriate as a single source of information on which to base corrective strategies. Informal or teacher-made tests are sometimes appropriate tools for surveying student knowledge but these tests also have their advantages and disadvantages.

Informal Testing. Informal tests in science include nonstandardized tests supplied with the science textbooks, content or group reading inventories, and traditional teacher-made tests. In classes where textbooks provide the core of the science program, the tests that accompany the science textbooks can assess both content covered and some of the important science skills. If teachers closely adhere to the instructor's guide and if the textbook tests are directly tied to the major concepts and intended instructional objectives of the book, then the test results can provide meaningful data. The key to the effectiveness of textbook tests is the manner in which they are used. When used for grading purposes alone, their value is negligible, but when used for prescriptive purposes, the results of these tests can identify both content and skills in need of direct instruction.

Although several published content or group reading inventories are available, their use is limited because of content restrictions and lack of teacher familiarity with such tests. Teachers can construct their own content inventories. In their simplest form content inventories include skill-specific questions about the content of the science materials currently being used in a class. Students are asked to either read or listen to the material and then, without review, answer 12 to 14 skill-specific questions about the material. The number of questions answered may reflect students' knowledge of the actual content, while the types of questions that they can and cannot answer may yield clues to some problematic skills and point to areas for further diagnosis. Although not every science skill can be assessed with this format, reading, listening, analysis, prediction, classification, generalization, and evaluation can be at least lightly tapped. Cloze inventories can also be used to check comprehension of content texts, but these only indirectly test understanding of the content itself or the science skills.

Traditional teacher-made tests are paper/pencil tests that assume proficiency in reading and writing for students to respond. Some teachers draw many of the questions from the tests that accompany the particular textbook, adding and deleting according to the material actually covered in class. Some teachers may include measures of several science skills as well. Teachers who do not use a basal textbook but focus instead on process skills must measure the skills as they have been taught. When assessing process skills, a useful diagnostic aid is a checklist such as the one in Figure 3.1. Regardless of the exact content of the tests, if they include provisions for stimulus/response variations according to the needs of the students and also tap the science skills, then analysis of the results could provide direction for programming to meet special needs in science. Unfortunately, although conceivable, this is seldom the case. However, when analyzing available data, the results of classroom testing should certainly be scrutinized for instructional implications.

Interviews. Interviews are another method of screening students' science interests and achievement. The two sources of pertinent data are past teachers and the students themselves. When interviewing past teachers, key questions to ask are: How much time was spent studying science? What was the content of the program? What was the usual format of science lessons? What was this student's typical performance? Which of the science skills were the strongest? What particular skill problems did you note? Which topics were of greatest interest? What did you find best facilitated performance? If available, a checklist of skills and topics might assist both the interviewer and the responding teacher to identify the critical elements of a science program for a particular student.

Interviewing the students themselves can often provide data not available through other means. According to the abilities of target students, several approaches might be appropriate. One option is to construct six to ten short-answer or open-ended questions involving a specific topic in science. For example: How do we know what the surface of the moon is like? Have you ever seen a picture of the moon's surface? How is the moon different from the earth? Why would someone want to know about the moon? What would you like to learn about the moon? Asking content-direct questions of individuals or small groups will provide a limited but direct indication of which students have some background and perhaps interest in a particular topic. Direct pretest interviews can be used to determine the

FIGURE 3.1   Checklist for Detecting Special Needs in Science

Student's Name_____ Observer's Name_____ Date(s)_____

SKILLS	STUDENT BEHAVIORS	OBSERVED	REPORTED	COMMENTS
Information Acquisition:				
Observation	• Attends to stimuli • Distinguishes relevant features • Describes observations • Other:			
Listening	• Attends to stimuli • Understands details • Listens critically • Other:			
Reading	• Recognizes and understands word meanings • Comprehends details • Makes inferences • Reads critically • Other:			
Study	• Works independently • Organizes for study • Follows a routine • Locates additional information • Other:			
Directed Experimentation	• Follows directions • Observes and describes • Draws conclusions • Other:			
Information Processing:				
Organization	• Organizes self and materials • Sorts and groups data • Follows a plan • Other:			
Analysis	• Identifies unique features • Compares and contrasts • Describes relationships and patterns • Other:			
Measurement	• Chooses correct instruments • Selects appropriate methods • Understands basic math- ematics involved • Other:			
Classification	• Identifies salient features • Groups by commonalities • Other:			

SKILLS	STUDENT BEHAVIORS	OBSERVED	REPORTED	COMMENTS
Prediction	• Anticipates relationships • Identifies cause and effect • Predicts outcomes • Other:			
Communication	• Orally explains understandings • Writes understandings • Demonstrates or performs understandings • Other:			
Integration:				
Synthesis	• Classifies information • Combines information into a new whole • Other:			
Hypothesis	• Predicts outcomes • States predictions • Other:			

Independent Experimentation	• Plans experiments to test
	  hypotheses
	• Conducts experiments to test
	  hypotheses
	• Other:			

Generalization	• Uses deductive logic • States scientific principles • Applies principles to other phenomena • Other:			

Evaluation	• Critiques the logic of information/
	  principles
	• Critiques the worth of information/
	  principles
	• Modifies conclusions when
	  appropriate
	• Describes personal relevance
	• Describes societal relevance
	• Other:			

Additional Comments:

Summary of Observations:

degree of familiarity students have with specific topics and identify topics of interest and the ones to emphasize. An alternate to constructing the questions is selecting the questions from a unit quiz in the textbook.

Adding questions about lesson formats and the science skills further extends the utility of a pretest interview. Such questions as these might be asked: Which types of science lessons do you prefer? Why? Which ones do you like least? Why? What helps you to learn about science? With which types of science activities do you have the most success? Why? With which types of activities do you have the most trouble? Why? Describe the science lessons that taught you the most; which parts of each lesson were most effective? Why do you think the lessons were so effective? Describe the science lessons that taught you the least; which parts of each lesson were least effective? Why do you think those lessons were so ineffective? Although the science skills might not be named, the responses to questions like these should suggest some of the skills in each of the three areas that are and are not problematic.

An orally administered science-interest inventory, either published or teacher constructed, can also add information to the interview process. Perhaps the simplest method by which to gain a rough estimate of topical interests is to present the table of contents of a science text that is compatible with students' reading levels; ask which three or five topics sound the most interesting and which ones sound the least interesting. Then have students explain the reasons for their choices. When several students work together, they might vote to decide on the first topic of study. Although there are a number of formats for determining interest, this one is quick, practical, and utilizes available resources.

Classroom Observation

Direct observation of students as they participate in classroom science lessons can often yield the most valid and reliable assessment data. Observations are particularly valuable for identifying the specific needs of special students. When the results of such observations are synthesized with information about students' interests and other available data, appropriate corrective plans can be made.

One convenient method for structuring classroom observations is to follow the behaviors and elements on a checklist while observing. A checklist, such as the example in Figure 3.1, helps to focus the observer's attention and also offers a convenient format for recording behaviors. Whether a checklist is detailed or general, it can be used by the teacher during science lessons, by an outside observer in the classroom, or even by interviewers to structure a teacher or student interview.

Although classroom observation alone can provide meaningful data for detecting special needs, it is when the findings of several observations are synthesized with accumulated diagnostic information that the most complete picture of students' performance emerges. Having diagnostic profiles of students in hand is the beginning point for selecting strategies that are most likely to correct individual students' special needs in science.

CORRECTION

The basic instructional approach that is amenable to individualization as well as compatible with the learning needs of many special students is carefully guided discovery. In this section, 14 basic principles of instruction are suggested to facilitate the mastery of science content and skills (see Figure 3.2). Most of these principles are appropriate for all learners but they are particularly important for teaching science to special learners. All can and should be implemented in a regular classroom setting as well as in special classrooms.

FIGURE 3.2 Fourteen Principles for Teaching Science to Special Learners

1. Use an activity-based format to teach concepts and skills
2. Choose important survival topics and apply them to everyday life
3. Use realistic and relevant experiments and examples
4. Establish the experiential base for each topic
5. Emphasize and directly teach vocabulary
6. Limit information to small, relevant amounts for each lesson
7. Provide generous review activities with each lesson
8. Integrate the study of science with that of other subject areas
9. Carefully structure the content and format of the program
10. Provide response prompts and teach self-monitoring
11. Encourage parents to reinforce the science program
12. Keep up with scientific advances
13. Build interest and enthusiasm
14. Both teach and adjust for specific skill needs

1. Use an Activity-Based Format to Teach Concepts and Skills

As noted in Chapter 1, mastery of science skills enables students to master science content both in the classroom and in later life. Since skills are best learned by doing, participatory experiences are essential for both understanding concepts and accomplishing the process skills. Such experiences may also bypass any weak basic skills special learners might have. Instead of fostering passive learning, guiding students to participate in discovering concepts creates active learners. Hands-on, interactive learning adds appeal to the senses and provides a reason to learn. Make generous use of focused and structured fieldtrips, simulations, nonprint media, and experiments. As an approach to teaching science, experimentation and laboratory study are too often either omitted or offered as supplementary tack-ons. When students are introduced to a topic by participating in demonstrations, tapes, and group experiments, motivation, interest, and self-esteem increase and students develop a sense of contribution and accomplishment. Cooperative learning groups can be used to facilitate this active learning; such shared learning also tends to promote social interaction, a much needed experience for special learners. When students provide input and become active participants in an event or classroom project, their understanding of concepts as well as their mastery and application of skills are likely to increase.

2. Choose Important Survival Topics and Apply them to Everyday Life

Since science skills are learned in the context of content and many of the special learners described in Chapter 2 can ill afford to waste valuable time learning inconsequential content, the selection of topics is another key variable in adjusting to students' needs. Special learners often require intensive and lengthy instruction, leaving teachers three choices: 1) Move very slowly through the science curriculum, covering all content and skills as much as possible; 2) select topics according to practical need and interest; teach the related skills and major concepts, establish the relevance for each, and then move on to the next important topic; or 3) delete nonessential topics, skim the less practical topics by emphasizing only major concepts, and teach the most practical topics and developmentally appropriate skills in depth.

Exercising the first option will mean that the students never reach the final topics in the curricular sequence, some of which may be important functional topics. The second option entails never mentioning some of the topics that students may encounter in newscasts or everyday conversation. To enable moderately to severely handicapped students to master the most vital functional concepts, this may be the appropriate course of action. The third option is the one advocated in this book for mildly handicapped students because it provides the widest coverage and the appropriate skills as well as the depth necessary for learning about real-life science.

Specific topics should be emphasized on a need-to-know basis. Much could be taught about any topic, but for special students, the basic concepts needed for survival and day-to-day functioning must be highlighted. Of particular importance to special students are the basic concepts involved in safety, health, and literate functioning. Emphasize the important while deleting the trivial. Choose current and practical topics from students' daily lives and from newspapers and newscasts. Consider the personal relevance of all scientific experiences in terms of the level and interests of the students. This may involve skipping a chapter or teaching only part of a chapter or unit. The selective use of content material can be helpful if relevant information is chosen. Later on, after mastery of the basic real-life concepts, it is sometimes possible to go back to more abstract and less critical sections of the material.

Careful topic and subtopic selection should not be construed as a leap-frog approach to the science curriculum but rather a meaningful, person-alized approach. When teaching about rocks, for example, begin with actual samples found in the neighborhood instead of metamorphic rocks that are foreign to the region. The local samples of rocks are more relevant and meaningful to the students than the rocks in the textbook, which students may never have seen. In regions where local varieties are limited, prepared collections of actual samples can be used. Not only are the samples interesting, but they are also kinesthetically appropriate for special students. Such an orientation requires teachers to view topics with an eye toward students' present needs and interests. Then, depending upon the nature of identified needs and interests, a topic may be introduced in specific terms or on a very general level, establishing a foundation for additional discussion later.

Certain of the topics presented in this book are inherently more oriented toward real life than others. For older special students (say, 13 or older) who are functioning at an elementary level, the topics that should probably be taught first and in depth are health and nutrition and work with machines. Next in importance are living things, prevention of infections, weather, and use of technology. Topics to emphasize when teaching younger special students include living things and health and nutrition. The topics that are less pertinent, such as ecological concerns and energy, might be skimmed, with the major concepts stressed. Topics that are nonessential, such as the earth and astronomy, should probably be saved for the end of the year, to permit in-depth treatment of the more practical concepts.

3. Use Realistic and Relevant Experiments and Examples

Closely related to activity-based learning and pertinent topics is the use of frequent hands-on experiences to illustrate what is being studied. Many scientific concepts can be demonstrated in one form or another. Establishing a realistic frame of reference for temperature, plants, electricity, wind, and thousands of other science-related topics makes sense only when the students have a concept to associate with or refer back to.

Examples that apply to the students' everyday life should be used regularly if the content is to become personally relevant to students. This may mean using the students' language to introduce concepts and then translating the ideas into scientific terms, although for some low-ability students, most of each lesson may have to be labeled with student, not scientific, language. Highlight the application and usefulness of each topic. Have students contribute personal examples, specimens, pictures, and experiences on a regular basis. Lessons are more interesting and easier to remember when personal relevance has been well established. Careful topic selection, relevant examples and experiments, and an activity-based format are important variables in establishing an appropriate experiential base.

4. Establish the Experiential Base for Each Topic

Special learners are frequently victims of assumptive teaching. Concepts are thrown at them, presuming their knowledge of directions and sizes and a wealth of background knowledge and past experiences: How would you describe sediment? What do I mean by the phrase "rotation of the earth"? Such questions should be preceded by specific examples and as many concrete illustrations as possible. Otherwise, instructional time may be wasted teaching mystery facts for an unrecognized purpose to confused students.

As an extension of assessment, measure students' prior knowledge of each topic before planning instruction. It is particularly important to identify the pre-existing concepts which will require expansion, modification, or change. This may mean taking time a day or two before beginning a lesson to determine what students know about a topic. Informal interviews and questions can be used. Assignments requiring students to bring in a sample of a leaf, food, or other object can provide a common ground for beginning the development of a new concept. If students have had numerous real experiences with the topic at hand, those experiences can be analyzed to reinforce the major concepts and perhaps discussed to provide secondhand experience for those students who have had little contact with the topic. Semantic maps, charts, and graphs of what is known about a topic permit students to see connections and patterns. When little or no prior knowledge exists, provide experiences both through experimentation and through vicarious exercises. Videotapes can be particularly rich sources of vicarious experiences, providing simultaneous sights and sounds that might not be practical or safe as real experiences. Building experiences sets the stage for learning, providing an important knowledge base and serving as a type of advance organizer, while identifying incomplete or erroneous concepts sets the stage for conceptual change.

5. Emphasize and Directly Teach Vocabulary

Learning science vocabulary means knowing more than how to pronounce terms and recite their definitions. The vocabulary of science carries the major concepts of each topic. However, some of the terminology is jargon and is unnecessary to the mastery of concepts. When possible, use functional language instead of technical terms. Begin with concrete referents and gradually add abstract terms. The accent should be on the functional language in order to both make the concepts understandable and manageable and to relate the ideas directly to the students' everyday lives. For example, when teaching about photosynthesis, it is not imperative that students master the terms chloroplasts and glucose, although many science experts would consider these two terms helpful to understanding the process. Instead of burdening special students with complex vocabulary and facts of little retention value, it is sufficient for some students to remember the basic notions: Plants make their own food through a process called photosynthesis, and chlorophyll and sunshine make the process possible.

Among the options for presenting vocabulary words are concept maps that graphically depict the relationships among terms, defining sentences, cloze-type activities in which a key term is deleted, or game formats that lead students to produce terms or match terms with definitions. However, regardless of methodology, the two to four terms that carry the major concepts should be emphasized throughout each lesson for these purposes: 1) before each topic is discussed as an advance organizer; 2) during the discussions and experimentation for clarification and elaboration; and 3) after study of a topic to summarize and review the major concepts.

Focused instruction should be provided for nontechnical words that are used in special ways. Studies have indicated that nontechnical vocabulary is often more difficult to understand than technical words with very specialized meanings. Such words as *lens, film, fuse, conductor,* and *mold* are examples of nontechnical words with multiple meanings. When students know a word in one context, it can be very difficult to accommodate new meanings to coexist for the same word or phrase. It is sometimes easier to assimilate new information (or special vocabulary) than it is to accommodate or expand existing meanings.

6. Limit Information to Small, Relevant Amounts for Each Lesson

Slow the instructional pace to match students' learning rates. Teach for mastery of concepts and skills, not coverage of material. Decide what is most important for each student within each chapter or topic. Begin with the most relevant by relating the topic to students' personal lives, stressing the importance, and providing experiences and examples to build and reinforce the information. Delete trivia and highlight the most relevant dimensions and features of a topic. Divide each task or principle into major concepts and their supporting ideas and information. As concepts are momentarily mastered, have students supply numerous personal examples and apply concepts to real-life situations.

7. Provide Generous Review Activities with Each Lesson

Relate each new topic to previously learned skills and information. Begin each lesson with a review of related concepts and their personal and societal relevance; build or reinforce students' experiences as needed. Repeat and review concepts often. Have students summarize everything in their own words and record them or have a peer take notes; guide students to develop charts and graphs to summarize information and concepts. Use numerous visual aids, topical summaries, taped overviews, and pictures or examples of projects displayed in the room to further reinforce important information. Vary the format of review experiences. Presentations that utilize puzzle, game, or learning-center formats can all be helpful. All reviews do not have to be teacher-directed question-and-answer sessions. The use of group projects and structured problem-solving sessions can help reinforce and apply what has been learned.

8. Integrate the Study of Science with That of Other Subject Areas

Rather than teach science as an isolated subject at a particular time each day, incorporate science topics into lessons in language arts, social studies, and mathematics throughout the day. This practice reinforces scientific skills and concepts and demonstrates the applicability of science to other areas as well. It is equally important to incorporate the other subjects into science lessons on a routine basis. Such integration offers special learners much needed review and repetition and models the generalizability of both skills and content.

9. Carefully Structure the Content and Format of the Program

Measures to insure the safety and health of all students, particularly special learners, are important considerations when planning and implementing science lessons. Classroom experimentation can be dangerous to the students and the teacher unless proper precautions are taken. Certain experiments are best demonstrated by the teacher (e.g., those involving flammable or poisonous materials). Safety assurance may also entail monitoring what students wear (e.g., safety goggles) and strict supervision of students as they experiment, even to the extent of soliciting the help of additional adults. Pairing or grouping special students with responsible peers is also helpful, especially if guidelines have been discussed with the peers.

Use a consistent format for presenting lessons and conducting demonstrations and experiments. Students need the comfort of knowing what to expect and the manner in which they will be asked to respond. The regular use of journals, tapes, and study guides all help build a pattern of structure. Always teach information the way students will be tested for mastery. If demonstrations, labeling, explanations, or multiple-choice items will be used as the criteria, be sure to use the same format to teach the material. The use of practice tests is also encouraged. A day or two before a test, give a practice test to be completed in small groups, orally, or individually, depending upon the particular criterion chosen. Discuss the correct responses and also answer questions about the appropriateness of student responses.

10. Provide Response Prompts and Teach Self-Monitoring

Give students specific feedback as they respond to questions. Self-monitoring involves having students determine just how they were able to solve a problem or arrive at an answer. Encourage thinking out loud to talk through a response. Praise correct responses, but counter by asking students: How did you figure out that answer? What made you select amoeba as the answer? That's possible, but what makes you think you are correct? Having students verbalize how they figured out an answer can give insight into how they are processing information. Of equal importance is the positive model students provide their peers when they explain how they came up with an answer.

Prompting or cuing for answers helps students think. Instead of concentrating on answers, provide verbal or nonverbal cues to answers. Helping students come up with their own answers takes longer but improves memory and class participation. For example, ask: What is the difference between orbiting and rotating? If no one answers, you could follow up by asking: Who can give me an example or instance when something has an orbit? What is it doing? Then ask for an example of something that rotates. Give clues to help students answer their own questions. Remember, after asking a question, it is helpful to wait 5 to 10 seconds before seeking more information. Think time or wait time used over an extended period can actually increase the number and quality of responses by getting students accustomed to answering, active participation, and utilizing teacher-provided clues.

Checklists are valuable self-monitoring aids for walking students through acquisition and processing of information and then integration of the concepts. Teach students to utilize checklists to guide their thinking as they work through new information and experiments. Begin by asking them key questions: Which features are the same? Which ones are different? As students become accustomed to answering your questions, shorten them to one or two words as oral questions or cues (e.g., Same? Different?) and then written cues. Use these cues to develop written checklists. As students use their checklists, have them verbalize the cues. Eventually, many youngsters will memorize the cues to the point that they no longer need the written checklist and can monitor and guide their thoughts as they approach new material.

11. Encourage Parents to Reinforce the Science Program

To reinforce and extend scientific concepts, broaden the experiential base, stimulate interest, increase generalizations, and establish relevance, encourage parents to supplement the school program with at-home activities. Although some parents may not respond, many parents of special students welcome such opportunities. To those who are receptive, suggest specific supportive activities. For example, the day-to-day responsibility for the care of a pet can render associated scientific concepts more meaningful than most teachers or textbooks. Similarly, responsibility for a home garden, whether located on a window sill or the last three rows of the "back forty," can teach much about plants. Other suggestions include involving students in pest control, keeping a monthly moon phase calendar, explaining health care as it occurs, and watching designated scientific programs on public television. An important point is to expand the reach of the science program by fully utilizing parental assistance.

12. Keeping Up with Scientific Advances

Remaining abreast of new developments in the field of science can be a constant struggle for teachers. However, presenting up-to-date scientific content is part of the professional responsibility assumed by teachers of science. Current content is important to all students, but for the special students who may have to struggle to master concepts, it is particularly important. What a waste of time and effort it would be for such students to labor to master erroneous or outdated information.

Science texts, even new ones, often contain outdated information. Scientific and technological advances occur at such a rapid rate that by the time the authors write and then revise their ideas and submit them to the publisher, the information can be as much as one- to three-years-old. And by the time the publisher produces the text, the content may have aged another year or two. How sad that four years after the first moon landing, one science teacher using a textbook with a three-year-old copyright taught her students that the United States might someday put a man on the moon—and how that must have confused her class, particularly the special students!

Although the information reported in professional journals might not be as current as that of popular news releases, the accounts are usually much more detailed and objective. Journal information is also typically two to three years younger than some of the content contained in textbooks. To stay current, teachers must closely monitor scientific advances reported in newspapers and broadcasts and also guide their students to do likewise. A classroom newsfile, compiled and updated by both teacher and students, is a convenient way to collect news. If the text of the selections is written at a level too far above students' reading levels, a skilled reader can dictate it on tape for later use at a listening center or the information can be rewritten at a less difficult level. Videotapes of newscasts that announce scientific advances can be used to present the information as well as to help make it come alive for students; the tapes can be edited to highlight the relevant and delete the nonessential content. In an era of so many important scientific advances happening so quickly, teachers and students can hardly afford to ignore new developments.

13. Build Interest and Enthusiasm

Unless students are interested in what they are studying, all of the previous suggestions are of little use. Teacher enthusiasm is a vital element for building interest. Give students a choice in what and how they learn. Present two options involving a new unit on energy: Would you like to begin with energy from the stars or energy from the earth? How do you suggest we begin? Why? Use discrepant events and anecdotes to encourage students' interest. Remember that active involvement promotes learning. Involve students not only in the actual activities but in each step of the planning process as well. Permit students to choose subtopics to explore in depth. Transmit an enthusiasm for science by bringing in nontextbook information about scientific and technological topics from other sources. Let students know about special shows on television. Videotape these shows and replay parts for further discussion and integration of topics when they come up in future lessons. It is often easy for both teachers and students to generate enthusiasm for new and novel scientific advances.

It is not unusual for students to perform above their established achievement levels when a topic of study is one with which they are particularly fascinated. Perhaps the most practical way to create interest is to establish the personal relevance and then the societal relevance of a topic. Understanding Me is always a popular topic and a critical component of the study of science by special students. Although such topics as dinosaurs, caves and rocks, weather, animals, and electricity are particularly interesting to many students, consider the increase in excitement when the implications and relevance of these topics are established. It is important to remember that the teacher's enthusiasm or lack of it can be contagious.

14. Both Teach and Adjust for Specific Skill Needs

Not only should the science skills be directly taught but they should also be circumvented as necessary. Certain of the science skills may be especially difficult for special learners. When a particular skill impedes the progress of students, either substitute a different skill or guide students through the thought processes for accomplishing the task.

In the discussions that follow, a few strategies are suggested for both teaching and adjusting for special needs in the three skill areas: information acquisition; information processing; and integration. Charts of the skills, showing which particular groups of special learners may exhibit problems, are presented with each discussion. Note that the skill needs marked for each special group were selected as likely correlates with the learning characteristics of that category; these needs are not necessarily representative of the categories or exclusive to them.

Information Acquisition Skills

As discussed in Chapter 2 and depicted in Figure 3.3, a number of special learners experience difficulty obtaining information when utilizing one or more of these skills. Reading about science is particularly difficult for many of these students, while directed experimentation is not especially problematic. However, in planning ways to accommodate special learners, the information acquisition skills are relatively easy to adjust by simple substitution of one for another.

Observation. A wealth of information can be derived from observations, but observation skills must often be developed and refined. Various sensory and learning

FIGURE 3.3 Information Acquisition Skills with which Traditional Categories of Special Learners Might Have Difficulty

SPECIAL LEARNER GROUP	OBSERVATION	LISTENING	READING	STUDY	DIRECTED EXPERIMENTATION
REGULAR/REMEDIAL STUDENTS					
Culturally Different		S	S	S	
Slow Learners	S	S	S	S	
SPECIAL EDUCATION STUDENTS					
Behavior Disordered	S	S	S	S	S
Hearing Impaired		M	S	S	
Language Disabled		S	S	S	
Learning Disabled	S	S	M	M	S
Mentally Retarded	S	S	M	M	S
Physically Handicapped			S		
Speech Disordered		S			
Visually Impaired	S		S	S	
Generic Handicaps	S	S	S	S	S

S = SOME of these students might have difficulty
M = MANY of these students are likely to have difficulty

handicaps can have a negative affect on the quality and the time needed to conduct scientific observations. When sensory abilities permit, these suggestions may assist students to observe carefully: Give students advance organizers that prepare them for the task at hand; state no more than three specific purposes for the observations to focus students' attention; if needed, ask specific questions to focus their attention to relevant details; give students clues as they observe (e.g., I see two other moving parts; I wonder about their purpose.); and lead students to verbalize their observations. When working with students who have attention difficulties, limit the length and scope of observation to a manageable unit.

Listening. Aside from textbook information assigned to students to read, much of the instruction in a typical classroom occurs as a listening exercise. Students who are easily distracted and those with hearing disabilities may not benefit from oral instruction; other students have specific problems remembering what they hear. It is not reasonable to expect students to listen attentively amidst too many competing noises; eliminate as many auditory distractions as possible before beginning a listening experience. Ways in which instruction can be adjusted include assisting students and skill substitution. To assist students to listen, try these ideas: Give students advance organizers to prepare them to listen; give them specific purposes for listening to focus their attention on the important content; ask periodic questions to refocus attention and generate discussions; pause and state or have a student state a subsummary to reinforce the content for those who listened and present it again for those who did not; occasionally pause and have students predict what will be said next; and limit the length of listening presentations. Have students who are too easily distracted to listen attentively in a group use headsets to listen to an audiotape of the vital content. Permit students who do not benefit from listening experiences to acquire the content by reading, observing, studying, and/or directed experimentation.

Reading. Some of the science instruction that occurs in classrooms requires reading, the very skill with which a large proportion of special students experience some degree of difficulty. Perhaps the bulk of the actual reading instruction that should be included in science lessons is mastery of the few most important vocabulary terms. As previously mentioned, recognition and understanding of as many of the key vocabulary terms as students can handle is central to understanding the content of a lesson. Teaching key prefixes and suffixes and their meanings as intact units to be recognized at sight offers students a particularly useful strategy for decoding scientific terms. When the reading level of the science textbook is so far above students' reading levels that little learning is likely to occur, either extra assistance or alternate methods for acquiring information must be provided. The best choice depends upon the skill level of the students and the resources of the teacher. To provide extra assistance, try these strategies: Give students an advance study guide to lead them through difficult text; use a felt marker to highlight (or guide students to highlight) only the most important terms and concepts in the textbook, and then cue them to read only the highlighted, essential parts; make an audiotape of the text for students to listen and follow along; locate a parallel text written on a lower reading level and have students read from it; use the book as reinforcement and follow-up material rather than initial presentation; or rewrite the most vital content at a lower reading level. Consider using as alternate methods of acquiring information observation, listening, directed experimentation, or a combination of the three to circumvent reading problems. Some alternatives are to present the text material orally; use captioned films, such as those for the hearing impaired (they often summarize major points), and then copy the captions for later reading experiences as follow-up; demonstrate concepts with model experiments while students observe and then discuss the findings; have students follow your directions to perform the experiments themselves; or use pictures, films, or interactive videotapes to present the information.

Study. Study is usually an independent activity and as such should utilize the information skills that are the easiest for the individual student. Study and research can be of several types: additional reading, observation, listening, or directed experimentation. Study in the classroom often includes reading. When given a choice, special students are likely to avoid reading if it is one of their skill weaknesses. Two adjustments required for special students to study to broaden and deepen their knowledge: 1) Present information in several formats so that students can choose the skill on which to rely; and 2) directly teach students at least a few rudimentary study skills. Their study must often be supervised and discreetly directed if they are to succeed.

Directed Experimentation. Few adjustments are needed for special students to perform experiments under the direction of the teacher. Beyond the teacher's careful selection of experiments that are safe and direct instruction in the handling of the materials, often the only accommodations that need be offered are focusing and verbalization. During experimentation, the teacher should prompt, question, and stress key features to assist students to focus on the most important details and also verbalize the description of events, guiding students to follow suit.

Information Processing Skills

Of the skills involved in processing scientific information, communicating orally or in writing present the most difficulty for many special learners. Least problematic is measurement, an arithmetic skill that can be directly taught. As portrayed in Figure 3.4, students with speech disorders are least noted for exhibiting weaknesses in these skills.

Organization. Organizational skill is especially important to understanding isolated bits of scientific information because organizing data increases utility. Two strategies are useful for assisting students to organize and can be implemented in cooperative learning group settings: 1) a chart on which students record information as they encounter it and 2) questions designed to organize and clarify data. For both techniques, teacher-constructed and labeled grids are helpful, with the exact labels depending on the nature of

FIGURE 3.4 Information Processing Skills with which Traditional Categories of Special Learners Might Have Difficulty

SPECIAL LEARNER GROUP	ORGANIZATION	ANALYSIS	MEASUREMENT	CLASSIFICATION	PREDICTION	COMMUNICATION		
						SPEAK	WRITE	PERFORM
REGULAR/REMEDIAL STUDENTS								
Culturally Different						S	S	
Slow Learners		S		S	S		S	
SPECIAL EDUCATION STUDENTS								
Behavior Disordered	M			S		S	S	
Hearing Impaired		S			S	S		
Language Disabled		S		S	S	M	M	
Learning Disabled	M	S	S	S	S	S	M	
Mentally Retarded	S	M	S	M	M	S	M	S
Physically Handicapped							S	S
Speech Disordered						S		
Visually Impaired	S	S		S				S
Generic Handicaps	S	S	S	S	S	S	S	S

S= SOME of these students might have difficulty
M = MANY of these students are likely to have difficulty

the content and the abilities of the students. If the students themselves are capable of reading and writing either the information on the chart or the answers to the questions, then the written record should serve as a roadmap for processing and integrating the concepts. If reading and writing are problematic, several pictures can be placed in each grid and the students instructed to mark the correct pictures. If only writing is a weak skill, students can discuss and orally state or tape record the information for a teacher or peer to write on the form. Once they become accustomed to the organizational charts, many students begin to rely on them for periodic summaries and as a self-monitoring guide.

Analysis. Analysis is the learner's formative evaluation in the science learning cycle. The purpose of analysis is to take stock of what is known, what else needs to be known, and what strategies are available to obtain additional information. Students must identify unique features, relationships, and patterns to compare and contrast data. Either of the previously mentioned organizational charts can serve as the stimulus for analysis. Using a chart, the students can be asked to state or write the answers to these three questions: What do I know now? What else do I need to know? What is the best way to find out about this? When students have difficulty answering the questions, walk and talk them through the process by thinking aloud. Then guide students with key questions (e.g., What is the most important characteristic of birds? How are birds and bees related? Do you see a pattern? Compare and contrast what you know about birds and bees.). When the answers require measurement, classification, prediction, and/or communication, strategies suggested for those skills should be used.

Measurement. When particular types of measurement are taught concurrently in science and arithmetic classes, each lesson can reinforce the other. Regardless of the particular target to be measured, three elements should be stressed: choosing the unit of measure, selecting the tool with which to measure, and deciding on the method for interpreting the measurements. Demonstrated options can assist students to accomplish each task. Present three to five options from which to choose each element; demonstrate or have students demonstrate measurement with each option; discuss the logic of each; and then decide on the one that is most logical. If necessary, guide students through the logic by asking key questions. When choosing the unit of measure, ask: Which unit is the easiest to understand? Which one do you think is most often used? Why? Which one would be the easiest to explain to a peer? Then guide students through the think-aloud process to decide. For the measuring tool, ask: Which one looks the easiest? Which one is easiest to use for this task? Which one does the job the fastest? Which one is most likely to be available to other people who want to do the same thing? Again, have students think aloud as they choose. For interpreting results, ask: How would you explain this to a friend? What is most important about your measurements? How can you decide what this means? As students think aloud their responses, prompt them as needed with additional questions until they have selected each element and defended their choice.

Classification. Classifying information is one of the most powerful strategies available for sorting and understanding concepts. Using concrete objects greatly assists students in classification and provides opportunities to demonstrate key terms (e.g., *most, least, better, best,* and the like). The use of a standard set of prompts can guide students through the sorting process and eventually lead them to use the prompts to accomplish the task independently. Ask questions or write the questions for students to answer while they observe. As students become accustomed to the routine, questions can be abbreviated to only the key words, such as these: Alike? Different? Most important likenesses? Important differences? Term for likenesses? Term for differences? Depending on the skills of the students, the terms or even key pictures for the categories may have to be supplied. In this case, abbreviated questions might be: Alike? Different? Most like this group? Most like that group? It may be helpful to have students orally defend their answers or if needed to have a peer defend their answers.

Prediction. Prediction relies heavily upon students' pre-existing concepts and prior experiences with the target elements or with similar objects or events. Logical predictions set the stage for formal hypotheses. Students who have limited experiences or who have particular difficulty predicting may need to begin by making wild guesses and then, after a relationship has been established or an event has occurred, by reasoning backward to discern how they could have predicted the outcome. A variation of the demonstrated options described for teaching measurement is also useful for improving prediction skills. Begin by having students summarize what they know about the topic (they may use an organizational chart if it is available); then present three to five options from which to choose the best prediction; prompt students to give reasons why each option might be correct (this will usually narrow the choices); then, after a relationship has been established or an event has occurred, reexamine each option to see why it was or was not correct; discuss what students had to know and how they could have made the correct prediction, thinking aloud as needed.

Communication. Whatever the form, the primary purposes for students' communication in the science class are to enhance their understanding, share data to clarify patterns, and demonstrate their knowledge. Three communication formats are commonly used: speaking, writing, and demonstrating, or performing. Many special students are likely to have weak writing skills, some have speaking difficulties, and a few have trouble demonstrating their understandings. An excellent strategy for facilitating the communication of special students is to offer them their choice of communication channel. When speaking is particularly difficult, ease the students' burden: Give them an outline as a speaking guide; ask oral questions that require one- or two-word responses; present a selection of answers from which students choose; permit students to write their answers instead of say them (or select one of the writing options); or have students actually demonstrate using concrete objects. When writing is difficult, adjust the stimulus/response format to simplify the task: Provide partial sentences that require one- or two-word responses; give students a selection of answers (either words or pictures) to mark; permit students to answer orally instead of in writing (or select one of the speaking options); or have students actually demonstrate using concrete objects. When demonstrations are problematic, offer speaking or writing as communication options.

Integration Skills

Because of their complexity, integration skills are particularly difficult for many special learners. Generalization and evaluation, two of the most important science skills, are perhaps the most problematic. As indicated in Figure 3.5, neither physically handicapped nor speech-disordered students are especially noted for weak integration skills.

Synthesis. Since synthesis is a critical thinking skill, requiring the meshing of known information into an integrated whole, both information acquisition and processing skills are involved. The same charts that were suggested for organization can be extended to facilitate synthesis. Following the charting of data on a labeled grid, guide students to summarize each column, row, and/or category as appropriate; if needed, have them mark out details with a felt pen and substitute summary terms or pictures; then help them answer the first question recommended for analysis: What do I know now? As an advance organizer for hypothesis, add the question: What could it mean? As

FIGURE 3.5   Integration Skills with which Traditional Categories of Special Learners Might Have Difficulty

SPECIAL LEARNER GROUP	SYNTHESIS	HYPOTHESIS	EXPERIMENTATION	GENERALIZATION	EVALUATION
REGULAR/REMEDIAL EDUCATION:					
Culturally Different	S			S	
Slow Learners	S	S	S	S	S
SPECIAL EDUCATION STUDENTS:					
Behavior Disordered	S			S	S
Hearing Impaired	S			S	
Language Disabled	S			S	S
Learning Disabled	S	S	S	S	S
Mentally Retarded	M	M	M	M	M
Physically Handicapped					
Speech Disordered					
Visually Impaired			S	S	S
Generic Handicaps	S	S	S	S	S

S= SOME of these students might have difficulty
M = MANY of these students are likely to have difficulty

with previous strategies, walk and talk students through the process, thinking aloud and prompting as needed.

Hypothesis. To guide students to develop formal predictive statements of hypotheses lead them to review their answers to the synthesis questions, particularly What could it mean? Discuss the answers and think aloud as the teacher or a student critiques the possibilities. Some of the strategies suggested for prediction may be helpful. Refine the statements of possibility to produce three or four predictive statements, or hypotheses. Students who have special difficulty may need teacher-prepared statements from which to choose hypotheses.

Independent Experimentation. When working with special students, the degree of independence may be relative to their ability levels, the maturity of their judgment, and their work habits. These factors help determine the amount of teacher guidance needed. For the planning stage, begin with the three or four hypotheses developed as described; present or have students design (depending on ability) three choices of experiments to test each hypothesis; think aloud the critique of each experiment as a means of assisting students in their choices. Prompt students with such questions as: What do you think it will prove? Why? Do you think it is possible to perform in this classroom? Explain. Do you think it is practical? Why? Do you think it is safe? Explain. What information might it provide? When one experiment is chosen for each hypothesis, review the selected experiments to identify the one that would test all chosen hypotheses, again prompting and guiding students. For the conduct of the experiment, pair students, designating one the researcher and the other the director; have students verbally rehearse the procedures before actually beginning. Include in the rehearsal appropriate special precautions. During experimentation, have the director verbalize the procedures while the researcher implements them. After the experiment, have the students take turns describing the procedures and the results (if possible). All experiments should be closely supervised by the teacher; the descriptions should be monitored as well so that the teacher can fill in as needed.

Generalization. Generalization is particularly difficult for some special students, who often need to observe proof of applicability to many examples. When a principle is demonstrated with one example, have students predict and hypothesize using strategies such as those suggested, critiquing each prediction and hypothesis. If needed, help students demonstrate through repeated experiments the generalizability of the principle. Repeat the predict-and-verify process as often as is necessary (and practical). At the conclusion of each experiment, think aloud and prompt students with questions to emphasize the clues to appropriate generalizations.

Evaluation. Like generalization, evaluation is problematic for a number of special students. Both skills require sophisticated and critical thinking. For conceptual change to occur, evaluation must focus on two features of science: logic and worth. To assist students in evaluating logic, compare the logic of their old ideas with the logic of the new ones; walk and talk them through the entire process by which generalizations were made, using the strategies recommended for each skill. To help students evaluate the worth of particular scientific information and principles, guide them to identify personal value first and then societal value. Lead them through the thinking process by using a standard set of prompts not only to direct their thinking but also to furnish a self-monitoring aid. Orally ask or write questions such as these: How can I use it? When will I use it? What good will it do me? Where will it help me? Why will it help me? Who else might it help? As students become accustomed to the routine, abbreviate questions to only key words: How? When? What? Where? Why? Who else? Using students' answers to these questions, construct or have them construct statements of personal and societal relevance.

SUMMARY

To detect special needs in science, observe students learning and working in their science classroom; a checklist of skills is a useful tool for this purpose. Add to the diagnostic data with a synthesis of school records, the results of testing, and interviews of both the target student and his or her past teachers. Use the resulting diagnostic profiles as direction for choosing corrective strategies.

To correct special needs in science, use a carefully guided discovery approach. A number of principles of corrective instruction may facilitate the mastery of both the content and skills of science: Use an activity-based format; choose topics that apply to everyday life; use relevant examples and experiments; establish a sound experiential base; emphasize science vocabulary; limit information and provide frequent review; integrate science with other subjects; structure the program; teach self-monitoring and provide prompts; involve parents; stay current; and build interest and enthusiasm. Of these principles, perhaps the use of an activity-based format to teach concepts and skills and the selection of real-life topics are the most valuable for teaching special students.

The final corrective principle, teaching and adjusting for special skill needs, is particularly important for accommodating the needs of special students. Several strategies are suggested for such adjustments. For corrective instruction in the information acquisition skills, the major theme is permitting the interchange of stimulus/response formats. Guiding students through the thinking process with the aid of questions, modeling, and prompts is the recurring suggestion for corrective instruction in the information-processing and integration skills.

The suggestions contained in this chapter are not intended to be exhaustive but rather to provide a framework for correcting special needs in science and selecting topics, skills, and activities from the chapters that follow.

REFLECTIONS

1. Teaching science to handicapped students is considered by some teachers and parents to be superfluous; they believe that the academic program should focus instead on more basic skills, particularly reading and writing. Under what circumstances do you agree? Disagree? Defend both sides of the issue and then state and justify your stand.

2. In Chapter 1, several factors are suggested as important considerations when selecting science topics for particular students. Review those factors and then rank them in order of their importance for teaching normal elementary students; for remedial instruction of adolescent students; for young handicapped students; and then for adolescent handicapped students. How do your rankings change according to student ability and age? Which factors do you consistently rank high, regardless of student ability or age? Why? Compare your rankings with those of a peer. Consider the values reflected in your rankings.

3. Three groups of science skills are described in Chapter 1. In each grouping, decide which one skill you want to emphasize in your class and justify each choice. Then identify the one skill in each group that you think should receive the least emphasis, and again justify your choice. Compare your choices with the science skills that are emphasized in most science classrooms in the schools in your area.

4. In Chapter 2, the science needs of special categories of students are described. Contrast the special problems of regular/remedial students and special education students. Which categories cite the most dissimilar problems? Which groups have the most similar problems? Are there specific problems that are common to most groups? Why or why not?

5. One of the special categories of learners is *teacher disabled.* Why and how do you think this occurs? Estimate the frequency of occurrence of students becoming teacher disabled in all subjects. How often do you think this happens in the area of science? Compare and then justify your estimates.

6. The third chapter suggests 14 instructional principles to help special learners master the content and skills of science. Randomly select a science lesson from the teacher's edition of an elementary science textbook; independently or with a peer, analyze the lesson to identify the use of these instructional principles.

7. Particular difficulties in science tend to vary according to the student population and the biases and perceptions of individual teachers. Interview a highly skilled regular education teacher to determine his or her perception of the degree and incidence of specific problems in science as well as ways to detect and correct them; then discuss the detection and correction of any special problems that are not mentioned in Part I. Follow a similar procedure to interview an exemplary special education teacher.

8. Planning appropriate science lessons for special learners requires careful consideration of each student's skill needs and the topics or concepts that should be emphasized. Select a hypothetical special learner; using the discussions of special learners, the instructional principles, the suggested strategies for cor-

recting each skill, and hypothetical diagnostic information, modify a lesson from a science textbook for that student. Repeat the process for an actual special student, using diagnostic information available from the school and taking the content for your lesson from the science book currently in use in the student's classroom.

9. Actual lessons taught in the classroom with real students often differ dramatically from lessons planned on paper, no matter how carefully they are prepared. Teach the science lesson that you designed for the special student. As you teach, note the learning characteristics, skill needs, and interests of the student for consideration in planning future lessons.

10. A number of science and special education textbooks are pertinent to the science needs of special students. Compare and contrast discussions in these sources with the information in this section:

Abruscato, J. (1988). *Teaching children science* (2nd ed.). Englewood Cliffs, NJ: Prentice-Hall.

Cain, S. E., & Evans, J. M. (1984). *Sciencing: An involvement approach to elementary science methods* (2nd ed.). Columbus, OH: Charles E. Merrill.

Carin, A. A., & Sund, R. B. (1985). *Teaching science through discovery* (5th ed.). Columbus, OH: Charles E. Merrill.

Corrick, M. E. (Ed.) (1981). *Teaching handicapped students science.* Washington, DC: National Education Association.

Gega, P. C. (1990). *Science in elementary education.* (6th ed.). New York: Macmillan.

Hadary, D. E., & Cohen, S. H. (1978). *Laboratory science and art for blind, deaf, and emotionally disturbed children: A mainstreaming approach.* Austin, TX: Pro-Ed.

Harlan, J. D. (1988). *Science experiences for the early childhood years* (4th ed.). Columbus, OH: Charles E. Merrill.

Jacobson, W. J., & Bergman, A. B. (1987). *Science for children: A book for teachers.* Englewood Cliffs, NJ: Prentice-Hall.

Kameenai, E. S., & Simmons, D. C. (1990). *Designing instructional strategies: The prevention of academic learning problems.* Columbus, OH: Charles E. Merrill.

Lapp, D., & Flood, J. (Eds.) (1989). *Content area reading and learning: Instructional strategies.* Englewood Cliffs, NJ: Prentice-Hall.

Mercer, C. D., & Mercer, A. R. (1989). *Teaching students with learning problems* (3rd ed.). Columbus, OH: Charles E. Merrill.

Polloway, E. A., Patton, J. R., Payne, J. S., & Payne, R. A. (1989). *Strategies for teaching learners with special needs* (4th ed). Columbus, OH: Charles E. Merrill.

Schulz, J. B., Carpenter, C. D., & Turnbull, A. P. (1990). *Mainstreaming handicapped students: A guide for classroom teachers* (3rd ed.). Boston: Allyn and Bacon.

Smith, L. J., & Smith, D. L. (1990). *Social studies: Detecting and correcting special needs.* Boston: Allyn and Bacon.

Wolfinger, D. M. (1984). *Teaching science in the elementary school: Content, process, and attitude.* Boston: Little, Brown.

Wood, J. W. (1989). *Mainstreaming: A practical approach for teachers.* Columbus, OH: Charles E. Merrill.

Zeitler, W. R., & Barufaldi, J. P. (1988). *Elementary school science: A perspective for teachers.* White Plains, NY: Longman.

PART II

LIFE
SCIENCE

Life science is probably the area of science that is of the most immediate value to special learners. Topical content is vital to the understanding and care of self as well as to socialization and healthful living. Part II includes some of the traditional life science topics and also extends to health-related topics, such as nutrition and understanding illness. Although all skill areas are called upon, listening and communicating and particularly observing, predicting, and generalizing are stressed as facilitative skills. Developmentally, the content of this section is particularly appropriate for use as an introduction to science.

For special learners, a strong grounding in life science is particularly necessary. Each chapter in Part II contains information of high personal value and relevance for students. Thus, sections in these chapters are longer than others in this book because of their importance to students' well-being and social and personal growth. The longer treatments permit inclusion of additional suggestions for reinforcing targeted skills using familiar content.

In Chapter 4, we briefly discuss the three traditional categories of life: plants, animals, and the human body. Since these topics are quite broad, a number of key issues are deleted, most notably sex education, an important subtopic of the study of the human body. Because of the wide range of age and ability levels of special students and the controversies surrounding when, what, how, and to what extent sex education should be presented as well as who should provide the training, this subtopic is not considered in this book. Instead, to teach special students about sex, we suggest applying the principles in Part I to structure the particular policies and sex education curriculum adopted by the local school system.

Chapter 5 focuses on ecological concerns. Ecology is approached from the stance of personal safety as well as responsibility. Land, water, and air are first considered separately and then combined in the treatment of the interdependence of living things and ecology.

In Chapter 6, we present five aspects of health and nutrition, including diet and exercise. The chapter opens with personal hygiene because of its contributions to health and to social acceptance by peers. Both the dangers and the benefits of psychoactive drugs are emphasized. This chapter concludes with a discussion of recreation and safety.

Understanding illness, a major health and self-care topic, is the emphasis of Chapter 7. Although we have divided the chapter into three sections, it is appropriate to combine or overlap information about causes, treatment, and prevention, while maintaining a focus on one of these concerns.

For surveying students' needs for concentrated instruction in certain life science topics, interviews, informal questioning, and classroom observations are recommended diagnostic techniques. Beyond the requirements of the school curriculum, individual student needs must be a major consideration due to the importance and relevance of these topics. Interest surveys are useful for identifying specific subtopics for study. Special skill needs can be observed initially using a checklist, such as the one in Figure 3.1, and then confirmed during the ongoing process of diagnostic instruction. Skills to emphasize include observing, listening, predicting, communicating, generalizing, and to a lesser extent classifying, analyzing, and evaluating.

The topics in Part II are especially appropriate for using personal and high-interest comparisons to relate the content to students' existing knowledge and experiences. Many students have a reasonable understanding of living things, although the content associated with the human body and interdependence may need to be adjusted dramatically for individual needs. In most instances, health and nutrition and understanding illness must be directly taught but with emphasis carefully varied according to the age, ability level, and prior knowledge of the individual special students.

CHAPTER 4 /
LIVING THINGS

1. PLANTS

DETECTION Mastery of key concepts may be difficult for students who:

- Do not observe carefully
- Have difficulty classifying
- Have limited experiences growing or caring for plants
- Cannot explain the value of plants to animals and humans

Description. Teaching and learning about plants involves a mixture of classroom and outdoor activities. Associated topics include seeds, roots, food plants, flowers, soil, and other types of vegetation. Because many teachers are comfortable with this topic, students may be familiar with much of the content but may not have exercised all of the skills.

Special Problems. Skills involving observation, classifying, measuring, and particularly evaluation are important for mastering the concepts and content of plant study. When these skills are weak, students may have problems recognizing distinctive features and analyzing plants. Limited exposure to nature and to different plants narrows the knowledge base on which to build new learning and inhibits interest. Prior knowledge of the value of plants facilitates progress: Students from rural areas may have a better appreciation of both food and other cash crops than do students from urban areas; those accustomed to abundant ornamental plants tend to enjoy the purpose and beauty of decorative plants. Students who have never had full responsibility for the care of their own plants may view plants differently than do those with gardening experiences. Without ample real and vicarious experiences, higher level, interdependent concepts are apt to be difficult to master.

Instructional Implications. The study of plants interests students and teachers alike when hands-on experiences are used. Highlighting local flora and crops, particularly food crops, emphasizes the relationships between concepts and the surrounding world and plants and the students themselves. Numerous films, such as the classic time-lapse productions by National Geographic and Disney, can be used as demonstrations. Rural students can share and compare their knowledge and samples in class. Where natural settings for growing plants are limited, nearby atriums, greenhouses, and local experts can provide experiences. Effective instruction provides abundant experiences growing seeds, bulbs, and cuttings and then manipulating conditions and measuring and charting growth. Students can be guided to grow local plants outside the classroom window while ongoing studies of growing plants easily can be conducted in a classroom setting.

CORRECTION Modify strategies for topical and learning needs:

1. *Plant Vocabulary*
     Skills: Observing; listening; reading; communicating
     Limit direct instruction to 3–4 of the most important words for each lesson,
     reviewing old terms each time a new lesson is begun. Embellish students'
     understandings of the most basic terms such as *water, soil, air, light,* and
     seeds by discussing and demonstrating numerous variations of each term.
     Adjacent to plants growing in the classroom, post labels for each part and
     then post daily comments about the parts or the progress of the plants;
     discuss each comment as it is added.

2. *Plant Names*
     Skills: Observing; reading; analyzing; classifying; communicating
     Determine the types of trees, flowers, and indoor plants that are common to
     your area. Present samples and/or pictures and names and have students
     locate the plants in places outside school. Develop a list of local plants,
     adding to the list descriptions and the places where specimens were seen.
     Guide students to describe plants and to analyze their similarities, differ-
     ences, and structures. Have students make small-group or class plant
     booklets of cut-out pictures or photos and printed names with descriptions.
     These booklets can serve as reference books to be added to later.

3. *Plant Families*
     Skills: Observing; analyzing; classifying; evaluating
     Provide or have students find actual samples of leaves or products of several
     types of local trees or food plants; match each sample with a picture or
     specimen of the complete plant. Cue students to observe carefully and
     classify by asking compare and contrast questions: Which one is taller? How
     is this one different from the last one? Can you find 3 ways in which these
     plants are the same or different? Then have students sort the samples
     according to similarities. To extend concepts, guide students to discover how
     each plant is useful to themselves and/or others.

4. *Food Plants*
     Skills: Observing; studying; classifying; predicting; hypothesizing;
             generalizing; evaluating
     Begin by displaying samples of fresh fruits and vegetables. Encourage
     discussion about how they are grown and which foods are grown in the
     region where the students live. Have students predict how each food is grown
     (e.g., above ground, below, on stalks, on trees, and so on), and then verify
     their predictions. After identifying a few foods that are grown locally, have
     students gather information about the plants by observing, listening,
     reading, viewing tapes, or study and research. Form teams or pairs of
     students to search for answers to target questions about regional conditions
     that permit the plants to flourish and then chart their answers. To integrate
     concepts with social studies, guide students to discover the other regions to
     which the local foods are shipped. Repeat the activity for students' favorite
     produce that is not locally grown, but have students determine why the foods
     are not grown in their region.

5. *Food Supply*

> *Skills:* Observing; studying; analyzing; classifying; generalizing; evaluating
> Using the food charts developed for Activity 4, guide students to add food prices from advertisements to identify the change in prices of certain foods over a period of weeks or months; chart and display the information. Prompt students to identify the effects of weather, disease, and seasonal growing periods on prices. Display samples of fresh produce for students to examine or have students grocery shop with their parents. Guide students' observations and compare changes in quality with price changes. Then lead students to chart the times for the best price and quality of several foods. Give older students a wallet-size personal copy of the chart.

6. *Seeds We Eat*

> *Skills:* Observing; classifying; synthesizing; generalizing; evaluating
> Begin by showing students seeds that are safe and good to eat (e.g., a variety of unshelled nuts or sunflower or pumpkin seeds). Guide students to group the seeds by type. Have students taste the meat of each type of seed. Ask: Which types of seeds look the most alike after they are opened? Which one do we spread on bread? Which one has the hardest shell? Which seed would we have to crack the most of to get a pound? Which one tastes best to you? Why? Later, have student teams identify the regions in which seeds are grown, required growing conditions, and when prices and quality are best, and then chart their findings as in Activities 4 and 5. Food pods and pod fruits can also be included or used as follow-up for this experience.

7. *Seeds and Growing Plants*

> *Skills:* Observing; directed experimenting; measuring; predicting; all
> integration skills
> Choose 2–3 different kinds of seeds for students to examine and feel. Discuss and compare size, shape, weight, and texture. Next show pictures of mature plants grown from similar seeds in soil. Provide checklists for planting, caring, and feeding of the plants. Be sure students understand the 4 things seeds need to grow: water, air, food, and warmth. Assign students the responsibility for growing 1–2 soil cups containing 1–3 seeds each. Have students chart water, air, food, and warmth conditions. Help students set up a chart for weekly growth measurements. By having growing areas in several parts of the classroom, different rates of growth may also occur. (At this point, teach photosynthesis to students who can handle it.) Later, repeat the project but have students select the seeds, design the conditions, formulate the hypotheses to test, and evaluate their results.

8. *Plants as Medicine*

> *Skills:* Observing; reading; studying; analyzing; classifying; synthesizing;
> evaluating
> To introduce the concept of using plants as medicine, bring an aloe vera plant to class, break a leaf, and have students examine the sticky substance inside. Show pictures or actual samples of commercial products that contain aloe vera (soap, cosmetics, ointments) and discuss the purported benefits. Check the labels of patent medicines, consult local physicians, and

have students quiz their parents to identify additional medicinal plants. Bring in samples that are locally grown. As in previous activities, guide students to identify and analyze the plants and their benefits and then determine how each can be useful to themselves.

9. *Dangerous Plants*

    Skills: Listening; studying; analyzing; classifying; synthesizing; generalizing; evaluating

    From a local nursery, obtain a list of poisonous and harmful plants indigenous to the area and also include popular houseplants. Post a chart that includes a picture of each plant. Assign 1–2 plants to pairs of students; guide them to search for information that tells where the plant is typically found, the particular part of the plant that is harmful, the effects of contact or ingestion, and treatments to counteract ill effects. (Consult the local poison control center.) Have students tape record or write their data to post on charts. Categories might include: Picture; Plant Name; Where Seen; Bad Part; Effects on Me; Effects on Pets; Treatments. Personalizing effects makes the danger more understandable and memorable. Leave charts posted and have students record their sightings of the plants as they occur and review the dangers.

10. *Parks and Nurseries*

    Skills: Observing; organizing; analyzing; classifying; predicting; generalizing; evaluating

    Before planning a trip to a park or nursery, invite a resource person to explain what is done there and the types of plants involved. Guide students to prepare questions ahead of time. To prepare for the fieldtrip, help students develop an outline to guide them while they tour (what to look for and what questions to ask). Also plan who will be in charge of taking notes and pictures and writing the thank-you note. Assign students the task of identifying 1–3 plants they consider the most desirable based on beauty, utility, hardiness, cost, and care. Arrange for a guide to accompany the students during the tour to help them fill in their outlines as they go. Later, have students discuss and defend their choices of desirable plants.

11. *Reliance on Plants*

    Skills: Studying; analyzing; predicting; synthesizing; generalizing; evaluating

    To stress the reliance of humans and animals on plants, play No Plants. Set up a simulation in which all plant life is destroyed. Have teams of students decide what people and animals will eat, what will happen to the air and ground, how fish will breathe and eat, and/or where birds will live. The complexity of the simulation depends upon the knowledge and abilities of the students, but numerous options and types of activities are possible. Have teams present their solutions to peers to evaluate.

12. *Extra Practice.* • To extend Activity 7, have students order seeds from a catalog, plant them outside the classroom window, and monitor conditions and growth. • To extend Activity 4, take students to visit a food-producing area to observe and interview growers to discover how to grow a particular food.

2. ANIMALS

DETECTION Mastery of key concepts may be difficult for students who:
- Do not observe carefully
- Cannot classify or predict
- Have had few experiences with domestic or farm animals
- Cannot explain the interdependence of humans and animals

Description. The study of animals can be one of the most interesting topics that students encounter in science. Animals are particularly easy for most students to classify because of prior familiarity and understanding of some of the more common species. Concepts to be built include the differences among and within animal species, their basic needs, their adaptations to their environments, the nature of the relationship between animals and humans, and the responsibility of humans for animals. Additional concepts to consider are vertebrates and invertebrates, carnivores and herbivores, and for advanced students detailed characteristics of the various animal groups, orders, families, genera, and unfamiliar species.

Special Problems. Students who have difficulties understanding animals are often those who have had limited real experiences with domestic or farm animals. Children who live in urban areas and have not owned or played with pets are often less knowledgeable than those who live in rural areas or who own pets. However, since at least some types of animals are or can become an important part of the daily experiences of most children, weak skills need not interfere with understanding if observation, classification, analysis, and prediction skills are directly taught and topical relevance emphasized.

Instructional Implications. Understanding animals contributes to the overall understanding of life. Responsibility for the care of pets or farm animals is an important facilitative experience. These experiences should be provided in the classroom and parents should be encouraged to provide similar experiences at home. Assuming responsibility for the care of a nonjudgmental and responsive animal can be a therapeutic activity that teaches children a variety of positive attitudes and is reported to enhance self-concept in many cases. Such care also emphasizes the personal relevance of animals to the students involved. When handling animals in the classroom, it is important to stress humane treatment and then supervise the students to insure that neither animals nor students are injured. Students who live in rural areas often view animals differently than do those who live in urban areas; these differences should be discussed, with emphasis on the interdependence of humans and farm, wild, and domestic animals. Students also need to know the circumstances under which animals should be avoided. Experimentation is seldom advisable (and in some cases is illegal), except perhaps in demonstrations such as how behaviors are learned and then only under strict supervision and controlled conditions. Important learning experiences include the care and observation of pets, snails, crickets, worms, fruit flies, amphibians, and the like to identify, analyze, classify, and study, predict, and chart behavior.

CORRECTION Modify strategies for topical and learning needs.

1. *Basic Animal Vocabulary*
    Skills: Observing; listening; reading; communicating
    Teach vocabulary words as they occur in class discussions, using proce-
    dures described in Chapter 3. At the most basic level, these words might
    include: *big, little, feet, number words, color words, animal sounds, live,
    breathe, hair, fur,* etc. As students progress, teach additional and more
    technical terms in context.
2. *Animal Names*
    Skills: Observing; listening; analyzing; classifying; communicating;
        generalizing
    Ask: What is an animal? How do you know one when you see one? Then, as
    students name animals and their characteristics, draw or display a picture
    of each. Ask students for an explanation of how they know each is an animal.
    Guide them to discover the characteristics of animals by comparing the
    examples. Later, have students collect pictures of animals from magazines,
    newspapers, or discarded texts; display, discuss, and label all pictures that
    students bring, emphasizing distinguishing features.
3. *Animal Classification*
    Skills: Observing; analyzing; classifying; communicating; generalizing
    Using live animals or pictures of familiar animals, guide students to first
    compare, then contrast, and finally classify animals. Provide group (or class)
    labels such as Mammals, Birds, and Reptiles. Place a picture or name of an
    example with each label and then question students until they describe a few
    characteristics of each group; list several of their key descriptive words for
    each group. Emphasize similarities and differences of structure and func-
    tion across and within categories using graphic aids such as Venn diagrams.
    After a few animals are placed in each category, guide students to summarize
    the characteristics of each group and then generalize their findings to new
    examples. Follow similar procedures as students add pictures or names to
    each group. For future reference, record the information on audiotape and
    post a summary chart.
4. *Animal Homes*
    Skills: Observing; analyzing; classifying; communicating; synthesizing;
        generalizing
    Ask: What do you have to have to live and be safe in your home? What do you
    want to have that will make you comfortable in your home? Lead a
    discussion of the students' basic needs for shelter and their wants for
    comfort. On the board, a transparency, or a chart, list or illustrate their
    suggestions under either Need or Want. Next, ask: How do you think animals
    decide where to live? What do they want to be comfortable? Using a familiar
    animal as an example, make a list of needs and wants. Then, show films of
    animals in their natural habitats. Chart each animal's needs and wants.
    Lead a discussion of why animals choose to live with their own kind by asking
    why different animals would not live together (e.g., prairie dogs and birds;

zebras and goats; or tuna and cats). To extend the activity, consider fieldtrips or videotapes of: • a walk around the neighborhood or in the woods to observe the homes of birds, squirrels, rabbits, etc.; list characteristics of the observed homes and compare to students' lists • a visit to the zoo to compare the students' lists with the provisions made for the animals there; then evaluate the zoo homes • a visit to a pet store to observe and evaluate the temporary homes there.

Use this activity periodically throughout the school year to increase students' awareness and understanding of the basic needs of animals and to compare and contrast the needs of animals and humans. This activity can also add to the study of communities and societies in social studies.

5. *Animal Friends and Foes*

Skills: Observing; predicting; communicating; generalizing; evaluating
Read aloud a news article or story, show a film, or tell of an incident in which a human was harmed by an animal. Then ask: What caused this accident? How could it have been prevented? To bring out points—such as animals that are typically friendly to humans, the importance of the animals' past experiences, the state of the animals' health, and most importantly people's behaviors that encourage animals to be friendly—read aloud short stories for emphasis. Use probing questions such as: Why would animals want you for a friend? How do you know which animals could be your friends? Which animals should you avoid? Why? As each point is discussed, restate it and then chart it under such headings as Animal Friends, Animal Foes or Enemies, How to Make Friends, What Makes Animals Unfriendly, or perhaps When Animals Are Sick. Encourage students to find related incidents or stories to tell, read, or have you read. Guide students to summarize each incident and add to the chart; then summarize the chart to generalize simple rules for handling animals. As an ongoing project, this activity builds important survival concepts that special students need to know.

6. *Animal Care*

Skills: Observing; listening; analyzing; predicting; communicating;
generalizing; evaluating
Tell or read aloud an anecdote about the consequences of not knowing how to care for an animal (e.g., the child who fed her pet rabbit so much lettuce that the rabbit became ill). Then, plan a visit to a pet store, zoo, or farm, or have a resource person bring a few animals to the classroom. To prepare for the experience, read to students about the needs and characteristics of the chosen animals; guide students to develop a list of questions to ask and points to observe that will help them conclude how to care for the animals. Later, guide students to develop a simple list of rules for animal care. Next, describe situations that the students might encounter or present real problems, such as: • If you can prove you know how to care for a puppy, Jim will bring his puppy to visit our class next week. • I will bring a guinea pig to serve as the classroom mascot if you can describe exactly how to care for it. • A baby bird has fallen from its nest; what should you do? How can you find out? • A bird has a broken wing; what should you do? • Angel's dog

followed her to school; what should she do? Why? • Have you ever had a problem caring for an animal? Tell about it.

Guide the students to list the steps they should follow to solve each problem. At a learning, center provide the tools for students to find the needed information (e.g., films, audiotapes, questions to ask resource people, etc.). To avoid overwhelming students, investigate the care of only 1–2 animals at a time; then repeat the activity with new animals. Classify each new animal as it is discussed and add its picture or name to a classification chart.

7. *Animal Mascot*

Skills: Observing; measuring; predicting; generalizing; evaluating

As an extension of the study of animal care, adopt an animal as the class mascot. Prior to the young pet's arrival, present films, books, tapes, and the like that discuss the characteristics, needs, and wants, of the animal and what constitutes responsible care. Summarize important points with the students, prepare a home for the mascot, and post Rules for Care of Our Mascot at a center. Plan who will take care of the pet during holidays and at the end of the year. Then, once the mascot is settled, assign care duties as well as observation tasks that include measurement of sleep, play, growth, and behavior changes and then prediction and hypotheses.

8. *Animal Inquiry Center*

Skills: Observing; studying; measuring; communicating; synthesizing; hypothesizing; generalizing; evaluating

Place at a supervised center an ant farm, an aquarium with fish, a snake, or insects, or a cage with a rabbit or gerbils. Provide a time each day for 1–3 students to observe the animals for 5–10 minutes; plan feedings, wake-up, or arousal periods for the animals to coincide with observation times. Designate a specific purpose for each observation, and give students a checklist of elements to analyze. Activities at this center are the heart of animal study in the classroom; the possibilities for teaching and reinforcing essential skills and concepts are limited only by the age, interest, and ability levels of the students and the purposes set.

9. *Extra Practice.* • To extend Activities 2–5, ask students to watch for animals on TV and either list or have a family member list the animals and some key characteristics to share with classmates. • Have students make up a story about their favorite animal, tell or write the story, and post it for peers to read. • Encourage students to add incidents to a file of Special Tips for Activity 5 (e.g., Eye contact may make a menacing dog attack.). • Have students develop problems to solve or observation tasks for Activities 7–8. • Have students interview a resource person about the care of animals and report to peers. • As an extension of Activity 8, have students study, measure, and write or tape record the behaviors of pets at home; plan times for sharing the findings.

3. THE HUMAN BODY

DETECTION Mastery of key concepts may difficult for students who:

- Demonstrate limited self-awareness
- Display poor health and hygiene habits
- Have difficulty analyzing
- Have problems hypothesizing
- Cannot explain the value of understanding the human body

Description. This is probably the most relevant topic for all students, but it is especially critical for special students. Understanding the human body lays the foundation on which to build health and safety concepts and lifelong practices. Basic topics include the study of bones, muscles, senses, organs, systems, and although not covered here sex education. The information is often technical; descriptions and explanations of body systems, parts, and functions can be difficult to simplify, particularly for establishing personal relevance. Recognizing and describing related functions of body parts, reading and study, and communicating ideas about the human body are often difficult for students to express.

Special Problems. Because the human body is so complex, many adults understand relatively little about it and special students know significantly less. Misconceptions abound, particularly in the minds of students who receive little or no accurate information from home. Students who display poor health and hygiene habits are likely to experience particular difficulty mastering the content because of competing concepts. Adult oversight, stemming from the supposition that the complexities of the body are too far over the heads of youngsters, may be the cause of insufficient background knowledge. Physically or medically handicapped students may be knowledgeable about their specific problems but not necessarily informed about the body in general. The particularly difficult vocabulary and personal nature of the information make some students and adults uncomfortable. For example, the use of chicken muscle and bone for study may alarm some students to the point of avoidance. Using raw chicken requires additional care to see that students wash hands thoroughly and do not eat the meat.

Instructional Implications. Although the human body is worthy of years of intense study, both content and lessons can and should be based on the students' need to know and experiential backgrounds. Help students understand that the body contributes to an overall positive sense of self and is the basis for developing good health and safety habits. For the information to be useful, concepts must be directly related to each student personally. The extensive use of simple, concrete examples and manipulative models to provide visual, hands-on activities for students facilitates mastery. For example, both structure and function can be clearly illustrated by using various types of disarticulated skeletons. It may be necessary to explain many body-related functions in simplistic terms. Labeling of information and frequent oral or written student feedback is recommended.

CORRECTION Modify these strategies for topical and learning needs.

1. *Body Builders*

    Skills: Observing; analyzing; classifying; communicating

    Much of the terminology involving the human body is specialized. Many common examples should be used to explain ideas, parts, and functions of the body. Terms also should be directly associated with pictures to show relationships, concepts, and personal relevance. Such words as *circulation, joint, nose, ear, eye, skin, leg, hand,* and *muscle* can be related by picture or personal identification. Internal organs and systems can be demonstrated using models, simple drawings, examples, or videotapes of some of the excellent programs on a cable medical network. (Delete the sound to avoid the technical dialogue.) By using a straw to represent a blood vessel or a door hinge to represent a hinge joint, students will develop concrete ideas to relate to terminology and concepts.

2. *Which Bone?*

    Skills: Observing; studying; analyzing; classifying; communicating; generalizing; evaluating

    Bones are the support system of the body. Demonstrate how students can carefully position their fingers to locate different bones in their bodies (e.g., ankle, chin, knee, elbow, and so on). Then, display a model or diagram of the skeletal system. Use Velcro tabs or pins to place namecards on the skeleton to label specific bones. For associative practice, try oral cloze exercises in a game format by having students follow your prompts to place the labels on the appropriate bones and also discuss both function and relevance: The large bone between your wrist and elbow is called _____?_____; you need it because _____?_____; without it you could not _____?_____. For extension, have students think of a certain number of activities that could not be conducted if particular bones were injured. Encourage discussion in a playful manner, but emphasize structure and function.

3. *Muscle Power*

    Skills: Observing; analyzing; predicting; generalizing; evaluating

    Concepts to stress include: Muscles can only stretch and pull, not push; they are used to move the body and, in general, work in pairs or groups to move the skeleton; systematic use strengthens muscles; and overuse causes pain. Use several different sizes of rubber bands to illustrate the varied sizes and shapes of muscles and to demonstrate the pull-not-push action. For example, use a thin, small rubber band and a thicker, longer band and ask students: Which band do you think would work better in a leg? How would it work? Point out where muscles can be felt, such as on the calf portion of the leg, have students move that muscle, and then describe the action. Use pictures and diagrams to emphasize that muscles are somewhat like several bands stretched over the body and to reinforce the actions as students move. To illustrate how muscles are strengthened, gently stretch new rubber bands until they become flexible; overstretch the bands to illustrate why muscles become sore with overuse. Verbalize your muscle actions as you move about the room and encourage students to do likewise.

4. *Using Your Senses*

    Skills: Observing; directed experimenting; analyzing; predicting; classifying; generalizing; evaluating

Establishing the relevance of sensory organs is usually no problem because their functions can be readily observed and personally experienced. There are a variety of ways to provide practical experiences using the 5 senses of tasting, touching, seeing, hearing, and smelling, but in each case, the role of the senses in acquiring information should be stressed. As a matter of good practice, identify and then avoid students' known allergies and dietary restrictions. Accompany each experience with diagrams to depict parts and functions, working models or videotapes to illuminate concepts, and labels and verbalization of the process occurring, first by the teacher and then by students. Conclude each experience with verbalization of how each sense contributes to acquiring information, self-knowledge, and life enrichment.

    Taste. To illustrate the 4 different tastes (sweet, salty, sour, and bitter), use 4 containers of water with additives such as salt, sugar, lemon, and vinegar. Dip a cotton swab into each liquid, apply to the tongue, and ask students to identify each taste. Provide diagrams showing the 4 regions of the tongue that detect different tastes (tip of the tongue for sweet; front sides salty; back sides sour; and back center bitter). Have students follow the diagram as they repeat the tasting to verify.

    Touch. Create a Touch Box or Feeling Bag filled with several textured objects; have students take turns describing and then guessing what they feel inside the box or bag; conclude with discussions of how touch assists them to understand.

    Sight. Show a black-and-white picture and a color picture of a similar scene or object and have students discuss and compare. Shine a flashlight across the room with the lights off and then with the lights on; discuss why the light seems brighter in a dark than in a lighted room. Next, have students observe in a mirror the change in their eyes as you move a light toward them; lead a discussion of the purpose of changes in size of the eye's pupil with a question like: Why do you wear sunglasses? Follow with lessons on eye safety and care.

    Sound. Begin with a discussion of the sounds students consider the most pleasant and unpleasant. Use a variety of supervised experiments to demonstrate that vibrations cause sound and to introduce the concepts of quality, pitch, and intensity and the causes of their variance. Stringed musical instruments, rubber bands, tuning forks, small objects on a drum, and simple flutes can be manipulated for illustration. Guide students to verbalize what is occurring in each case. Then present a diagram of the ear and verbalize each step of the auditory perception process as students repeat their experiments. Conclude with lessons on the long-term effects of loud music or industrial noises and proper care of the ears.

    Smell. Demonstrate the function of smell in tasting by having students compare taste when they hold their noses and when they do not while eating; discuss the implications for eating something pleasant or unpleasant or for tasting when students have a cold. Call attention to the odors from the school cafeteria and identify the ones that make students hungry and those that do not; discuss associations and effects on appetite. Have students smell several perfumes and then discuss why the latter fragrances are not as distinct. With some students, this also may be a good point at which to introduce discussions of unpleasant body odors and personal hygiene.

5. *Organs*

Skills: Observing; listening; directed experimenting; evaluating
The specific organs selected for study depend on the needs of students; of particular interest and importance are the brain and lungs. Lessons for most organs can be presented much the same as this one for the heart.

The Heart. The key idea to stress is the central role of the heart to all that the human body does. Explain that the heart pumps blood all over the body. Display pictures and diagrams to illustrate the parts and their functions, introducing such terms as *atrium, valve,* and *ventricle,* if appropriate. To demonstrate the action of the heart, use a silent videotape from a cable medical network. As students view the tape, supply your own dialogue to fit the ages and abilities of students; while viewing, have students feel their own beating hearts. Have the school nurse help students listen to their own hearts through a stethoscope. Have students compare pulse rates after sitting quietly, running, and walking.

6. *Systems*

Skills: Observing; analyzing; predicting; evaluating
Complex systems should be taught in as much detail as students can handle and need to know for maintaining health and safety. Both filmed simulations and simple demonstrations with common objects may be used as in this presentation of the circulatory system.

Circulation. Important concepts are the functions of the system: to distribute food and oxygen throughout the body; to fight disease; to regulate body temperature; to remove waste; and to interact and help maintain the functions of the heart and lungs. The power of the system can be illustrated by the vast amount of information revealed by a single blood sample (e.g., SMAC test) and can be presented by a local nurse or physician. Microscopic study of blood is usually of interest to students. A clear straw can be used to illustrate how blood travels through the body and what happens to circulation with distortion or blockage.

7. *Extra Practice.* • Have students find pictures of other items that function much like the bones in the human body. • On a regular basis, feature a secret taste, touch, sight, sound, or smell for students to identify and then confirm. • To extend the study of organs and systems, have students collect news articles about discoveries to record or write for peers to retell in their own words. • Invite a local physician or nurse to visit the class; have students prepare a list of questions about the proper care of organs or systems and then take turns asking 1 question each. • Guide students to make human models where they use their bodies as parts. • Help students use clay to create models of organs or systems and then tell how they work.

CHAPTER 5 /
ECOLOGICAL CONCERNS

4. LAND

DETECTION Mastery of key concepts may be difficult for students who:

- Do not observe carefully
- Have difficulty predicting, generalizing, and/or evaluating
- Have very limited experiences outdoors
- Are unaware of land preservation strategies
- Cannot explain the value of land to self and society

Description. The study of land preservation involves responsible care for ground areas of soil, rock, or earth as well as trees, grass, crops, and vegetation. Students need not be avid campers or nature lovers to appreciate the reasons for better land use. Improper methods of farming, mining, and waste disposal, irresponsible construction practices, harsh weather, inadequate precautionary measures, and careless use of land for recreation all contribute to the problems of contamination, erosion, and destruction of land.

Special Problems. This topic is difficult to teach because the time span from cause to visible effect is often lengthy and because land abuse includes acts of omission as well as commission. Immediate interests interfere with some students recognizing that what is done today will affect others tomorrow. Predicting and visualizing consequences about future effects of current land usage is not easy. Because in many cases the students themselves will not experience the effects of current land usage, they may resist instruction. Students from farming communities are often more attuned to soil conservation than are students from urban areas. Students with untrained observation skills may not notice the effects of previous land misuse or connect the effects with an unseen cause. Unless consequences are demonstrated and directly related to cause, students may not consider this topic important.

Instructional Implications. Begin by using familiar and local examples of land abuse—situations that are obvious and that negatively affect students or someone they know. For example, the mudpuddles that linger for several days on the playground and the consequences of fire or severe weather should be considered before examples that are less familiar. The connection between cause and effect must be illustrated as clearly and concretely as possible. Scaled-down or simulated experiments (e.g., dig out a small area of the playground to simulate strip mining) offer quick demonstrations of cause and effect. For this topic, societal relevance is the dominant concept, with personal relevance primarily limited to feeling good about oneself as a responsible citizen. Integrated study of land preservation with social studies lessons is logical and may facilitate recognition of societal implications.

CORRECTION Modify strategies for topical and learning needs:

1. *Building Land-Related Vocabulary*
   Skills: Observing; analyzing; communicating; synthesizing; generalizing
   Select a topic each week or 2 and post pictures showing positive and/or negative land use practices: landfills, irrigation systems, drainage projects, and other constructive land projects and/or litter, erosion, dump sites, and additional examples of land abuse. Post 2–3 key words under each picture. Discuss the picture using the vocabulary. After a few pictures and words are displayed, review by going back to previously posted pictures and tying these into a new picture problem or solution.

2. *Changing Shapes*
   Skills: Observing; studying; classifying; predicting; communicating; evaluating
   In most communities, the appearance of the land has changed over time and continues to change. Locate old pictures of the community. Have students guess the area depicted in each picture. Next, show photos of the same locations as they presently appear. (Take photos or have the class visit the locations.) Discuss the changes and predict future changes. Then have students evaluate the changes in terms of appeal, usefulness, and preservation or destruction of the land. Take photos at regular intervals of any local building, mining, or farming projects currently in progress and have students discuss, compare, and evaluate why land use varies at different times and the effects the changes will have on their lives.

3. *Types of Soil*
   Skills: Observing; analyzing; measuring; evaluating
   Bring to class samples of different types of soil, such as sand, clay based, garden soil, and others. Have students compare the textures and appearances. Use a magnifying glass for careful examination. Assist students in taking notes, analyzing, and discussing differences in color, weight, density, smell, texture, moisture, and composition. The extent of analysis should be determined by the knowledge and ability levels of students and the sophistication of the classroom equipment.

4. *Moisture Retention*
   Skills: Observing; directed experimenting; measuring; predicting; generalizing; independent experimenting; evaluating
   Assist students to prepare soil containers with which to determine moisture absorption. First, cut the bottom from several pint-size milk cartons. Then place each carton on a doubled paper towel and set the towel-bottomed cartons over a piece of screen, such as the type used in screen doors and windows. The screen should be resting on a glass jar or beaker to permit students to see how quickly water seeps through each type of soil. Next, using samples of different soils taken from the area surrounding the school, the students' homes, and their community, pack a 3–5-inch layer of soil in each milk carton. Add 4–6 tablespoons of water to the top of each soil sample. 1) Measure how long the water takes to soak through and drip to the bottom;

2) determine which type of soil seems to absorb the most water; and 3) identify which type absorbs the least water. Guide students to analyze the soil in each carton to determine factors that contribute to absorption. Then give students a choice of several settings (e.g., lakebed, beanfield, roadbed, landfill site, and playground) and have them decide, based on water absorption, which soil sample would be best suited for each. Guide student teams to develop and conduct soil experiments and then share and compare results.

5. *Soil Analysis*

Skills: Observing; studying; directed experimenting; analyzing; classifying; predicting; all integration skills

Soil must often be modified to obtain the proper content and balance for growing particular plants or crops. Invite a soil analyst from a local farm agency to explain soil analysis and demonstrate the process by involving students in the analysis of the soil from their schoolyard. Before the visit, have students suggest 3–5 specific flowers and crops that might be grown outside the classroom window. After the soil analysis, have the speaker describe the soil modifications, weather conditions, and care required to grow the chosen plants. Have students critique the value of soil analysis to plant growers and then evaluate the needed soil modifications to decide on the flower and crop most likely to flourish. Later, guide students to grow a few samples of each. Encourage independent experimentation by systemati- cally varying the soil modifications.

6. *Soil Conservation*

Skills: Observing; directed experimenting; analyzing; predicting; generalizing

Use a clear plastic cup as a planter and punch 2–3 small holes in the bottom. Fill the cup with soil and a very small plant or a few seeds. As the plant grows, encourage students to observe how the roots grow in the soil and hold it together. After several weeks, loosen the soil from around the sides of the glass and carefully remove the plant. Then discuss the soil clinging to the roots and the concept that crops, trees, grass, and root systems help hold the soil and keep it from washing away. Have each student identify 3–5 places in the community where vegetation is preventing erosion. Have students photograph, draw, or describe orally or in writing each of his or her sites to share with peers. A game format also can be used wherein each student orally describes the sites for peers to guess.

7. *Land Preservation*

Skills: Observing; listening; reading; analyzing; communicating; hypothesizing; generalizing

As a food source, for recreation, and for environmental reasons, natural settings must be visited, seen, and enjoyed to be appreciated. Fieldtrips, films, pictures, and TV programs can be used to develop a positive point of view. Involve students in talking about "what could happen if . . ." or why preservation of the local park or forest is helpful to people and animals. Note that sportsmen, commercial developers, and employees who depend on land usage often view land conservation differently than do farmers, campers, or environmentalists. Have students debate the most appropriate land usage from both viewpoints. For example: Is destroying a park to build a hospital an appropriate use of land? Ask students to suggest alternatives: How would removing the largest trees from the mountainside affect your life in the valley? Who would favor the logging project? Why? What about cutting trees from the forest to make way for a new and shorter road? Draw the content for debate from real or hypothetical local issues. Have students evaluate the conclusions in terms of immediate effects and long-range effects on people, animals, and plants.

8. *Misuse of Land*

   Skills: Observing; studying; organizing; communicating; synthesizing; generalizing; evaluating

   Display videotapes or photos of specific scenes in the local community showing litter, abandoned cars, burned property, waste dumps, and other unkept or misused property. Have students first consider the implications of such scenes in terms of present and future consequences, including air and water contamination and appearance. Then guide them to consider ways to improve existing conditions. If they are unable to think of solutions, suggest 2–3 ideas and have them decide which would be the best.

9. *Waste Recycling*

   Skills: Observing; studying; analyzing; all integration skills

   As a class or independent project, recycling activities can improve local conditions, increase awareness and commitment, raise money, and actively involve students in the learning process. Since recycling projects are also important lessons in citizenship, they should be paired with lessons in social studies. Present the concept of recycling as a solution to some types of land abuse. Beginning with the trash can in the classroom and moving to garbage from the school cafeteria, students' homes, and litter along the roads to and from school, have students identify the types of trash that can be recycled instead of left to litter or contaminate the land. Videotape some local scenes, including the local garbage dump, for additional examples. As students identify each item, guide them to investigate its recycling potential through study, analysis, and interviews. Use news items to present the array of possible projects (e.g., garbage for fuel or organic matter for fertilizer) and consider inviting resource people to explain different recycling processes. This may be a good point at which to discuss trash that cannot be recycled and will not rapidly decompose (e.g., certain types of plastic). Then have students decide on a manageable large-group project or a few small-group projects recycling items such as aluminum cans, paper trash, or glass bottles, and determine how any revenues will be used. Environmental improvements, not earnings, should be emphasized.

10. *Extra Practice.* • Have students retell orally or in writing news reports about the effects of weather on land. • Assign pairs of students to develop scrapbooks of Land Gifts showing the natural resources that come from the land; use the scrapbooks as a stimulus for extended land study. • Have student teams develop Gifts to Land scrapbooks depicting what the students themselves are doing to preserve land in the local community.

5. WATER

DETECTION   Mastery of key concepts may be difficult for students who:
- Have only experienced clean and plentiful water
- Demonstrate problems observing, analyzing, and/or predicting
- Are unaware of water pollutants
- Cannot describe the importance of clean water to self and society

Description. Clean water is essential to health and is a topic that students usually enjoy studying. Content includes the study of water sources, uses of water, evaporation, pollution, purification, and the water cycle itself. To narrow the scope of study to the most essential consumer elements, this section primarily focuses on the use of water as a source of drinking and everyday use. Instruction also can be integrated with water-related topics such as the study of living things, recreation, natural resources, and transportation. Important skills include observation, directed experimenting, analysis, measurement, classification, prediction, and all integration skills.

Special Problems. Even though water is essential for sustaining life, many people take for granted the availability of clean water. Many students and adults as well are unaware of where the water they use comes from, the nature of its quality, or what is happening to water supplies worldwide. Some of those who are aware may be unwilling to assume responsibility for monitoring, maintaining, and improving water supplies. When pollution is a major and documented threat to the welfare of humans, animals, or plants through the contamination of a well on the farm, a nearby fishing lake, or a river supplying local homes, remedies are sought. However, the average consumer usually judges water by surface not scientific qualities: When drinking water looks, smells, and tastes good to a person, concern is usually minimal irrespective of the quality of the water; conversely, an obvious taint to the look, smell, or taste of water, no matter how harmless, often receives immediate attention. Thus, concern for clean water typically develops from a personal concern for satisfaction and comfort, health, and safety. Students from uninformed or unconcerned families may lack essential background knowledge and attitudes. The major interference with concept mastery stems from indifference toward water, a seemingly free and plentiful element.

Instructional Implications. From one perspective, water may be easier for students to learn about than air because water is more tangible. Since students regularly see, smell, taste, and touch water, they are aware of their experiences with it. It is important to focus first on local water concerns and issues. Clean water, water supplies, and energy-related uses of water should be explained in terms of immediacy and value in day-to-day events. Water problems in other regions can be used to accent the problems that students may face in a few years. Students must be led to realize their roles and responsibilities as consumers and custodians. Numerous demonstrations and hands-on experiences should be used to teach concepts such as water changing form, the interrelationship of water and air, and ways to keep water clean.

CORRECTION Modify strategies for topical and learning needs:

1. *Water Words*
      Skills: Listening; reading; predicting; synthesizing
      Begin a class listing of water-related words to be used in reading about and
      discussing water. *Air* could be used along with *Water* as headings and then
      related words listed under either heading. A middle heading could be used
      for words that can be associated with both water and air (e.g., Pollution,
      Contaminated, or Conservation). Under*Water*, list words like *purifying,
      evaporation, erosion, table* or *cycle, acid rain, reservoir, filtering, settling,* and
      dissolves as they are studied. As each word is listed, guide students to state
      what each means personally or how they will use the concepts; list 1–2 of
      these meanings beside each term and display the list.

2. *Water Sources*
      Skills: Observing; studying; predicting; communicating; generalizing
      Ask: Where does your water come from? Move from immediate sources to
      actual sources such as wells, lakes, and springs. Use the chalkboard to
      sketch the chain beginning from, for example, the school water fountain
      back through a pipe to the town watertower or perhaps a water treatment
      plant and nearby river. Guide students to construct a similar map for their
      water at home. This is a good point at which to introduce the interaction of
      plants, animals, humans, and the water cycle (see Activity 3, Topic 7).

3. *Drinking Water*
      Skills: Observing; listening; directed experimenting; analyzing;
                 classifying; evaluating
      Help students understand and judge differences in drinking water by
      conducting an informal taste test. Use samples of bottled water, spring
      water, or other safe treated or natural water. Then obtain a sample of the
      drinking water in the school. Label the samples but do not disclose which
      is which at first. Have students compare the samples for color, clearness,
      smell, and taste. Then ask students to rate or rank the samples, chart their
      findings, defend their ratings, and discuss differences.

4. *Water Purity*
      Skills: Observing; analysis; communicating; generalizing; evaluating
      Have teams of 3 students collect water samples from at least 3 sources, such
      as home, school, and a mudpuddle. Have all team members view samples
      under a microscope. Then designate one team member as Describer, a
      second as Artist, and a third as Recorder. The Describer should again view
      each sample and orally describe what is seen, while the Artist sketches the
      sample from the description; the Recorder should retell on tape or write a
      summary of each sample. After all samples are analyzed, the sketches and
      recordings should be compared. Although the school samples are from the
      same source, differences will be noted because of variance in the time and
      exact locations of samples and perceivers' tastes. Guide students to identify
      and then evaluate impurities through demonstrations and directed study.
      To extend concepts, invite a resource speaker as in Activity 10 or use this
      activity to introduce certain chemicals or single-cell life.

5. *Evaporation and Impurities*

   Skills: Observing; directed experimenting; predicting; generalizing

   To illustrate that some water impurities cannot be seen or smelled, mix 2 teaspoons of salt in a quart of water for students to taste. Fill a plate with the salt water and let it stand for a day or so. Direct students' attention to the evaporating water and the salt crystals left. Guide them to speculate about events and then view the crystals under a microscope. Explain that salts are only one type of mineral often found in water and that the potential danger depends upon the type and quantity of salt. (Lightly explain evaporation, but focus on the water contents.) Ask: Does your water contain any salts? How can you find out? Guide students to repeat procedures using local water.

6. *Purifying Water*

   Skills: Observing; directed experimenting; synthesizing; evaluating

   Have a student add a tablespoon of dirt to a glass of water and stir. Ask: Would you like to drink this? Why? How could this happen to your water? What else could get into your water? How? Cover the glass of dirty water and let it stand undisturbed until the next day. Then ask: What happened to the water? Where is the dirt? How could what you have just observed be used to improve water? Stir the water and pour it through a water filter into another glass. Direct students' attention to the dirty filter and clarified water. Guide students to conclude the implications for water treatment plants and then evaluate the use of home water purifiers.

7. *Uses of Pure Water*

   Skills: Observing; studying; classifying; communicating; generalizing

   Begin by citing 2 uses of pure water (e.g., making ice, cleaning contact lens). Ask students to name other uses and then name uses for which dirty water is adequate (e.g., cleaning the driveway). Keep a list on a chart. Have students add to the list by studying or observing at home. Then list products that contain pure water. Conclude by discussing and then ranking products by greatest need in a simulated water shortage.

8. *Conservation Concepts*

   Skills: Observing; studying; analyzing; communicating; generalizing

   After giving a few examples, help students think of ways in which they personally can help conserve water and limit water pollution. Begin with examples of local places and situations: Alison left the water fountain on; what should you do and why? Guy needs to throw out the dirty water after washing the boards; what should he do and why? Angel put her mouth on the water fountain; what should you do and why? Then move to larger issues that affect the total community. Conclude with a review of the situations and the impact of students' actions on themselves and others.

9. *What If . . .?*

   Skills: Listening; analyzing; predicting; synthesizing; generalizing

   Use a problem/solution format involving potential water pollution to help students consider options for preventing potential or existing pollution.

When possible, present real problems of local significance or use simulations. For example: A proposal for building a new bridge would mean cutting through many acres of a protected wetland area. The river would be diverted at one point and a new road built along a riverbank area known for slides and erosion. Along with 2 other bridges that already exist, the new one would enable the town to double its capacity for traffic from across the river. What problems might the new bridge cause? Could more traffic increase pollution or other inconveniences? Can you think of better alternatives to building a new bridge?

10. *Personal Appearances*

Skills: Listening; organizing; communicating; synthesizing; evaluating
Invite a local person from a water treatment facility or health department to speak in class. Ask the resource person to bring both pictures and actual samples to class and specify the knowledge and ability levels of students and particular points to emphasize. Help students develop a list of questions to ask and designate which students should ask specific questions. Before the presentation, arrange questions in logical order and then give all students copies of the questions, leaving partial blanks for answers; also make a copy of the questions on a transparency. During the presentation, as answers are stated, have students record them in the partial blanks, focusing on content, not mechanics; after the presentation, have students ask any remaining questions and record the answers on their pages as you model the process on the transparency. When the speaker leaves, guide students to use their answers to retell the major points in their own words.

11. *Water Pollutants*

Skills: Observing; analyzing; classifying; all integration skills
To illustrate ways in which water becomes contaminated, show pictures and discuss disposal of waste that may be destined for bodies of water. Follow with photos of situations that contribute to water pollution in the local area. Sewage disposal plants and practices, disposal of factory waste, chemical waste in sealed containers close to water sources, and even candid shots of individuals as they dump trash beside or in local waterways could be shown and described as potential polluters. In each case, have students identify the picture or photo, tell as much as they know about it, and describe what they personally might do to remedy the problem and avoid the tainted water. If possible, have students visit the sites of the photos and conduct interviews to verify pollution and the methods used to control it. Consider taking water samples for analysis and experimentation. Guide students to develop a list of local practices that are the most problematic to themselves and others. Post the list and seek additions throughout the year. As students discover them, ask them to draw, describe, and/or photograph additional local scenes that may cause water pollution.

12. *Extra Practice.* • Have students explain or predict how dangerous liquids might leak from sealed containers into the water supply. • Have teams investigate advantages and disadvantages of adding fluorine to water. • Modify these activities to study air, land, energy, and natural resources.

6. AIR

DETECTION Mastery of key concepts may be difficult for students who:

- Have limited experience observing or studying about the air
- Do not observe carefully
- Have problems analyzing, predicting, or generalizing
- Demonstrate a limited knowledge about air and its importance
- Cannot explain the importance of clean air to self or society

Description. The study of air includes learning about what is in this colorless gas, its uses, and the things that pollute it. Many students take air for granted because it is always there and is not typically seen or felt. To understand air, students are required to observe carefully, analyze, predict, generalize, and evaluate both the personal and societal relevance of clean air.

Special Problems. Two major reasons to become knowledgeable about air involve pollution and comfort. Students who live in relatively unpolluted areas, like some rural areas, may not think much about the air. Fresh air has a natural smell and a clean, clear appearance. When this changes, people begin to notice. Because air is not easy to see or touch, students may tend to find its existence difficult to understand. An empty glass is not empty because it is full of air; this sounds like double-talk to some students unless concrete explanations can be provided. Difficulty is also caused for students who do not understand that oxygen is needed for humans and animals to breathe and that plants use carbon dioxide from the air to make oxygen. Air that is visibly contaminated (e.g., smog) or that has the unpleasant odor of chemicals from a nearby factory is much easier for students to conceptualize than is air laden with unseen pollen or odorless chemicals. Students who have experienced difficulty breathing because of allergy-, physical-, or infection-related problems are generally more aware of the importance and existence of air or oxygen.

Instructional Implications. Since each human breathes approximately 10,000 liters of air daily, the quality of that air is a major issue. Students living in nonurban areas may feel that clean air is not their concern. However, polluted air has brought acid rain and unhealthy elements to even remote areas of the world. Personal relevance must be established in order for students to understand the need and importance of clean air. The uses of air, the effects of air under pressure, the sight and smell of polluted air, and the effects of polluted air on plants, animals, humans, and even nonliving matter should be clearly demonstrated. Because air itself is always invisible, and some pollutants are not readily observable, the visible effects of pollution may not be instantly apparent; extra demonstrations and observation and study across time may be required for understanding to occur. Structured group work and experimentation are key elements for building these and other concepts such as air all around us, in water and holes, taking up space; air replacing water or water replacing air; and the necessity of air to life.

CORRECTION Modify strategies for topical and learning needs:

1. *Vocabulary Development*
   Skills: Observing; listening; classifying; generalizing
   Introduce parts of air such as nitrogen (78%), oxygen (21%), and carbon dioxide (.03%) on a bar or pie graph. Students can be taught that air contains different gases, even though they cannot be seen. Then introduce waste products that pollute the air. Words such as *smog, smoke, fog,* and *acid rain* can be listed on cards and displayed beside pictures showing their existence or results. Pictures of a smog-covered skyline or effects of continuing acid rain would be appropriate. Have students add pictures of their own to the bulletin board or display. Mix the cards and ask students to match the pollutant with the right picture. Be sure to include pictures involving causes (smoke, gas fumes) to be matched with results (smog, watery eyes) and teach for concepts, not memorization.

2. *Vocabulary Maps*
   Skills: Listening; organizing; predicting; classifying; synthesizing
   Print on the chalkboard or a transparency 2–4 words such as smog, smoke, pollen, or whatever pollutants are common to the local area. Then list a possible cause or source of each type of air pollution, explaining each as presented. Guide students to match the results with probable causes. Be sure to discuss what can be done about these causes.

3. *Air as Matter*
   Skills: Observing; directed experimenting; measuring; communicating
   To illustrate that air exists even though it is not usually seen and that it takes up space, have students feel an uninflated balloon. Blow up the balloon and note the difference. Ask: What changed the shape of the balloon? Have students feel the air escape when the air in the balloon is released. In cooler weather, have students exhale while they are outside and observe their breath. Ask: What is coming out of your mouth? Why do you think you can see the air when it is colder? Discuss the effect of temperature on air.

4. *Uses of Air*
   Skills: Observing; listening; analyzing; generalizing; evaluating
   Ask students to name items or find pictures of ways air is used. Actual items or pictures of hair dryers, fans, shoes, tires, balls, and mini-vacuum cleaners can be used as examples. Then ask students to pick an item that uses, moves, or holds air; demonstrate (if possible) and describe the function of the air and of the object; and state the value of the air to the object and the object to themselves. Make a chart of the pictures or names and descriptions and add to it as new uses are found.

5. *Air Pollutants*
   Skills: Listening; predicting; communicating; predicting; synthesizing; generalizing; evaluating
   Take photos of items that contribute to air pollution in the local area. Cars, cropdusters, large factories, smokestacks, dry cleaners, service stations, refinishing shops, and chimneys could be shown and described as possible

sources of air pollution. Have students identify each picture and tell as much as they know about it. Then name a problem, such as strange smells or smoky areas, and have students identify the picture(s) that could be the source of the problem. Ask questions such as: How can you tell that the air from this source is polluted? What effects might this air have on plants? What effects will this air have on you? How can you avoid the contaminated air from this source? What can you do to improve the air? Guide students to develop plans for avoidance and improvements. This information can be added to the charts developed for Activity 4.

6. Air Alert

Skills: Observing; analyzing; classifying; predicting; communicating; generalizing; evaluating

Use photos of local scenes that probably contain contaminated air, but do not picture the source of pollution. Some of the pictures should show hazy or smog-filled skies, but some should depict no obvious pollution (cotton field, downtown street, field of flowers, local schoolyard, dusty construction site, or the like). Guide students to predict the pollutants that are probably present and hypothesize their sources. Then have students rank the pictures according to most and least dangerous to themselves and to others. If possible, have students visit the scenes to observe (from a distance!) and/or telephone to interview residents or business owners to verify pollution and sources. After the visit, rerank the dangers. Be sure to talk about the causes and what can be done about the pollution they see in the pictures. Add the information to the charts in Activities 4 and 5.

7. Clean Air

Skills: Observing; analyzing; communicating; generalizing; evaluating

Guide students to identify locations with clean air and the reasons the air is clean. Begin by showing photos, drawings, or films of both clean and contaminated sites. Include 2–3 pictures taken inside a home, a business, and a classroom. As with Activities 5 and 6, have students analyze the pictures to identify sources or evidence of pollution. Stress the absence of sources of pollution and also introduce and explain indoor or car air-filter systems. Consider displaying a used filter from an air conditioner or heating unit. Have students examine the debris in the filter to identify the pollutants that have been removed from the air. Extend the filter concept to other settings, such as a park or forest area, and compare the air there to that in their school or neighborhood. Guide students to develop an oral or written list of safe places to go.

8. Air Pollution Log

Skills: Observing; analyzing; measuring; generalizing; evaluating

Have students use data logs to document air pollution that they observe. Over a 2–3 week period, have students make a daily record of the air quality at a certain time and place. Guide them to develop their own simple descriptors (e.g., *clear, foggy, hazy, frosty, dusty, smoky,* and the like), with descriptors determined by the area in which the students live. If appropriate, also ask students to keep track of the smell of the air, using descriptors such as *none*, *some*, and *lots*. After several days of recording data, help students analyze and evaluate what they have learned.

9. *Air Pollution Monitors*

Skills: Observing; listening; communicating; generalizing

Have students watch for newspaper stories, radio and TV reports, magazine stories, and personal sightings of air pollution. In many areas, cable TV programs routinely report the pollution index in great detail; if possible, show a tape of one such program to demonstrate the type, use, and interpretation of available information. Ask students to provide documentation for each sighting. For a TV story, record the time, date, and station; for printed stories, list the title, date, page number(s) and source. Then have students share their findings either orally or in written form. Keep a class Air Monitor's Report on a bulletin board. In addition to common smog, include reported measures of pollen and noise pollution.

10. *Identification of Noise Pollution*

Skills: Listening; reading; classifying; communicating; hypothesizing; generalizing; evaluating

Have students listen for a variety of noises around them. Make a list of the sounds they hear in the classroom, during a short trip outside, or during a specified period of time. On the chalkboard, list the sounds students name, guide students to discuss and critique each noise in terms of its value or harm to people or animals in different situations, and then classify each noise as good, bad, or questionable. Discuss sources and reasons for each sound and what students can do to avoid the bad noises or decrease them. This is a good time to evaluate the noises of the classroom and guide students to develop new class rules.

11. *Investigative Inquiry*

Skills: Reading; organizing; communicating; generalizing; evaluating

After several activities that culminate in identifying local sources of air pollution and the ones most likely to affect students negatively, select 1–3 methods of controlling or preventing a particular type of air pollution. Then help students construct group letters asking for details about what a company or agency is doing about air pollution. Include 3–4 specific questions in each letter. For example, letters could be sent to car manufacturers, local and national governmental agencies, and specific companies located in or nearby the area. When responses are received, guide students to evaluate the effectiveness of each remedy; also share replies orally and display copies of the letters and responses.

12. *Extra Practice.* • Assist students to read about or contact governmental agencies to learn about laws regulating air pollution and report to peers. • Compare air pollution data logged to identify seasonal differences in the type and frequency of air pollution. • Add the pollution remedies and their effectiveness discovered in Activity 11 to the vocabulary maps in Activity 2. • Have students collect and share pictures of the evidence of air pollution or of methods to prevent pollution; use these pictures to extend Activities 5, 6, and 11. • Adapt activities from Chapter 9.

7. INTERDEPENDENCE OF LIVING THINGS

DETECTION Mastery of key concepts may be difficult for students who:

- Do not observe carefully
- Exhibit difficulty communicating and generalizing
- Cannot explain mutual dependence of life and environment
- Demonstrate little concern for preservation of nature
- Cannot explain the value of the environment to self and society

Description. As one of the most relevant areas of study, the interdependence of various life forms and their interaction with the environment can be related to the study of a variety of other topics, such as the earth, natural resources, food chains, weather, the balance of nature, and so on. In addition to the plants, animals, and humans themselves, the preservation of habitats, food sources, essential life-sustaining elements, and adaptations are important concepts for maintaining different ecosystems. Involvement in this broad area of study utilizes all the information acquisition and processing skills. For the content to become more than a grouping of ideas to be studied and forgotten, personal and societal relevance must be clearly and firmly established.

Special Problems. Understanding ecosystems presupposes mastery of a large number of concepts about the separate units and how they function. A limited background of real experiences or inadequate academic training is likely to limit understanding. The actions of some families suggest a lack of environmental awareness that is reflected in the attitudes of students. The stands of students' families on such issues as hunting game versus protecting wildlife; economic progress versus preserving land, water, and air; or individual responsibility for preserving and improving the environment also tend to influence students' attitudes. When those attitudes are negative, students may find this topic especially difficult. Immediate surroundings also shape knowledge and attitudes; students from sparsely populated areas are likely to be somewhat informed about the preservation of wildlife and the balance of nature, while students from urban settings may consider the topics remote and uninteresting.

Instructional Implications. This is a complex topic, difficult for most students and especially for special students. Considerable teacher direction may be required to guide students through the most relevant relationships. Instruction should begin with examples that are familiar and meaningful to the students. This may mean starting with the cutting of firewood, the environmental balance of the classroom aquarium, or even the needs of personal pets. A familiar reference provides students something with which to compare less obvious situations. The interdependence among life forms and nature is clearly illustrated in the various cycles that replenish necessary elements; the depth of study should of course be varied according to student needs.

CORRECTION Modify strategies for topical and learning needs:

1. *Vocabulary Building*
   Skills: Observation; listening; reading; communication
   Review the vocabulary words used in studying air, water, and land. Relate each new term to the students themselves (e.g., Nitrogen is the major element in the air that *you* and *your cat* breathe.). Have students take turns describing each term's personal meaning and later draw or paste pictures under each term to illustrate its personal meaning.

2. *Picture Concepts*
   Skills: Observing; listening; reading; studying; organizing; classifying; predicting; generalizing; evaluating
   Create a Problems and Solutions scrapbook. Designate each left page a "problem" page and each right page a "solution" page. Begin with a list of events that might create environmental problems: floods, volcanoes, fires, droughts, logging, hunting, and building. Have students find or draw pictures of people, animals, plants, and places that might be affected most by each type of problem, paste the pictures under each problem event, and then take turns describing the effects. Then guide students to suggest solutions to these problems and paste appropriate pictures on each facing right page. Each 2-page format can be extended to include: additional examples throughout the year; personal photos of problems or solutions; written descriptions and explanations; and news clippings of similar events in the local community. Share the scrapbook as a picture-telling book with other classes or with families.

3. *Interdependence Cycles*
   Skills: Observing; studying; directed experimenting; organizing; predicting; communicating; all integration skills
   Plants and animals, through their interactions with the environment, continuously recycle raw materials that are necessary to maintain life now and in the future. Interruption of any part of a cycle is also likely to change or interfere with life and the environment. Diagrams or flowcharts, as detailed as the students' need-to-know and ability levels can handle, can be used to depict the interrelationships, walk students through the cycles, and serve as self-monitoring checks as students study 4 interdependent cycles: air, water, land, and food cycles.
   Air Cycle. This cycle is less complex than the others. Begin by presenting and discussing the components of air required by humans and animals and by plants: oxygen; carbon dioxide; and nitrogen. Choose directed experiments to demonstrate the release of carbon dioxide by animals, humans, and fires and the release of oxygen by plants. During each demonstration, display and verbalize the diagram for the particular event in the air cycle. Then display and verbalize the entire diagram, noting that even as they discuss it the students are contributing to the cycle. Also briefly sketch and mention the contribution, through the decay of plants and animals, of the carbon cycle to the carbon dioxide in the air. Relate the respective air needs

to common practices, such as taking oxygen for breathing problems, talking to plants to make them grow, or closing the doors during a fire, and then evaluate the practices. Evaluate the effects of a change in the animal, human, fire, and plant ratios.

Water Cycle. Begin with the broadest concepts: bodies of water, evaporation, then precipitation. Select a directed experiment to demonstrate evaporation and then present the diagram of only this part of the cycle. Display the diagram and verbalize the cycle each time precipitation occurs. Next, with or following the study of plants, use a similar procedure to introduce and study the second phase of the water cycle: precipitation, plants, transpiration, then precipitation. Display, verbalize, and often refer to both subcycles. Then, with or following the study of respiration, present the role of animals and humans in the water cycle: precipitation and bodies of water, animals and humans, respiration, then precipitation. Review and verbalize all 3 subcycles regularly.

Land Cycle. The nitrogen cycle is primarily a land activity. Present nitrogen as the the major component of the air breathed by animals and humans. Explain the importance of nitrogen and demonstrate its presence in air through directed experimentation. Then, as in teaching the other cycles, display a diagram and verbalize the cycle, starting with the nitrogen present in the air and tracking it to soil, plants and animals, soil, and back. Consider also the role of lightning, bacteria, and algae in converting nitrogen to usable form. Conclude by discussing the uses of nitrogen in fertilizer, cleaning agents, and common chemicals and its dangers in some forms.

Food Cycle. Food chains are complex but can be simply illustrated using familiar examples. Present diagrams for aquatic, farm, and woods environments. Simplify terms as *producers* and *primary* or *first, second,* and *third consumers* or *eaters* and *scavengers.* Display and verbalize the cycles for selected cafeteria menus and then cover the woods cycle. Conclude by discussing the effects of disruptions in the air, water, or land cycles on food supplies.

4. *Protection Alert*

   Skills: Observing; listening; organizing; communicating; generalizing
   Invite local resource people to explain their experiences or jobs protecting people, animals, and land (humane shelter officers, forest and zoo personnel, county agents, and/or zoning officials). Have each guest present local issues. Prepare students by having them view videotapes of related newscasts and then guide them to prepare questions to ask. Record or film the visit for later use and review. Have students summarize key ideas or dictate a group story about the visit.

5. *Issue Debate*

   Skills: Listening; studying; organizing; communicating; analyzing; predicting; synthesizing; evaluating
   Form a classroom Board of Land Use or Nature Committee composed of 3–4 students. Guide peers to develop requests to take before the board. For example, present a request to bring a new industry to the area, such as a lemonade stand in the middle of the football field, or propose planting a

ragweed patch outside the classroom window. Help committee members prepare their questions and applicants prepare their defenses. Issues to present also might include simulations of actual applications placed before local boards. Conclude with questions such as: Why does it matter what type of factory or plant a request involves? How does the location of the property affect the decisions? What effect do the needs of local people have on decisions? Why do we need boards to regulate land use? This activity also can be paired with lessons in social studies to simulate, for example, how certain requests would likely be received in other regions or countries.

6. *Survey of Concern*

    Skills: Listening; reading; directed experimenting; organizing; classifying; communicating; all integration skills

    Organize students into pairs or teams and have each team select the ecological issues it wants to investigate. Guide teams to prepare 3–8-item questionnaires to survey the knowledge of students and teachers about specific ecological matters. Use categories of responses to organize results and make them easy to interpret. Help the teams decide on numbers and categories of students and teachers they will interview and hypothesize which ones will know the most about ecology. After the data are collected, guide students to organize, synthesize, and interpret their results by categories and dictate or write summaries of their findings. Use the summaries as news releases for the school paper or to post on a school bulletin board. Some results may indicate the need for additional investigation of factors that influence knowledge of certain groups.

7. *Concerned Citizens*

    Skills: Listening; reading; organizing; communicating; synthesizing; generalizing; evaluating

    Help students organize a resource file of names, addresses, and brief descriptions of community and national organizations that are interested in improving ecology. The file might include: fire departments; fish and game services; zoos; garden clubs; park services; the Environmental Protection Agency; the Audubon Society; the Sierra Club; and the National Aeronautics and Space Administration. Begin by guiding students to develop a form letter or interview form. Request from each agency specific information about activities in the surrounding community. Then assign a pair or team of students to contact each organization by telephone or letter. Have the teams display information they receive and orally report services and local activities of their assigned organization while peers evaluate the services. Pair these activities with social studies lessons.

8. *Extra Practice.* • On a poster, list key environmental legislation along with pictures to reflect sites or examples affected by each act; include the Clean Air Act (1970), Ocean Dumping Act (1972), Noise Control Act (1972), and Toxic Substance Control Act (1976); have students add brief descriptions and updates. • Tape environmental programs from local educational TV channels for students to view in part or whole to reinforce concepts. • Have students report to peers any local news stories that might interrupt one of the interdependence cycles.

8. PERSONAL HYGIENE

DETECTION Mastery of key concepts may be difficult for students who:

- Do not observe carefully
- Display weak organization skills
- Seldom appear to be clean
- Wear rumpled or dirty clothing
- Have offensive body odors
- Exhibit offensive personal actions

Description. Personal hygiene involves learning proper habits for cleaning and protecting the skin, hair, nails, teeth, mouth, eyes, and ears. These habits in turn form the foundation for building good grooming skills. Hygienic habits include not only body cleanliness but also clean personal habits such as using a tissue versus picking one's nose, wiping carefully after going to the bathroom, and refraining from nailbiting, thumbsucking, and picking at sores. While a proper diet and exercise also are related to personal hygiene, this section deals with developing health habits and cleanliness. Nutrition and exercise are considered as separate topics later in this chapter.

Special Problems. Many students are unaware of appropriate personal hygiene habits because they have not practiced proper hygiene at home. For some types of handicapped students, personal care may be somewhat difficult. Limited mobility, inadequate vision, or poorly developed coordination can make mastery of basic hygiene care a tedious and sometimes embarrassing process for untrained or uninformed individuals. Poverty, although unfairly blamed much of the time, is a very real cause of infrequent bathing in some situations for economic and practical reasons: the cost of soap, water, and heating the water prohibits numerous baths; cold houses make bathing uncomfortable; and crowded homes necessitate taking turns bathing. Finally, some cultures view cleanliness differently and simply do not prioritize bathing as others do.

Instructional Implications. Hygienic habits are not only important to health but also to social acceptance by peers. Due to the very private nature of some aspects of personal hygiene, topical content and the context of interventions must be carefully selected. Modeling and training experiences should be conducted in a manner that is sensitive, appropriate, and manageable for handicapped or uninformed students. Having family members participate in selected experiences at home will often help reinforce the need and provide the support for acquiring positive personal habits.

CORRECTION Modify strategies for topical and learning needs:

1. *Helping Hands*

    Skills: Observing; listening; communicating; generalizing

    Select the key vocabulary words for a particular lesson or unit. When studying teeth and gums, such words as *plaque, cavity, tartar, flossing,* and *toothbrush* might be used. Print each word on a card shaped like a hand, giving students a Helping Hand in learning concepts. Pronounce each word while displaying the card. Ask students to pronounce the word several times while you talk about it, discuss its meaning, and use pictures or examples. Have students state how they will personally use each word and then pin the card and its picture on a board.

2. *Community and State Resources*

    Skills: Observing; listening; reading; synthesizing; generalizing

    In many communities, people representing local health departments, hospitals, private physicians, school nurses, dentists, manufacturers, and others offer free demonstrations, school kits, and printed material explaining the proper care of skin, teeth, eyes, and ears. Take advantage of these materials and determine which products or procedures are appropriate for particular students. Welcome personal visits, loaned tapes, and free literature. In advance of each visit, outline for the speaker the students' needs; present background concepts through reading, listening, and demonstrations to the students; and guide students to prepare questions to ask. Later, guide students to record the key points.

3. *Clean Air and Clean Breath Poster Ads*

    Skills: Listening; reading; communicating; analyzing; synthesizing; generalizing; evaluating

    Guide students to make "smoke machines" (i.e, simulated cigarette smoking) with filter paper to see the results. Then provide printed, film, and personal interview information about problems associated with smoking. To encourage students to develop healthy attitudes, help them collect or make up phrases to increase their awareness of the unclean nature of smoking (e.g. Smoking pollutes us all! or One tip you don't need is a filter tip.). Make 2–3 page- or poster-size ads that offer a message about smoke pollution or general health and smoking. Include pictures and phrases or statements to make a point. Display ads in the school halls.

4. *Skin Tests*

    Skills: Observing; reading; analyzing; communicating; predicting; generalizing

    The skin protects the body and senses, helps warm and cool the body, and helps get rid of wastes. Three simple experiments can be used to illustrate the vital functions of the skin. After having students examine their skin under magnification to analyze appearance, lead them to discover the functions of skin by directing them to perform 3 activities. 1) To demonstrate the protective function of skin, have students remove the skin from their piece of cooked chicken at lunchtime. Point out the exposed parts and then guide students to infer the protective qualities of skin. Ask for personal examples of events in which skin protected the students. 2) To demonstrate the sensory function of skin, have students close their eyes and explain what and how they feel as the teacher or a peer touches their hand with string, ice, or modeling clay. Experiment and see if the hand is more or less sensitive than the nose or finger. 3) Before illustrating the temperature control and excretory functions of skin, have students tell everything they know about perspiring: what it is, when it occurs, how it occurs, and its purpose. Fill in or correct missing or erroneous information. Then wet the backs of students' hands—or better yet, catch them sweating—and have them blow across their moist skin and then blow across dry skin to compare the feelings. Repeat the questions about perspiring, emphasizing the purpose. For older students, mention the 2 types of deodorants, odor neutralizers, and odor and perspiration inhibitors, and evaluate them.

5. *Needed Skin Care*

   Skills: Observing; listening; reading; measuring; classifying; synthesizing; hypothesizing

   Highlight skin care by having students select ads for skin-care products, such as soaps, creams, lotions, ointments, and clothing. Guide students to classify products as necessary or superfluous as they describe the conditions under which each would be needed and the purpose it would serve. Discuss the basic care of skin: keeping it clean and moist, treating wounds; maintaining proper diet and exercise; and protecting it from scrapes, extreme temperatures, and too much sun. Then have students make a poster showing necessary products for skin protection. As an extension, have students dictate or write short ads or slogans for selected products.

6. *Clean Clothes*

   Skills: Observing; listening; communicating; generalizing

   To emphasize both health and social reasons for cleanliness, display a very dirty white sock. Ask: Would you like to wear it? Why or why not? What about it do you not like? Would you want your best friend to wear it? Follow a similar procedure with a dirty football jersey. Explain that clothing is another layer of protection, much like skin; when pleople wear dirty clothes, others sometimes avoid them because of odor and unattractive appearance. Emphasize that people usually prefer being friends with people who wear clean clothing and whose skin is clean. Have students discuss reasons for not wearing the dirty sock over a cut foot and keeping the skin clean around a cut. Display clean clothing and ask students why they would prefer it over dirty clothing for themselves or their friends. Conclude with neat dressing: Have students demonstrate how to rearrange their clothing to make it look sloppy and not as clean and then how to make their clothes appear neater.

7. *Hygienic Grooming Tips*

   Skills: Observing; classifying; communicating; generalizing; evaluating

   Students are sometimes more concerned with the social aspects of hygiene and grooming than with the health aspects. Since the objective in teaching these topics is to develop hygienic habits, regardless of the students' motives, highlight the social implications. Guide students to construct a Health and Grooming Tips poster to list additional topics as they are studied; include pictures and explanations to provide visual reminders of each topic and brief reviews. To avoid embarrassing anyone, use as a negative example a pet (either one that is routinely kept in the classroom or bring a friendly dog in need of a bath), but make careful arrangements for the proper care of the pet (and the students) during demonstrations.

Hair Tips. Display the pet and invite students to observe, touch, and smell its hair; ask them to describe what they do and do not like about the hair. Lead them to suggest that the pet's hair should be washed and brushed or combed. After students have washed their hands, guide them to list the reasons why they prefer clean, groomed hair on the pet and then on themselves and others, stressing social and health reasons. Help students develop guidelines for how and when to wash their hair.

Dental Tips. Borrow a large model of teeth from a local dentist; smear the teeth with a dark color of preserves and let them dry overnight. Carefully position and hold a *very* friendly pet so that the students can quickly see its teeth and smell its breath. Guide students to conclude possible reasons for the pet's bad breath (e.g., teeth not brushed; no mouthwash; tooth, sinus, or other infections) and discuss the consequences of bad breath, first for pets and next with emphasis on people. Then, using the sticky model of the teeth and a regular-size toothbrush, have students take brief turns demonstrating and explaining how they think the teeth should be brushed. Point out the need to remove the preserves to prevent decay and bad breath while demonstrating proper brushing. Note the effort and time required. Have students wash their hands and then follow your brushing model using their index fingers as brushes. Give them individual charts to record and compare when and how often they brush.

Nail Tips. Manicure the nails of one hand but leave the nails on the other hand dirty, uneven, and/or with unsightly polish. Have students critique your nails and suggest ways and reasons to improve; be sure the handling of food is stressed. Demonstrate the use of nail clippers, files, and white nail pencils on yourself. Then have a manicure party by guiding students to use the files and pencils (not clippers) on themselves.

Habits Tips. Have teams of students respond to if/then statements about the consequences of unhealthy and socially offensive habits: If you bite your nails, then . . . ; If you pick your nose, then . . . ; If you always scratch yourself, then . . . Lead the teams to compare and discuss their responses, highlighting both social and health consequences. Then discuss why people develop the habits and how to substitute better habits.

8. *Extra Practice.* • Help students read different shampoo labels to compare ingredients, directions, and prices; they should conclude that most of the ingredients and directions are similar, but prices vary widely. • Holding a Helping Hands word card in each hand, have students take turns telling partners what they know about each term. • Extend Hygienic Grooming Tips to caring for animals and how and why they clean and groom themselves.

9. DIET

DETECTION Mastery of key concepts may be difficult for students who:

- Are too thin or too fat
- Do not eat a balanced lunch
- Are often sick
- Have difficulty classifying and generalizing
- Have family histories of diet-related problems
- Cannot explain the value of proper diet

Detection. This topic includes information about the importance of maintaining a proper diet of basic foods, limiting intake of certain foods, and developing a life-style that includes appropriate amounts of food and exercise. Problems may involve both overeating and/or excessive dieting or even compulsive or abusive behaviors, such as anorexia, bulimia, and acute obesity. Another concern is the student who is overfed but undernourished. The main objective of this section is to suggest strategies for actively involving students with appropriate content. While information acquisition and processing skills are necessary, it is the integration of ideas and appropriate behaviors that is required to achieve some degree of practical and healthful life-styles.

Special Problems. Poor habits developed and even encouraged at home are a major cause of eating problems. The values of some cultures are at odds with good nutritional practices. In some families, the problems stem from the need to economize on food and/or inadequate knowledge of nutrition. Some adults knowingly elect to follow unhealthy eating patterns, choosing convenience and pleasure over health. When students are fed junkfood at home, encouraged to buy it at school, and then see teachers and older students following similar dietary patterns, the role models and habits are confirmed. Most students are not concerned about proper nutrition; attractive appearance, physical abilities, convenience, and pleasure often seem more important. Certain students overeat because they either do not acknowledge the problem or they feel out of control, while other students almost starve themselves to achieve the look popularized by the media. Not just any balanced diet is appropriate for students who are allergic or hypersensitive to certain foods; the problem foods must be identified and eliminated from the diet. And finally, some students, because of inactivity or handicapping conditions, may require special diets and careful monitoring.

Instructional Implications. Individuals with eating disorders may require professional assistance and counseling. Replacing old, unsatisfactory habits with better ones is often a long-term process. The teacher's role is to model and encourage healthy eating habits and to tailor nutritional information to individual needs. Where changes in dietary habits are needed, always consult a medical expert and a student's family before suggesting a plan. To be successful, dietary programs must be supported and continued outside of the school setting.

CORRECTION Modify strategies for topical and learning needs:

1. *Healthy Terms*
   Skills: Observing; listening; directed experimenting; analyzing; communicating; generalizing; evaluating

   When presenting new diet vocabulary, do so in a positive and pleasant manner. A discussion of the basic food groups, for example, becomes more meaningful if several edible samples are presented with the vocabulary words. Place terms on cards with sample pictures and also post the new words under pictures that accurately reflect the appropriate food group. Have students take tiny bites of a sample each time they pronounce and explain the meaning of a term. Have students decide which sample in each food group they like best and then find a picture of the particular food to paste on their individual word cards.

2. *Home Habits*
   Skills: Listening; measuring; classifying; communicating; experimenting

   As food groups and special habits are discussed, have students try to include a few of the items in their diet outside school. This may require contacting family members to inform them of the schedule of study and foods. In some cases, parental cooperation will not be available. However, in many homes, family members want to help and may even gain valuable information for the entire family. For example, designate a New Food Week during which students are to taste a new food in each food group, rate the food in terms of appeal and nutritional value, and orally report the results to the class. Or have students try a new food in a specific food group, rate it, and report results. Have students keep a record of the foods they eat, particularly those representing a specific target food group.

3. *Food and Health Relations*
   Skills: Listening; reading; analyzing; classifying; generalizing; evaluating

   When studying about essential nutrients or food groups, follow a 4-step plan: 1) Guide students as they add favorite foods to the lists for each category; 2) use pictures of the source or foods suggested; 3) always match the nutrients (proteins, carbohydrates, fats, vitamins, minerals, and water) with foods, sources, or supplements; and 4) have each student evaluate the value of the food to himself or herself. By adding personal reference information students will find it easier to remember information.

4. *Food Families*
   Skills: Listening; observing; classifying; communicating; synthesizing; generalizing

   Print categories such as *Milk, Meat, Fruit and Vegetable,* and *Bread and Cereal* on the chalkboard. Then, on index cards, print the name or use a picture of each specific food. Hand out the cards and have students go to the board to hold the card under the appropriate category. Using a game format, award a point for each correct answer. If a wrong category is selected, the card should be handed over to the competitor(s). Also ask students to name foods of their own that fit in the categories they correctly identify.

5. *Breakfast Club*

    Skills: Listening; organizing; communicating; evaluating

    Because eating a nutritious breakfast is so important, ask your students to join a Breakfast Club. Keep a daily class record showing who eats breakfast (including the teacher) and featuring My Favorite Breakfast menus each week. As a group activity, discuss and evaluate at least 1 person's breakfast each day. Include an incentive system to reward those who improve their breakfast habits.

6. *Try It First*

    Skills: Listening; organizing; directed experimenting; communicating; all integration skills

    Students and some adults are at times very reluctant to try unfamiliar or different foods. To help students become more accepting of different foods, plan a special theme food day or week (e.g., International Day; Breakfast Day; or Vegetable Week). Have students bring samples (at least 1 bite for everyone) of a special food they enjoy. If circumstances prevent some students from contributing, bring ingredients to school and have those students help you prepare samples to share. Ask each student to explain the origin of his or her special food, the caloric and nutritional values, and its food group. After each tasting experience, have students rate and rank the foods. If appropriate, also ask for the recipes to share. Integrate lessons with social studies and mathematics.

7. *Food and Drink on TV*

    Skills: Observing; listening; directed experimenting; analyzing; classifying; communicating; generalizing; evaluating

    Ask students to analyze food commercials on TV and radio. Have them count, describe, and critique the types of foods and brands they see advertised the most often. Categorize the information and discuss why certain products are advertised during particular programs and the types of advertising techniques that are used. Ask such questions as: Are all products of equal nutrition? What kinds of food and drink are advertised during your favorite programs? What age of audience is the ad directed toward? What techniques are used in the ad? Which is your favorite ad and why? How much attention is focused on nutrition? Or assign students a designated time period to watch commercials. Conclude by having student teams develop advertisements for healthy food products and present them to peers.

8. *Food Analysis*

    Skills: Observing; reading; studying; analyzing; classifying; communicating; generalizing; evaluating

    Because much of the food that students eat is preprocessed, the labels must be read to determine content. Display 3–4 popular products with relatively uncomplicated ingredients. Explain the labeling requirements and then list on the chalkboard or a transparency the ingredients in each product. Then, depending on the ages and abilities of students, consider these activities:
    • Guide students to study and research to identify the cosmetic ingredients

added for color, texture, consistency, smell, and so on and then evaluate their value. • Compare the ingredients and prices of different brands of the same product to evaluate which is the most nutritious and which is the best buy; also have students compare the flavors if appropriate. • Compare the ingredients of different products, say, 3 processed snacks, to evaluate which is the most nutritious. • Have students analyze several types of juice to evaluate the proportions of real juice and added nutrients that are needed for nutritional value.

9. *Food Journals*

   Skills: Listening; reading; analyzing; classifying; communicating; all integration skills

   To reduce the tendency to eat too much of certain foods and not enough of other foods, guide students to keep an individual interactive food journal. Demonstrate the process as a group process after a favorite lunch at school. In addition to the amount, frequency, and types of food consumed, have students write about the texture, flavor, and nutritional value. (If written expression is a particular problem, permit students to dictate their entries to a tape or peer.) Have students write entries for everything eaten each day, including snacks; classify what they eat by categories you provide (depending on age and ability levels); and then submit the journals at regular intervals. For a journal to be an interactive 2-way dialogue, the teacher regularly must read it and write comments to which the students respond. Teacher comments might include: How much liver did you really eat? I'll bet you enjoyed that! Mmmm, that makes me hungry! Where did you get the fudge? Which basic food group was missing on Monday and Tuesday? or You must have been in quite a hurry! After the first week, have students analyze their eating patterns and guide them to suggest the changes they should make. Pair students to develop slogans to help them remember the changes: Check the Labels; Toast on Tuesday; or Peaches, Not Pie.

10. *Extra Practice.* • When introducing food groups, try featuring different foods each week; include samples to taste and check with the cafeteria (if available) to see if the order of your food choices should be changed to go along with their menu. • Invite a nutritional expert to visit and discuss proper diet with the class. • Periodically send notes home suggesting appropriate snack foods, particularly for students who show up in school with candy and other high fat or salty snack foods. • As a teacher, set the example by eating healthful foods when you are at school. • When special seasonal foods are available, bring samples to class for students to try; be sure to have students classify their food according to food group and or nutrient group. • To go along with reviewing TV commercials, have students use a checklist to measure or rate advertised foods and drinks according to their nutritional value. • Have pairs of students exchange food journals and interact by writing or sharing audio tapes as in Activity 9.

10. EXERCISE

DETECTION Mastery of key concepts may be difficult for students who:

- Exhibit a dislike for physical activity
- Appear overweight and/or underdeveloped
- Do not observe or listen carefully
- Have difficulty generalizing and evaluating
- Cannot explain the value of exercise to health

Description. Exercise should be considered along with proper diet and rest and with particular attention to appropriate exercise. Physical activity is generally accepted as a basic ingredient for healthy growth and development. For nonexceptional and for handicapped students in particular, emphasis must be placed on proper phasing or working toward optimal limits of physical activity. Proper amounts of exercise can help students feel better, fall asleep more easily, and have more energy. Depending on physical capabilities and existing levels of fitness, students can benefit from developing habits of regular exercise that involve using a variety of muscles and the respiratory system. An additional bonus of regular exercise is that a student's mental attitude is often improved.

Special Problems. Habits of healthy and regular exercise reflect positive attitudes and expectations of the potential benefits. Students who come from families that prefer sedentary activities may require additional convincing and instruction before they subscribe to the notion that exercise is healthy. Although many parents and school personnel recognize the importance of exercise, there is a tendency to protect handicapped students for fear of causing physical injury. While this is a potential risk for all students, the avoidance of physical activity carries with it a greater risk in terms of limited muscular and motor development. Some types of physical and medical handicaps prohibit students from engaging in certain kinds of exercise; these students require adaptive physical education as specified by physicians and other specialists.

Instructional Implications. Research findings indicate that a lack of physical activity is related to respiratory and circulatory problems even in children and young adults. The healthy body/healthy mind concept has been documented as a valid tenet for healthful living. Before beginning any type of exercise, medical personnel should be consulted to establish 1) a schedule for gradually building tasks and time spent in physical activity by all students and 2) an outline of appropriate activities and schedules for individual handicapped students. Students often can be eased into an exercise regime by gradually exposing them to limited exercise and introducing noncontact sports or games, such as swimming or dancing. Along with exercise, good nutrition and rest should be incorporated into any physical fitness program. The activities that follow are designed to suggest cognitive experiences that encourage the development of healthy bodies through exercise.

CORRECTION Modify strategies for topical and learning needs:

1. *Word Captains*
   Skills: Observing; listening; reading; directed experimenting;
        communicating
   As new words are introduced, used in demonstrations, and repeated by students, ask a student to be captain of a particular word. Print the word on the board with the student's name beside the word and also give the student the word on a card. During discussion and at others times during the day, take the opportunity to use the words and call on each captain to pronounce his and her word and show the word to others. Use the captains throughout the day. For example: All word captains with words beginning with *j,* please stand and display and demonstrate their words *(jump* and *jog).* To build in needed review and repetition, rotate word captains so that each word is supervised by a different student each day.

2. *Beginning Exercise*
   Skills: Listening; reading; analyzing; communicating; evaluating
   To personalize a physical fitness study, help students analyze their individual physical interests and needs. Then guide students to write a group letter to the President's Council on Physical Fitness, Department of Human Services, 5600 Fishers Lane, Rockville, Maryland, 20852. The letter should include mention of the particular aspects of physical development and fitness in which individual students are interested. It also should request information about the program sponsored by the government. Contact can also be made with local representatives for the Special Olympics, YWCA, and YMCA if your community has such programs. Feature replies on a bulletin board along with copies of the original letters of inquiry. On an individual or paired basis, help students analyze the replies to extract the information that applies to their needs and develop plans to implement a personalized physical fitness program.

3. *See and Do*
   Skills: Observing; directed experimenting; synthesizing
   When teaching a new movement or exercise, instead of standing or facing students, position yourself beside or with your back to students so that they can easily follow your movements. Guide students both verbally and visually. After several demonstrations, if needed, move behind individual students and physically help them follow a pattern or movement. Always be positive and encouraging by using verbal comments.

4. *Target Walks*
   Skills: Observing; listening; directed experimenting; analyzing;
        measuring; predicting; synthesizing; generalizing; evaluating
   Target Walks involves a simple concept: Always set a goal or objective for daily walks. For example, here are 6 ideas for using Target Walks:
        A. Today we are going to see how long it takes us to walk from point A to point B. Do you think it will take longer than yesterday's walk from C to D? Why?

B. Which is the shortest route to point A? Let's plan 2 routes and then measure and compare the distances. Here are the routes; which do you predict will be shorter?

C. Today we are going to the library to watch a film about walking. However, instead of taking our usual route, we will take the longest possible route to the library; who can suggest the best way to go?

D. As we are walking outside today, raise your right hand each time you pass a tree (or bird, flower, student, etc.) on your right, and raise your left hand if it is on your left.

E. Since it is raining today, we will take our walk inside; our mission is to walk so quietly that no one else in the building will notice us. How can we be that quiet?

F. Count the number of steps you take during our walk; begin counting as you step through the classroom door and end when you return to your seat.

5. *Movement Melodies*

> *Skills:* Observing; listening; directed experimenting; analyzing; generalizing; evaluating

Most students find it difficult to sit still when they hear music. As students listen to taped music, insist that they try to sit still for a few minutes and imagine how they should move and dance to the music. Tell them to visualize themselves making the movements. Then invite individual or pairs of students to demonstrate their movements for others to follow. After everyone has had a turn, have students decide which movement best matches each part of the music. From the selected movements, develop an exercise routine. Have students perform and evaluate the routine to identify the muscles that are involved in the actions. Have students suggest modifications each time the routine is performed.

6. *Video Versions*

> *Skills:* Observing; directed experimenting; organizing; communicating; synthesizing; evaluating

Have students view a videotape of a popular exercise routine and identify the features that make them want to exercise while watching. Then have them plan and make their own exercise videotape. For each exercise, use a different student to lead the others. Begin each exercise by having the leader explain and demonstrate a particular exercise or movement before working with the whole class. When the tape is completed, have students critique it, suggest improvements, and retape as desired. Later, have students watch their tape as they practice the exercises.

7. *Fitness Opportunities*

> *Skills:* Listening; studying; classifying; communicating; generalizing evaluating

Share advertisements, flyers, or other information about an exercise opportunity available in your area (e.g., water parks, skating rinks, swimming pools, or skateboard parks). Have students either recall or bring in lists of places and events that involve exercise or some type of physical fitness experience. Have students analyze, discuss, and evaluate each contribution and then vote on their top 3–4 choices.

8. *Exercise Journal*

Skills: Observing, listening; communicating; organizing; measuring; synthesizing; evaluating

Have students try several different exercises and then vote on the one that they most enjoy. Have them record in an Exercise Journal the amount of time they devote to performing the exercise over an initial period of a week. Read and respond to the journal entries, writing comments and questions. Then have students track and record in their journals all the types of exercise in which they engage, concluding each entry with an evaluation of the activities described. At regular intervals, correspond with students through their journals and also have pairs of students exchange journals. The journals are motivational and provide meaningful writing experiences. They also serve as an excellent diagnostic tool for identifying individual needs.

9. *Original Seated Exercises*

Skills: Observing; listening; directed experimenting; generalizing; evaluating

While sitting at your desk, demonstrate simple hand, arm, neck, and back exercises. Have students join in. Assign students to groups of 2–3 to invent 1–2 exercises that easily can be done while seated. Have the groups demonstrate their new exercises and lead their peers in performing them. Guide students to identify the muscles affected, the conditions under which each exercise would be useful, and the potential benefits.

10. *Fitness Builds Energy*

Skills: Observing; listening; directed experimenting; communicating; generalizing; evaluating

Select a time during the afternoon when several students appear tired. During a 3–5 minute interval, lead the class in a few different arm, hand, neck, and leg exercises. Keep the movements simple, light, and of short duration. Next, have students sit erect, inhale, and then exhale 6 deep breaths with you. Have them describe how they feel. (Many will feel more energetic than before the light movement.) Lead them to discover the results of their exercise and then identify the circumstances under which they should use similar activities.

11. *Cautious Supervision*

Skills: Observing; predicting; independent experimenting; evaluating

Begin by talking with parents to identify any exercise restrictions for each student. Constantly monitor students during exercise; even minimal signs of discomfort, pain, or unusual behavior are cause to discontinue an activity. Guide students to develop a list of symptoms that indicate when exercise is not appropriate and then use their list to monitor and regulate their exercise.

12. *Extra Practice.* • Have students take turns setting the purpose of Target Walks. • Invite athletes from a junior or senior high school to demonstrate several exercises they use on a regular basis. • Ask students to bring their own favorite music to use during brief exercise periods; have them explain their choices and tell something about the artist(s).

11. PSYCHOACTIVE DRUGS

DETECTION Mastery of key concepts may be difficult for students who:

- Have experienced pleasure using psychoactive drugs
- Demonstrate a limited knowledge about drugs
- Are unwilling to communicate about drug use
- Have difficulty predicting, generalizing, and/or evaluating
- Cannot explain the dangers of drug abuse to self or society

Description. Psychoactive drugs alter the way in which the mind and body function, a deliberate and healthy alteration when necessary and taken properly. However, when illegal drugs are taken and/or when the drugs are unnecessary, drug use is illicit and unhealthy. *Illicit drug use* involves use of a drug intended for someone else or in a way other than its intended purpose (e.g., taking diet pills to get high), use of a substance to produce drug-type effects (e.g., sniffing glue to get high), or taking drugs that are prohibited by law. Frequently abused drugs include prescription and nonprescription drugs, alcohol, tobacco, and the caffeine commonly found in coffee, tea, and other drinks. Drugs prescribed as medicines as well as common over-the-counter medicines can be harmful and even deadly when not used properly. Fumes from paint thinner, glue, and other products can cause dizziness, headaches, and eventually damage to organs in the body if abused over a long period of time. In addition to alcohol and tobacco, at least six major categories of drugs are associated with abuse problems: *depressants, stimulants, hallucinogens, narcotics, marijuana and hashish,* and *solvents.*

Special Problems. Misuse of drugs often occurs when students want to belong or fit in with a group. Sometimes curiosity or rebellion causes students to experiment to just see what drinking or smoking is like. Taking medicine prescribed for someone else or not following the prescribed dosage can cause unwanted effects. One major cause of frequent drug use is a desire to escape from problems—a desire that can be temporarily accommodated by taking one of the psychoactive drugs. Because psychological and/or physical addiction to many drugs may result when they are used improperly, even casual use can lead to a desire for more. Special students are not immune to drug abuse. Low self-esteem or a need to be a part of the group are a particular concern for some of these students. Drug abuse can be problematic for students regardless of background, race, religion, family influence, or cognitive ability.

Instructional Implications. Two of the greatest influences affecting drug use are a student's network of family and friends and knowledge of the potential effects. Because of the wide availability of illegal drugs and the prevalence of illicit drug use, most students will at some time have an opportunity to experiment with various drugs. The primary focus of instruction should be on building awareness of the effects of improper use of drugs as early as possible, and then reinforcing that awareness on a regular basis. The proper use of drugs also should be stressed.

CORRECTION Modify strategies for topical and learning needs:

1. *Advertising Drug Jargon*
    Skills: Listening; reading; classifying; communicating; synthesizing
    Begin by using vocabulary that can be easily related to uses and products students may already be familiar with. Bring to class newspaper inserts from discount and drug stores that often appear in the Sunday paper. Ask students to cut out coupons or sale advertisements about different types of drugs. Magazine advertisements can also be used. Have students glue each coupon or ad portion on an index card. On the opposite side, label the card specifying a product or drug type. Additional information can be added, such as contents or potential effects. Have students use the cards to practice each word, confirming their pronunciation with the picture on the back. Use posterboard to create a master board with 2–3 headings at the top and card pockets below each heading. This example has 3 main headings:

    Over-the-Counter   *Tobacco*   *Alcohol*

    _____   _____   _____

    _____   _____   _____

    Have students form teams and draw cards to match the drug pictured in the proper category. If appropriate, use 5–6 categories, such as types of drugs (e.g., stimulants, depressants, narcotics). Give extra credit for additional information, such as contents or potential problems.
2. *Reasons Not To . . .*
    Skills: Listening; reading; analyzing; communicating; generalizing; evaluating
    For topics of particular importance or high interest, help students construct a list of Reasons Not to, or posting on a bulletin board. Guide students in developing their list based on reading and discussions. A list for smoking could include: Reasons Not to Smoke
    • Smoking is unhealthy.
    • Smoking causes bad breath.
    • Smoking is expensive.
    • Smoking hurts my eyes.
    • Smoking smells bad to nonsmokers.
    • Smoking causes fires.
3. *Consequences of Drinking*
    Skills: Observing; listening; reading; generalizing
    Some students view the consumption of alcohol only from a short-term perspective. Use stories and films to relate the short-term and potential long-term consequences of alcohol abuse. Share information about tragic situations involving drinking and driving, loss of friends and jobs, and health problems caused by excessive use of alcohol. Take time to solicit personal contributions from students who wish to share what they have learned or heard about drinking alcohol. Conclude by having each student develop a Reasons Not to Drink Alcohol list as in Activity 2.

4. *What to Do?*

> *Skills:* Listening; studying; predicting; communicating; synthesizing; generalizing; evaluating
>
> Roleplay situations in which students must decide whether or not to take drugs. Have 1–2 students act out each scene while peers watch and evaluate their decisions. Simulations might include: A friend offers to share a beer; you find a bottle of prescription medicine on the floor; a stranger offers a cigarette; you forgot to bring your allergy pills, but a friend offers you one of his; someone you know offers you $2 for every pill you sell for her; a friend or relative shows up at a party, acting crazy and smelling like alcohol; you have medicine for a cold but can't remember how many of your prescription pills to take and how often; or you have a bad headache and you know where your parents keep the aspirin. Ask students to suggest similar situations they know about for their peers to roleplay. The particular type of simulation to use depends on the ages and abilities of the students. However, exercises like these provide experience making decisions in a safe environment and practice for real situations students may confront.

5. *Expert Information*

> *Skills:* Observing; listening; organizing; evaluating
>
> Having professionals from law enforcement or drug abuse centers talk about and show actual drugs to students can have positive and dramatic effects. Contact the local police department or a clinic and request that an expert visit the class to share information about drugs that are prevalent in the area. Make arrangements in advance for a follow-up phone conference after the visit to clarify information. Before the visit, guide students to plan questions to ask. After the visit, as additional questions and ideas develop, have students plan the telephone interview, choose a spokesperson, and then make the call. If possible, use a speakerphone so that the whole group can participate.

6. *Drug Briefs*

> *Skills:* Reading; studying; organizing; analyzing; communicating; generalizing
>
> Demonstrate how to develop a 3–6 sentence newsbrief about a particular drug. Use topics currently being studied and talk students through the process. Include essential information about the drug and its effects. Have the students use their written or dictated briefs as sources for simulated radio or television broadcasts for class.

7. *Drug Safety At Home*

> *Skills:* Observing; reading; directed experimenting; analyzing; predicting; generalizing; evaluating
>
> Involve students in a project to survey drug safety at home. Before beginning, send a note home to inform family members what will be happening. Then ask students to get a responsible adult to help them conduct a safety inventory. This includes listing over-the-counter drugs, prescription drugs, sources of caffeine, tobacco products, solvents, and cleaning products that

may be potentially harmful. In addition to the listing, note the location in which each substance was found and the adequacy of safety measures (out of reach of children or sealed properly). Pair students to evaluate the drug safety in their respective homes and then suggest an improved plan.

8. *Caffeine Alert*

   Skills: Observing; studying; analyzing; measuring; communicating; all integration skills

   List the major sources of caffeine: coffee, tea, certain carbonated drinks, and chocolate. Have students tell how each product makes them feel and why they enjoy it. Ask students to keep daily diaries of their use of caffeine foods and drinks for a 5-day period, including how they feel as they make each entry. Then have them abstain from all caffeine use for a second 5-day period and record their feelings as they did for the first period. Guide students to analyze and compare their diaries. Then discuss the problems that are commonly associated with this stimulant and have students evaluate the use of caffeine.

9. *Good Drugs*

   Skills: Listening; analyzing; communicating; generalizing; evaluating

   Have student volunteers list any medicines they are currently taking, the reasons for taking them, and their source. Have peers observe, interview, and keep a medical chart for each student who is taking medicine, recording appearance, energy, mood, and obvious symptoms and the type of medicine, dosage, and any side effects. As each student recovers or maintains his or her health, evaluate the effectiveness of the medication as a group experience. To balance the study of substance abuse, emphasize the positive features of drugs used properly.

10. *Drug Alternatives*

    Skills: Listening; studying; communicating; all integration skills

    Have students review the reasons for drug abuse: to feel good; to belong; to escape; to experiment; to relax; to relieve boredom; and to rebel. List the reasons the students dictate on a chart. Then, for each reason, have them suggest at least 3 alternative means of accomplishing the same goal. As each alternative is suggested, have students evaluate its effectiveness for someone their age, for someone younger, for someone older, and for an adult. List the best alternatives beside the reasons on the chart and leave it on display. Periodically ask for additional alternatives to evaluate and then list on the chart.

11. *Extra Practice.* • Have students interview non-smokers and former smokers and ask 3–4 questions about how they feel about smoking, why they quit smoking, and how they feel about being around people who smoke; follow a similar procedure to interview a reformed alcoholic. • Have students call or write for information from local resources for substance abuse; display the information received. • To focus on the legal drug distribution industry, have students interview a pharmacist to determine training, duties, and restrictions.

12. RECREATION AND SAFETY

DETECTION   Mastery of key concepts may be difficult for students who:

- Have had few opportunities for appropriate recreational activities
- Display weak social skills
- Do not listen carefully or observe events around them
- Have difficulty predicting and generalizing
- Are careless when playing
- Are inattentive or unusually active

Description. *Recreation* includes planned, supervised, and free play activities that occur both in and out of school. Whether such activities involve a large or small group or are engaged in as a solitary pursuit, when they are refreshing, amusing, or relaxing, they are recreational. The study of *safety* includes prevention of accidents as well as strategies for maintaining a safe environment at home, in school, and while traveling or playing. A number of first-aid concepts and the proper actions during emergencies are also issues for study. Both recreation and safety should be incorporated into the daily curriculum for all students regardless of age or ability.

Special Problems. Recreation is quite naturally an interesting topic to most students. The problems occur when activities are billed as recreational but are in fact neither refreshing nor enjoyable due to varying student interests and abilities. Physical problems, poor coordination, and weak social skills prevent some special students from enjoying group games and sports. Some special students are not adept at playing popular mental games, while others are not aware of the range of solitary amusements. The past experiences that students have had with certain activities influence the degree of present and even future pleasure they derive from them. Attempts to normalize special students can result in limiting recreational opportunities to those appropriate for their chronological ages rather than their interest or ability levels. Students who are inattentive and/or particularly active tend to overlook simple safety rules and precautions. A wealth of experiences enables students to identify potential hazards; students who have had limited experiences are unduly disadvantaged. Weak predicting and generalizing skills also interfere with the anticipation of danger. Some special students in particular have been protected from situations that might threaten their safety; while proper precautions are necessary, overprotection can turn into a handicapping condition itself.

Instructional Implications. Safe recreation and relaxation are important elements for maintaining the mental, physical, and emotional health of students and adults alike. Begin by asking students what they enjoy doing and then teach them strategies for doing it. When possible, emphasize educational recreation that is also enjoyable. Structure social interaction to insure acceptance and success. To develop safety habits, focus on activities that are of the most immediate interest and value to the students; then keep examples and experiences realistic and personally relevant.

CORRECTION Modify strategies for topical and learning needs:

1. *Key Terms*
    Skills: Observing; listening; reading; classifying; communicating
    To help students develop a meaningful vocabulary, associate terms with visual images, and review safety concepts, print the name of each recreational activity on a large and representative silhouette (e.g., a football when discussing that sport). Ask students to describe the types of accidents that might occur during the activity, identify the cause of each accident, and then propose rules for avoiding injury. As each rule is suggested, write or have a student write the rule on the silhouette. From the rules, select key terms to print on smaller silhouettes to give the students as their personal word cards. Have pairs of students use the cards to quiz each other by taking turns pronouncing each term, matching it to the large silhouette, and then describing its role in safe play. Pictures of objects can be used similarly, with words written around the object.

2. *Safety Rules*
    Skills: Listening; reading; analyzing; communicating; synthesizing;
        generalizing; evaluating
    Have the students themselves develop or modify safety rules and guidelines. First, have students identify all school rules that involve safety. These may include everything from not running in the hall to cafeteria rules to emergency evacuation procedures. These rules should be listed, discussed, and evaluated in terms of their contribution to each child's safety. Next, have students suggest modifications to the rules and even new rules that might improve school safety. List the improved rules and periodically review and refine them. Follow a similar procedure to evaluate and improve the safety features of existing classroom rules.

3. *Waiting to Happen*
    Skills: Observing; analyzing; predicting; communicating; generalizing;
        evaluating
    Use pictures from almost any source and guide students in looking for potential sources of accidents. Pictures showing toys on a step, an abandoned freezer, a batter swinging a bat, or people waiting to cross a busy street are examples of accidents "waiting to happen." In each instance, prompt students to predict the accident that might occur, the potential effects of the accident, and at least 2 ways to prevent the accident. Guiding students to predict potential problems before they happen and to plan ahead can be taught along with the discussion about each different safety area. Use pictures of all types of recreational activities, common household dangers, and product and appliance hazards to build a background for predicting and preventing accidents.

4. *Class Safety*
    Skills: Observing; directed experimenting; measuring; classifying;
        generalizing; evaluating
    Increase student awareness of accidents by keeping an accident chart for the class, such as this sample:

Weekly Accident Report   Date _____

BROKEN BONE	SPRAIN	SCRAPE	BRUISE	SUNBURN	CUT
Jerry	Angel Teresa	Sandy Tommy Guy	Sandy	Ocie Alison	Liz
Causes					
Treatment					
Prevention					

Add types of accidents as they occur. With each entry, guide students to identify the cause, treatment, and prevention. Periodically review the types of accidents and the frequencies with which they occur to identify needed modifications in safety rules or in the environment itself. As a variation, classify the accidents according to cause (e.g., fall, fight, or bite) and use the causes as headings for the chart.

5. *Mobile Safety*

   Skills: Observing; listening; reading; studying; analyzing; classifying; generalizing; evaluating

   Students use a variety of vehicles and equipment for recreational purposes: tricycles; bicycles; skates; skateboards; scooters; pogo sticks; surfboards; all types of motor bikes; automobiles; and the like. Whatever the particular equipment, 2 main areas are involved in its safe use: special safety features and safe operational techniques. Begin by having students describe, photograph, and/or draw a picture of their equipment or vehicle. Display pictures and prompt students to describe the safety features (e.g., reflectors, lights, flags, etc.), their purposes, and the types of accidents they are designed to prevent; then develop a list of rules for safe operation. Have students conduct a telephone or personal interview with the manager of a local store that specializes in the equipment to inquire about the special safety features and their cost. Guide them to plan what to ask and how to take notes during the interview. Compare and evaluate the safety features of several types and brands of equipment. Later, guide students to write to 2–3 major manufacturers of the equipment to inquire about special features, safety records, and cost of additional safety equipment they produce. Evaluate safety features to determine which company appears most interested in safety. Follow similar procedures for other types of recreational equipment (e.g., baseball gloves, football helmets, climbing bars, etc.). As needed, demonstrate and have students follow the model for appropriate safety actions, such as how to balance, roll, or fall.

6. *Seasonal Safety*

   Skills: Observing; listening; reading; studying; communicating; generalizing

   During different times of the year, specific safety measures should be reviewed. For cold weather, proper dress and walking on ice and snow or winter sports safety would be appropriate. For the spring and fall, water safety (including boating, swimming, or fishing) or an emphasis on soccer, football, baseball, or track may be appropriate. Encourage students to dress the part during a Safe Sports Day and feature safety lists, show-and-tell about injuries or near accidents students have had, and a poster display about safety advice for a specific sport or activity.

7. *Home Safety*

Skills: Observing; listening; reading; analyzing; communicating; generalizing; evaluating

As you discuss safety in the home, guide students to develop a 1-page home safety checklist. Include both potential hazards and safety equipment, such as fire extinguishers and smoke alarms, as well as a fire-escape plan and regular practice drills. Send a note to parents explaining that students are to use the checklist to evaluate the safety of their homes and requesting their assistance in the project. After completing the checklists, help students determine the most frequently occurring safety hazards and describe solutions, particularly for problems that the students can easily remedy. Send a copy of the proposed remedies to the parents and ask that they assist students to eliminate hazards.

8. *Accident Scrapbook*

Skills: Observing; reading; studying; analyzing; synthesizing; evaluating

Help students collect clippings from articles about accidents, focusing on the particular types that pose the greatest dangers to the students. Mount the pictures in a scrapbook along with a written analysis of the cause, treatment, and prevention, as in Activity 4. As the students themselves are involved in accidents, photograph the results (and the accident when possible), analyze the accident, and add to the scrapbook to personalize it.

9. *Emergency Contacts*

Skills: Listening; studying; organizing; communicating; generalizing

Begin by making a list of important people, departments, and telephone numbers that might be needed in school. Then assist students in developing a list of important numbers to keep at home. Telephone skills, using a phonebook, and remaining calm should be a part of the experience. Hold roleplaying sessions in which an accident occurs and students use a phone in class to call the appropriate person or department and provide the appropriate information.

10. *Extra Practice.* • Have students develop a personal list of a few important safety rules to follow for their special recreational interests. • Guide students to plan, practice, and then act out special safety procedures to be videotaped; use the videotapes for independent review and evaluation. • Invite members of local recreational groups to speak to students about safety tips for particular recreational activities; videotape the presentations for later review. • Have students read stories and books about various recreational activities and then evaluate the safety precautions described. • Have pairs of students contact the local Red Cross to obtain personal copies of first-aid brochures.

CHAPTER 7 /
UNDERSTANDING ILLNESS

13. CAUSES OF ILLNESS

DETECTION Mastery of key concepts may be difficult for students who:

- Are often ill and/or tired
- Seldom go to a doctor when sick
- Display unhealthy eating habits
- Have difficulty predicting and generalizing
- Do not follow basic hygienic practices

Description. Illnesses usually result from a physical or emotional shock to the body. Conditions that prevent the body from working properly are commonly referred to as *communicable* or *noncommunicable* diseases. Key concepts associated with communicable diseases are: introduction into the body of microorganisms causes infections; the types of microorganisms that are harmful to the body are protists, bacteria, protozoans, slime molds, and viruses; and most microorganisms are not harmful. Noncommunicable diseases are numerous and varied, but the major ones are cancer, heart disease, and even allergies. This section primarily focuses on how microorganisms are spread, where they live outside the body, health habits that influence illness, and common childhood illnesses, such as viral infections, chicken pox, and measles. Students also must be made aware that some adult illnesses can be traced back to childhood habits, heredity, and overall nutritional history.

Special Problems. Students who come from homes in which medical check-ups are infrequent and basic hygienic and nutritional practices are neither followed nor taught typically lack the experiential background that forms the foundation for understanding causes of illness. Some students avoid discussions of illness because of associated fear and discomfort. This topic is difficult for students to master for several reasons: The causes themselves often are not visible; the delay between cause and effect is highly variable; so many factors go into the cause/effect connection that prediction of illness is not certain; and much remains unknown about causes of some illnesses.

Instructional Implications. Early education of both parents and students is an essential step in understanding the causes of disease. The role of basic hygiene, nutrition, rest, and exercise as well as the emerging research on the influence of emotions and stress should be emphasized. The cause/effect connection must be clearly made; exploring cause, intervening variables, and effects of actual examples of students' illnesses can best illustrate the relationship. Be sensitive to students who are fearful of becoming sick, dying, or having to go to the hospital.

CORRECTION Modify strategies for topical and learning needs:

1. *Important Words about Illness*
    Skills: Listening; reading; classifying; predicting; communicating
    Begin by asking students to describe what they can remember about being
    ill. Print key words from their descriptions on the chalkboard. After
    discussion, divide the words into categories, such as symptoms or names.
    Then provide 2–3 headings, such as Mumps or Measles. If appropriate, list
    symptoms under each illness listed. After providing this frame of reference,
    have students read or listen to information about microorganisms. Include
    such terms as *protists* and *bacteria, protozoans,* and *viruses* and explain
    their roles in different diseases. Post review cards for each word and a brief
    description for future review. For *bacteria* and *viruses,* review cards could
    state:
        Bacteria: live in air, animals, people plants, soil, and water. Bacteria can
            be shaped like a corkscrew, round or rod shaped.
        Viruses: smallest microorganism that can live in many types of cells and
            keep cells from working normally. Viruses are small enough to live
            inside bacteria.
2. *How Microorganisms Spread Illness*
    Skills: Listening; reading; studying; organizing; classifying; communicating
    Help students develop a poster showing the manner in which microorgan-
    isms spread and the resulting illness. A partial display might look like this:

How Illness Spreads	*Results*
Air: sneezing, coughing, talking	colds, influenza, measles
Animals: biting	rabies
Contact: touching	colds, pneumonia, tuberculosis
Food: eating contaminated food	food poisoning, scarlet fever

3. *Specific Causes*
    Skills: Reading; studying; analyzing; communicating; generalizing
    Lead a discussion about familiar childhood illnesses, such as measles,
    mumps, flu, and ringworm. Provide sources in which student teams can
    locate information about which microorganism causes a specific illness and
    how the illness is contracted and spread. Also suggest interviews as another
    source of information. Have the teams write and record a 2–5-minute report
    on audiotape for sharing with other groups.
4. *Seeing the Unseen*
    Skills: Observing; studying; analyzing; communicating; synthesizing;
            generalizing
    It will be difficult for some students to understand just how small microor-
    ganisms are. Use analogies such as: 2,000 bacteria could fit on a pinhead.
    To explain that each type of microorganism is different, use pictures of each
    type and have students draw, color, and label 1 type of microorganism.
    Display the drawings for review. If appropriate, have students make smaller
    drawings on index cards and label by type on the back. To use the cards,
    show each drawing and have students identify the type and name 3 illnesses

it causes. To build verbal skills, name a type of microorganism and have students describe its appearance and name related illnesses. Later, if possible, have students match the cards with what they see as they view samples through an electron microscope.

5. *Magnifying Causes*

   Skills: Observing; listening; analyzing; communicating; generalizing; evaluating

   Ask students to select something in the room to examine under a magnifying glass. Have students describe how the object changes when magnified. Then have students magnify their hands, desks, books, and assorted objects in their desks to discover dirt and other foreign matter. Ask how what they see might be related to illnesses. Lead them to evaluate their environment and their everyday practices to conclude ways in which to impede the spread of illness in the classroom.

6. *Microscopic Study*

   Skills: Observing; listening; studying; directed experimenting; analyzing; communicating; generalizing

   Although students may not actually be able to see all microorganisms, the principles involved provide an excellent example for students. Obtain 1–2 microscopes and prepared slides from the science laboratory. To prepare original and safe slides, punch large holes in a strip of cardboard; put a strip of clear tape under the holes, place samples of dirt, water, and other appropriate materials on the sticky tape, and cover with an additional strip of tape. Discuss what the students see and how the microscope shows detail not visible to the normal eye. As in Activity 5, ask students how what they see might be related to causes of illnesses. Have students suggest other samples that might be associated with illness, examine the samples under the microscope, and discuss the relationship with causes of illnesses.

7. *Cover-up*

   Skills: Observing; directed experimenting; generalizing; evaluating

   To illustrate the necessity of covering their mouths when they sneeze or cough, have students cough while close to a mirror and then magnify the mirror to discover the droplets on it. Ask: Why should you cover your mouth when you cough? What do you think happens when you sneeze? Discuss the roles of coughing and sneezing in spreading illness. Then have students breathe on the mirror to frost it and examine the mirror under magnification. Ask: Why shouldn't you breathe in someone's face? Lead students to infer the role of breathing in spreading illness.

8. *Comparative Analysis*

   Skills: Observing; listening; studying; directed experimenting; analyzing; classifying; evaluating

   After students have used a magnifying glass and microscope to compare and analyze several samples, explain how people study microorganisms that are in the body of a person; when certain types of microorganisms are present and the person is ill, the microorganism may be the cause. Have a nurse, medical lab technician, or doctor bring samples, and if possible even small laboratory equipment to demonstrate how the microorganisms are detected. Later, have students judge the value of such analyses and the equipment itself and summarize their conclusions orally or in writing.

9. *Natural Homes for Microorganisms*

Skills: Listening; reading; studying; analyzing; communicating

Although microorganisms live nearly everywhere, harmful microorganisms are more likely to live in certain places. To inform students about these places, use pictures or descriptions of trash and garbage, dirty water, spoiled food, ill people, insects, and other scenes; ask students to describe the potential problems that may exist. Then have students analyze samples from a few of the settings, such as the school garbage or dirty water. Have students observe and record the changes in spoiled food (e.g., an orange slice) over a period of several days. Use magnification to highlight the gradual changes. If several samples are used, vary the temperature or moisture to compare changes. Identify the conditions and settings that are most likely to produce harmful microorganisms.

10. *Noncommunicable Illnesses*

Skills: Listening; reading; studying; classifying; communicating

Explain that, unlike communicable diseases, diabetes, heart and kidney disease as well as forms of cancer are not contagious. Another difference is that communicable diseases tend to appear suddenly while noncommunicable diseases form over a longer period of time as the result of unhealthy living habits or factors associated with heredity. Present information about diet, exercise, and harmful drugs as examples of potential causes of noncommunicable diseases. Then list 2 headings (Communicable and Noncommunicable) on the board. Name a disease and have students decide in which category the disease should be placed and why.

11. *Scientific Stories*

Skills: Listening; communicating; synthesizing; evaluating

Locate books in the school or public library that involve historical stories about the presumed causes of illness. Read the stories to the students for 5 minutes each day. Tell students to listen to identify the presumed cause and to explain why people thought it was the cause. After listening to the story, have students compare the cause in the story with what is known today about the cause and then evaluate the logic and accuracy of the cause cited in the story. Guide pairs of students to read and study about the people, diseases, and activities that were described in the story, and then compare information with their peers.

12. *Extra Practice.* • Have students keep a personal list of their illnesses and the probable causes. • Extend Activities 8 and 9 to include microorganisms that are helpful and essential to life. • Have students use reference sources to study microorganisms and report their research in small groups. • Invite a resource person to describe noncommunicable diseases that are associated with his or her family history.

14. TREATMENT OF ILLNESS

DETECTION Mastery of key concepts may be difficult for students who:

- Exhibit unhealthy habits of hygiene, nutrition, and exercise
- Know little about the causes of illnesses
- Are unfamiliar with sources and types of treatments
- Seldom seek medical assistance
- Have difficulty generalizing and evaluating

Description. When teaching about treatment of illness, the major concepts to emphasize are the patient's responsibilities, sources and types of treatment, and qualifications of service providers. The duties of the patient begin with the acceptance of responsibility for remembering symptoms and accurately reporting them, remembering to follow medical advice, and taking prescribed medication as recommended. Students should be aware of the sources where medical treatment is provided and the major treatment procedures, including drug therapy, diet control, physical therapy, surgery, and radiation as well as specific therapy for people who have emotional problems that are too big for them to handle alone. Finally, students should be aware of medical quackery and what to watch for from unqualified individuals who are well intentioned or perhaps more interested in making money than in helping people.

Special Problems. Medical treatment is primarily a family affair; students from families where treatment is seldom sought, practiced, or discussed often lack the experiential background on which to build concepts. Many people avoid this topic because they fear that the treatment will be costly, painful, and/or necessitate a change in old habits. Adults are not always aware of treatment facilities, sources of financial support, or the potential seriousness of certain health problems. Some students have been taught to be tough and not give in to aches and pains. In some families students are warned about particular treatments that did not help or were costly. A few families avoid the topic because of religious beliefs. The complexity and personal nature of this topic may make it particularly difficult or even inappropriate for young and low-ability-level special students.

Instructional Implications. Except for very basic principles, this topic may be too advanced for some special students. Essential elements of instruction include providing accurate information about the responsibilities of students and families, facilities and treatments available locally, and local sources of financial aid for medical services. Misunderstandings are easily adopted by students who listen to other students or poorly informed adults. Present positive views and discuss the treatment of illness as a way to improve the quality of life. Be particularly sensitive to families' rights to privacy, students' fears, possible conflicts with family beliefs, students who may be overconcerned with illness, and individual students who have had extensive medical treatment.

CORRECTION Modify strategies for topical and learning needs:

1. *Treatment Resources*
   Skills: Observing; listening; reading; communicating
   Present terminology in an upbeat, positive manner. Begin with your own treatment experiences and then relate those of famous people. Use a picture of a hospital or physician's office and post new words around this setting as they are discussed and explained. Post the words showing the general terms on top with the supporting or related words below. Partial listings for treatment of cancer and epilepsy might include:

Control of Epilepsy	*Cancer Treatments*
Medication	Chemotherapy
Warning signals	Radiation therapy
No contact sports	Surgery

   Have students illustrate the listings with cartoons that humorously depict the experiences; then have them share their illustrations.
2. *Home Treatment Inventory*
   Skills: Observing; studying; analyzing; communicating; evaluating
   Guide students to develop a checklist for inventorying treatment aids in the home. Ask parents to assist students in using the checklist to conduct an inventory in their homes. A partial inventory could include the following:
   Inventory of Home Health Care Products
   Are medicines stored safely?
   Have old prescription medicines been thrown away?
   Are emergency phone numbers easily accessible?
   Which of these items are available?
   Heating pad _____ Vaporizer _____ Humidifier _____
   Others_____

   Have students share their completed inventories, and if changes need to be made, use this list as a basis for deciding what is needed.
3. *Treatment Centers Update*
   Skills: Observing; listening; reading; analyzing; communicating
   Ask students where in the community people can go for medical help. List these and include 1–3 medical problems that might require treatment in a hospital. As facilities are mentioned, add these to the list. Include the school clinic, private offices and clinics, hospitals, minor emergency clinics, emergency rooms, and public health centers and clinics. Next, help students locate the addresses and phone numbers for facilities in their area. Then, assign student teams to contact the facilities to determine the types of services offered and the options for payment and/or financial aid. Provide a list of facilities for students to take home.
4. *What's Your Specialty?*
   Skills: Reading; studying; classifying; communicating; predicting
   Ask students what types of injuries or illness they think they might experience. As areas are mentioned, begin developing a Specialists Roster. From the more than 20 medical specialties, list those that students are most

likely to need, such as allergists, opthalmologists, orthopedic surgeons, otolaryngologists, and pediatricians. If appropriate, have students use a telephone directory to match physicians by name with their listed specialty. Have them compare the number of physicians listed for each specialty and speculate about the differences.

5. *Drug Therapy*

Skills: Analyzing; communicating; measuring; generalizing; evaluating

Drugs are the most common treatment to relieve discomfort and help the body fight infections. Ask students to describe medicines they have seen advertised on TV, the reasons people take them, how they know to take them, and how they know when to quit taking them. Prompt students to include the most common over-the-counter medicines, such as aspirin, cough syrup, stomach medicines, and antihistamines. Contrast these with medicines prescribed by a physician. Then prompt students to develop rules for assuming a share of responsibility for their medical treatment. Concepts to include are these:

- Do not take medicine you do not need or that is not prescribed.
- Do take your medicine as directed.
- Do tell your doctor when medicine makes you itch, nauseous, or dizzy.
- Do not share your medicine with anyone.

Conclude by contrasting the benefits of drug therapy with the dangers of drug abuse (see Topic 11, Psychoactive Drugs).

6. *Diet Control*

Skills: Listening; studying; analyzing; classifying; communicating; generalizing; evaluating

After reviewing the importance of nutrition and providing an overview of diet control, guide students to develop an interview form for collecting data on the use of diet to control various illnesses. First have each student respond to the questionnaire and then assign a certain number of interviews for pairs of students to conduct. Have students chart their findings, using headings such as Illness, Special Diet, and Results, and then evaluate diet control as a type of treatment for each illness.

7. *Physical Therapy*

Skills: Observing; listening; reading; communicating; generalizing

Demonstrate a simple massage on your hand and fingers and then have students follow your model to massage one of their own hands with the other. Explain that certain types of massage, heat, and exercise are used by trained physical therapists to help people move more easily and limit pain. Discuss the benefits of physical therapy for such illnesses as muscular dystrophy, multiple sclerosis, polio, arthritis, chronic back problems, and others that may be appropriate for the students. Have students suggest types of injuries for which physical therapy might be beneficial.

8. *Surgical Treatment*

Skills: Observing; listening; communicating; generalizing; evaluating

Present surgery as the treatment of choice when illness will not respond to drug, diet, or physical therapy. Begin by discussing minor surgery, such as that for ingrown toenails, removal of small foreign objects, and skin infections, and include laser, orthoscopic, and traditional surgical techniques. Be sure that students understand that the purpose of surgery is ultimately make the patient feel better. Show videotapes, such as the ones that physicians and dentists use to prepare young patients for minor surgeries. Read aloud one of the books written just for children to relieve their fear of hospitals and surgery (check with the librarian). Have students listen to discover the benefits of the treatments.

9. *Radiation Therapy*

Skills: Listening; analyzing; communicating; evaluating

If this activity is appropriate, explain radiation therapy as concentrated x-rays (much stronger than the ones used by dentists) used for the treatment of cancer to apply directly to tumors and sometimes before and after surgery to be sure cancer cells are destroyed. To illustrate how radiation is administered, shine a flashlight directly on a spot of a student's hand for 10–15 seconds, explaining that the x-ray is used in a similar manner to treat a specific spot in the body. Describe the side effects of radiation—hair loss, discoloration of the skin, and exhaustion—and have students weigh the merits of the therapy against the side effects.

10. *Emotional Treatment*

Skills: Observing; listening; reading; communicating; generalizing

Explain the roles and major differences between psychologists, counselors, psychiatrists, social workers, and other mental professionals in the local community. Direct several simulations about problems, such as a fight on the playground or losing a contest. Roleplay the part of the therapist (or have a visiting professional play the part) as students simulate patients attempting to resolve the problems you provide. Avoid personal problems of your students unless they offer no opportunity for embarrassment and are generalizable to most students and then only at the request of the involved student(s). After each simulation, have students critique the value of the therapy and suggest improvements.

11. *Medical Quackery*

Skills: Observing; listening; reading; analyzing; communicating;
       synthesizing; generalizing; evaluating

Present several make-believe and preposterous advertisements for products and services offering guarantees and cures for the class to evaluate and discuss why such claims may be false. Explain the meaning of *quacks* and that products promising miracles and quick cures are often sold through the mail, not through reputable retail stores or medical offices. Help student teams compile a list of such hypothetical products and services and their purported miracles. (Carefully avoid raising issues that may conflict with religious beliefs of some students.) Have the teams develop quackery ads for imaginary products and share with peers.

12. *Extra Practice.* • Have students roleplay calling a clinic and making an appointment for certain services. • As an ongoing activity, have students orally critique advertisements for medicines. • Invite treatment specialists to explain their methods and document their effectiveness.

15. PREVENTION OF ILLNESS

DETECTION Mastery of key concepts may be difficult for students who:
- Do not understand causes of illness
- Display unhealthy eating habits
- Do not follow basic hygienic practices
- Have difficulty predicting, hypothesizing, and generalizing
- Cannot explain the value of preventing illness

Description. Understanding ways to prevent illness presupposes understanding of the causes of illness. The major concepts revolve around the steps students can take to build their resistance or immune systems, including being immunized against the major communicable diseases; having regular medical check-ups; participating in a program of eating, exercising, and resting properly; wearing appropriate clothing; and limiting exposure to disease-causing microorganisms. Understanding how the body fights against disease by producing antibodies to combat infections is also an important concept.

Special Problems. Much like treatment of illness, preventing illness is mostly a family affair. Students who come from families who seldom seek medical treatment, are uninformed about causes of illness, and follow unhealthy hygienic and nutritional practices typically lack the experiential and knowledge base for understanding how to prevent illness. Many adults are not aware of all the steps that should be taken to limit the chances of becoming ill. As with understanding the causes of illness, students often have difficulty mastering this topic because of the variation in the delay between cause and effect. Students who have problems predicting and hypothesizing tend to experience problems mastering the content. In a school situation, students are constantly exposed to the communicable illnesses of their peers; when they too become ill, despite having taken seemingly proper precautions, they become confused. Students who have been taught to be tough sometimes fail to recognize the importance of the topic. While an overreaction to aches and pains is problematic for some students, reluctance to admit to feeling bad or trying to hide an illness is common for both youngsters and some adults.

Instructional Implications. To expand students' experiential base, routinely model, verbalize, and practice preventive strategies in the classroom. Regular reviews of the causes of illnesses and basic hygienic practices should be incorporated into instruction. Of particular importance is the emphasis on protecting others as well as oneself; a clear policy must be established for separating students with communicable illnesses from their peers. Both parents and students need to be informed about policy and about schedules for obtaining immunizations and other preventive steps, particularly during outbreaks of particular diseases. It is a good idea to introduce this topic by addressing prevention as it relates to one or more illnesses that are of particular interest to the students and their families.

CORRECTION Modify strategies for topical and learning needs:

1. *Healthy Words*
    Skills: Observing; listening; reading; communicating
    Vocabulary instruction should focus on 2 points: what students can do for themselves to prevent illness and what they can do for others. Ask students to remember the last time they were ill: How did you feel? What caused your illness? Could it have been prevented? How? What did you do to keep your friends from becoming ill? What other illnesses have your heard about? As students discuss these ideas print each sentence on sentence strips, but leave a blank in place of each key word (e.g. *immunization, sneeze, cold, mumps).* Print 3–6 key words that fit the sentences on separate index cards. Give each key-word card to a student. As the discussion ends, have 1–2 students hold up a sentence strip and ask their peers to decide which key word belongs in the blank. Then ask the student with the word to use a paper clip to clip the word card over the blank. Students should read or listen while the sentence is read and then decide if the word is correct.

2. *Identifying Sources of Diseases*
    Skills: Observing; listening; analyzing; predicting; communicating; synthesizing; generalizing
    To review some of the causes of illness, show pictures of potential hazards, such as a dog or cat, a snake, a mosquito or tick, contaminated food, and a poisonous plant from the local area. Discuss the different types of illnesses that can result from each of these sources and the treatments for each. Have students name 3 ways to prevent illness or injury from each source. (To avoid overgeneralizations about animals, review the activities in Chapter 4.) Then, using a game format, have pairs of students use the pictures and alternate naming the potential problem (e.g., bite, eating, touching), the possible result (e.g., rabies or infection, food poisoning or a specific disease, rash), the discomfort and inconvenience, the treatment, and methods of prevention.

3. *Simulated Antibodies*
    Skills: Observing; listening; directed experimenting; communicating; synthesizing; generalizing
    Describe the role of white blood cells in producing antibodies that work through the bloodstream to fight infections. Begin with an example such as a cut and a simplified description of the process whereby the white cells gather at the cut and begin to fight infectious microorganisms. Diagram the process on a transparency as you talk. Explain that a similar battle takes place with other harmful organisms that cause the flu or more serious illnesses. Give student teams copies of the diagram and have them simulate *on the paper* the battle as they roleplay the actions of miniature organisms, white blood cells, antibodies, and harmful microorganisms. Discuss how eating the right foods and getting plenty of rest facilitates this process within the human body daily. Be sure to note that much about the immune system is still unknown.

4. *Vaccine Battle*

> *Skills:* Listening; reading; studying; communicating; analyzing; synthesizing; generalizing
>
> As an extension of Activity 3, present the concept of vaccines as a "call to battle." Begin by asking students what would happen if a few invaders attacked their classroom on Monday, but on Tuesday, a much stronger group of invaders attacked. Lead them to conclude that they might be better prepared on the second day. Then explain that vaccines are available to help the antibodies mobilize to protect the body against specific invaders; a few invaders or microorganisms that cause infection are injected, the antibodies mobilize, and when the strong invaders attack, the antibodies are prepared to conquer them. The body is then protected from or immune to the invaders. Guide students to describe the the vaccinations, immunizations, or shots with which they are familiar and the illness each prevents. As each vaccination is described, have a peer follow your model to again describe the vaccine battle. Then guide students to develop a list of illnesses with corresponding vaccines. Conclude with each student compiling a personal Vaccine Battle Record.

5. *Preventive Behaviors*

> *Skills:* Observing; listening; reading; communicating
>
> Present a "how to" for preventing illnesses each week and build a list of proper behaviors for healthy living. After presenting 2–3, have students volunteer their suggestions for the following weeks. If appropriate, assign reading or listening that will lead to their determining another "how to" to share with others. Your list might begin with these:
>
> - Cover you mouth when you sneeze.
> - Turn away from others when you sneeze.
> - Wash your hands before you eat.
>
> Have students explain why each behavior is important and what it prevents.

6. *Resistance Team*

> *Skills:* Listening; studying; analyzing; generalizing; evaluating
>
> Begin a volunteer Resistance Team dedicated to developing positive health habits both personally and for those around them. Use stickers or an honor list for those who participate. Each member should keep a personal journal of the actions they take to stay healthy. Items such as hours of sleep each night, amount of exercise each day, types of foods eaten at each meal, and other health-related habits should be included. Periodically, have pairs of students swap journals and suggest improvements in the resistance measures. For extra credit, have students record the ways in which they persuaded others to improve health practices.

7. *Illness Report*

> *Skills:* Observing; listening; reading; analyzing; classifying; communicating; synthesizing; generalizing; evaluating
>
> Periodically, TV newscasts issue special reports on communicable diseases such as influenza. Develop a file of videotapes describing preventive measures (as well as causes and treatments) for particular illnesses with which students are likely to come in contact. Have student teams review appropri-

ate tapes. Guide the teams to take notes, summarize, and then present a 1-minute Illness Report to peers. As needed, help students telephone or write for additional information. Based on the report and any additional information that the students themselves must gather through study, have students conclude the appropriate preventive measures they should take to avoid the same illness.

8. *Preventive Mental Health*

   Skills: Listening; reading; communicating; synthesizing; generalizing; evaluating

   When reviewing causes of emotional illnesses, remind students that a major cause is letting problems pile up until they are unbearable. One way to prevent being overwhelmed is to find a way to vent. Ask students what makes them feel better when they are upset. Prompt them to include such outlets as talking to someone who really listens and understands, strenuous physical activities, recreational activities, laughing or crying, or even sleeping and being close to someone who really cares. Compare the venting to the forest ranger who puts out brush fires before they become forest fires. Have students describe in personal and confidential journals what worries them most at school and what they think they can do to prevent their worries from becoming larger. Offer them the option of sharing their journals with you, keeping them secret, or destroying each page after it is written. Have students mark the preventive suggestions that they want to share anonymously with the group. Present these suggestions as a stimulus for discussion to critique and improve upon.

9. *Healthy Friends*

   Skills: Listening; analyzing; communicating; generalizing; evaluating

   Introduce this activity by reading aloud or telling a synopsis of the story of Typhoid Mary. Ask: If you had lived then, would you have wanted to be Mary's friend? Why or why not? Lead students to conclude that good friends try to prevent others from becoming ill. Ask: What if Leonard has a sore throat and fever but he doesn't want to miss the Halloween party at school? He also wants to be a good friend. What should he do and why? How can you help keep your friends well? Prompt students to develop classroom guidelines for Healthy Friends. Include such concepts as these:
   * Don't get close to friends when you think you are getting sick.
   * When you get sick at school, go home.
   * Stay home from school till you are free of fever for 24 hours.
   * Don't let your friends come in to play when you're sick.

   Guide students to also include basic rules of hygiene. As rules are suggested, ask students to justify their importance. Insist that students share the rules with their families.

10. *Extra Practice.* • Use the sentence strips and key-word cards described in Activity 1 in a center for independent or small-group review. • As an extension of Activity 4, have students share their secrets for making shots less painful. • Have students tape an interview with the school nurse describing what can be done to stay healthy.

REFLECTIONS

1. The introduction to Part II presents a general overview of the topics discussed in this section. Now that you have considered each of the topics, what additional points would you emphasize or clarify in the introductory discussion? Why? How might your emphasis differ according to the ages and abilities of the learners? What additional topics would you add to this section? Why?

2. The relative importance of the topics in Chapter 6, "Health and Nutrition," may vary according to the region of the country, the experiences students have had, the ages of the learners and the degrees of their learning problems, and the philosophies of the teachers. Rank the topics in terms of your evaluation of their importance to a 7-year-old special student and a 13-year-old special student in your local region.

3. Preconceived notions often interfere with acquisition of new information. Along with one or more peers, consider the topics in Chapter 7, "Understanding Illness." What are some popular misconceptions associated with illnesses? List these and then decide on several strategies to overcome and replace the erroneous concepts.

4. Similar DETECTION behaviors are listed for several of the topics in this section. Analyze these behaviors for commonalities and differences across topics and explain your analysis. Then suggest additional behaviors that might indicate possible problems understanding the content of each topic.

5. The appropriateness of instructional activities varies with the age of the students. Identify five corrective strategies in this section that you believe would be best for teaching a 7-year-old student about ecology or illness. Which ones would be most appropriate for teaching the same topic to a 13-year-old? Defend your choices.

6. Textbooks determine the science curriculum in some teachers' classrooms. Review the second- and fourth-grade levels of the elementary science basal texts in use in the schools in your area. Compare and contrast the topical content of the life science sections in those textbooks with the selected topics in Part II. Justify any differences you observe. Then select a lesson from one of the textbooks and modify it for a real or hypothetical special student, incorporating into the lesson the principles discussed in Chapter 3.

7. Carefully structured questions help special learners focus on the most important concepts and guide their thinking. Construct such a set of questions about one of the life science topics; plan to use the questions as an advance organizer to introduce the topic and as a test of mastery after the topic is studied.

8. Observation, listening, and prediction skills are important facilitative skills for mastering many of the topics in this section. Review the recommendations in Chapter 3 for teaching these skills, and then plan how to teach these three skills to special learners as you teach the concepts for a life science topic of your choice. Practice teaching your lesson to a peer, and then, if possible, restructure your lesson for a specific special student and teach the lesson to the him or her.

9. Special students often require extra review activities in order to master a topic. Games can be used to interest students in a topic and then to review the concepts. Choose a life science topic and then develop a game that highlights the most important concepts. Try out the game with several peers and modify it as needed. Then, if possible, introduce and play the game with special students.

10. A number of resources about life science are available. Compare and contrast the topical, conceptual, and skills emphasis of these publications with the discussions in Part II:

Allison, L. (1976). *Blood and guts: A working guide to your own insides.* Boston: Little, Brown.

Bains, R. (1985). *Health and hygiene.* Mahwah, NJ: Troll Associates.

Ball, D. W. (1978). *ESS/Special education teacher's guide.* St. Louis: Webster/ McGraw-Hill.

Brandt, K. (1985). *The five senses.* Mahwah, NJ: Troll Associates.

Bybee, R., Peterson, R., Bowyer, J., & Butts, D. (1984). *Teaching about science and society: Activities for elementary and junior high school.* Columbus, OH: Charles E. Merrill.

Eugene, T. (1985). *Creatures of the woods.* Washington, DC: National Geographic Society.

Gega, P. C. (1990). *Science in elementary education.* (6th ed.). New York. Macmillan.

Herbert, D. (1980). *Mr. Wizard's supermarket science.* New York: Random House.

Nelson, L. W., & Lorbeer, G. C. (1984). *Science activities for elementary children* (8th ed.). Dubuque, IA: Wm. C. Brown.

Rinard, J. (1985). *Helping our animal friends.* Washington, DC: National Geographic Society.

Russell, H. R. (1973). *Ten-minute field trips: Using the school grounds for environmental studies.* Chicago: J. G. Ferguson.

Sabin, F. (1985). *Mammals.* Mahwah, NJ: Troll Associates.

Sabin, F. (1985). *Human body.* Mahwah, NJ: Troll Associates.

Smithsonian Family Learning Project (1987). *Science activity book.* New York: GMG.

Taylor, F. D., Artuso, A. A., & Hewett, F. M. (1973). *Exploring our environment: Science tasks for exceptional children in special and regular classrooms.* Denver: Love.

Terhune, J. A. (Ed.). (1987). *Health skills for life* (2nd ed.). Eugene, OR: Author.

PART III

EARTH SCIENCE

When presented in the right manner, the study of earth science can be of particular interest to special students. The content is especially appropriate for conducting experiments, projects, and small-group and independent studies on such topics as rocks, sources of water, and all types of weather. Although a variety of skills must be applied in learning the content, the highest priority skill areas include observing, analyzing, classifying, and generalizing.

When compared to the life science topics, most of the topics in Part III are not nearly so valuable to special learners; some of the topics may be, however, of great interest to particular students. Although all the topics affect in some way the present and future lives of students, perhaps the most obviously relevant are those having to do with weather.

Part III begins with a chapter on the earth and its geographic formations, including rocks, oceans, lakes, rivers, and forests. Rocks interest a number of students of all ages and abilities. The degree to which the other topics appeal to students often varies according to the extent to which they have traveled and the geographic locations of their homes. Because of the complexity of the concepts involved, the ever-changing nature of the earth is not addressed directly in Chapter 8, but study should be pursued by individual students who show special interest.

The subject of Chapter 9 is weather, ranging from temperature and precipitation to forecasting. Since these factors directly influence students' daily lives and even their social structures and customs, their relevance is comparatively easy to establish, particularly when study is paired with social studies lessons. The study of storms involves important safety concepts in regions where certain types of destructive storms are prevalent, while a general understanding of climate involves health concepts. The concepts of weather easily can be observed and applied to local conditions and events; thus, nature often furnishes the explanatory demonstrations.

Chapter 10 focuses on astronomy, an exciting area of study and one that is continually changing as new data become available and space exploration is expanded. Although these topics are not especially essential to students' personal safety on a daily basis, they contain current information that is often discussed in the news and by people of all ages. The thrust of this chapter is toward life in the future.

At least limited mastery of factual content, concepts, and skills are prerequisites for a deep understanding of earth science. To detect content needs, opportunities must be presented for students to exhibit mastery by demonstrating, experimenting, and participating in research activities. The ability to gather and analyze information is a key activity. The detection of skill mastery should be placed in the context of the particular topic or content material. Prediction skills, for example, can be screened more easily during the study of storms or weather forecasts than when studying rocks. Much of the assessment of content mastery involves the use of models, pictures, and other concrete examples.

An active, hands-on approach is advocated for the study of earth science. Students should be involved in doing as they listen and communicate with others. In addition to the target skill areas of observation, analysis, classification, and generalization, other skills are emphasized according to the particular topic. For example, measurement is stressed for dealing with temperature, while prediction is a vital experience for learning about weather and space exploration. The chapter about astronomy also is appropriate for encouraging creativity through classification or comparison of fictional/factual correspondences and prediction/verification activities.

16. LAND FORMATIONS

DETECTION Mastery of key concepts may be difficult for students who:

- Know little about local geographic formations
- Have had few opportunities to observe different geographic formations
- Do not observe carefully
- Have difficulty classifying and/or analyzing
- Experience problems generalizing

Description. One of the often criticized competencies of students and adults is their lack of knowledge about geography and matters related to land masses. A similar criticism has been extended to include their overall knowledge about major geographic regions in or surrounding the United States. This section includes ideas for developing skills and knowledge about important regions of the earth and the land and geographic formations associated with these regions. The major emphasis is on the continental United States although these concepts can be expanded to include any country or even other planets.

Special Problems. Knowledge of the earth's surface structure and vast differences across regions is not always given top priority in school curricula. Basic academic skills and more recently thinking skills and the arts have tended to receive more emphasis. Many adults are relatively uninformed about formations, geography and land history, or the continuing effects of weather and ecological abuses. Some programs emphasize space and technology at the expense of more basic concepts of earth science, leaving students without even rudimentary concepts. Students who do not observe carefully and those who have seldom traveled to areas with different formations are likely to have a weak foundation on which to build concepts. A final problem involves the actual content, which is beautiful and varied but typically not as exciting or interesting as some health and science topics.

Instructional Implications. To personalize the content, study should begin with the analysis of the formations within the region where students live and then expand outward. Whenever possible, activities should require active involvement. Since mastery of much of the content relies heavily on the analysis of a variety of different land formations, instruction should include guided observation of both the immediate area and a selection of pictures and films. Classification skills may need to be taught directly. To emphasize societal relevance, integrate study with social studies by carefully guiding students to conclude the sociological impact of various formations.

CORRECTION   Modify strategies for topical and learning needs:

1. *Earth Faces*

   Skills: Observing; listening; reading; analyzing classifying; communicating; evaluating

   If possible, visit and then use pictures and color maps of each type of local land formation (e.g., mountain, peninsula, desert). Label and post each picture or map. Have students select their favorite sites and justify their choices. Walk students through the process of comparing and contrasting similarities and differences in 2 pictures before having them follow the model to view films of and discuss other sites. Then have students identify other sites they would like to visit; provide visits by taking students to the sites or having them read or view pictures.

2. *Clay Concepts*

   Skills: Observing; studying; analyzing; synthesizing; evaluating

   Have students carefully study pictures of local or prominent land areas and then draw what they see. Have them explain which features they notice the most. Guide teams of students to make clay models of the land features, using their pictures and a raised relief map as references. Pair this activity with a social studies lesson to investigate the sociological effects of the land formations.

3. *A Concept of Scale*

   Skills: Observing; analyzing; measuring; communicating

   To help students develop a sense of the relative sizes of different land formations and areas, have them observe, feel, and describe the features of a designated area on a raised relief map. Next provide information about the dimensions of the features. Round off the numbers and make or have students make scaled cut-outs of specific sites. Then have students compare the sizes of different mountains, deserts, and other areas as well as the sizes of similar land types from different parts of the country. When possible, make comparisons using local landmarks and buildings as reference points to help develop a realistic concept of size and distance.

4. *Which Is Which?*

   Skills: Listening; reading; studying; analyzing; communicating

   Help students write 1–2 sentence descriptions of at least 4 different land areas. Place the descriptions on index cards. The same formations (e.g., islands or mountains) can be used several times but with descriptions written or dictated by different students. Form teams to take turns reading descriptions for others to identify.

5. *Extra Practice.* • Using a map, have students stick color-coded pins on examples of the formations as they are studied. • Check with tourism experts to obtain films or printed material showing nearby land formations. • Extend Which Is Which? by using descriptions of specific land areas, such as Mount St. Helens. • Read aloud descriptions from good travel books for students to summarize and then draw their visual images. • Have students compare one of the newer computer-generated maps of the local area to the site itself and to older, traditional maps.

17. ROCKS

DETECTION Mastery of key concepts may be difficult for students who:

- Have had few experiences with a wide variety of rocks
- Do not observe carefully
- Have difficulty analyzing and classifying
- Demonstrate limited knowledge about rocks and their importance
- Cannot explain the value of rocks to self and society

Description. Among the concepts to include are the characteristics of the major types of rocks, where they are found, and how they are changed. There are three families of rocks: igneous, sedimentary, and metamorphic. The most common and familiar rocks in each family are granite (igneous); sandstone, limestone, and conglomerates (sedimentary); and marble, quartzite, and slate (metamorphic). All three of the rock families are formed in a different manner but are changed by the effects of water, plants, and other natural forces. Rock families are subdivided by color, mineral content, or other features. The degree of detail and depth of study that is appropriate depends on the ages and abilities of the students as well as the number and variety of rocks that occur naturally in their immediate surroundings.

Special Problems. Because of the beauty of some rocks and the wide variety of shapes, colors, and textures available, rocks appeal to many students. It is typically not disinterest that creates problems but lack of opportunity. Students who live in areas where only a limited assortment of rocks occur naturally are denied the everyday free-play learning experiences that build a solid foundation for further study of rocks. In such areas, if teachers do not obtain sample kits, they too are handicapped by not having ready access to plentiful samples. Students who live in urban areas often have fewer contacts with rocks than do students who live in less developed areas. Even when the immediate environment is filled with rocks, students must observe carefully to detect and appreciate differences and commonalities in rocks. Difficulties analyzing and classifying interfere with content mastery. Students who only know rocks as pretty playthings may not fully appreciate the value of rocks.

Instructional Implications. Rocks should be studied in a hands-on fashion involving experiences with a variety of different rock samples. Students need plentiful opportunities to observe the different appearances and to handle and feel the textures and weights of various samples. Since no two rocks look exactly the same, opportunities for observing, comparing, analyzing, measuring, and classifying are abundant. As a record of the changes in the earth, rocks also present excellent opportunities to study the formation of the earth and its history. Good samples for study are often available in the cross-sections that are exposed where new roads are cut or where basements are dug. To personalize study, it is important to begin study using rocks that are familiar to the students. Interest and ability are important guides to the depth of study and number and types of experiments.

CORRECTION Modify strategies for topical and learning needs:

1. *Rock Displays*
    Skills: Observing; reading; studying; classifying
    Locate samples of different types of rocks, beginning with the ones that are found closest to the local area. Provide as reference sources books about rocks. As students study a particular type of rock, display it in a shoebox top and write its name and key features beside the sample. When students become familiar with the samples, remove a few, and ask students to match the stones with the correct names.

2. *Changing Rocks*
    Skills: Observing; listening; directed experimenting; analyzing
    To illustrate that water is a major cause of changes in rocks, first locate several smooth stones from a river or stream. Ask: What has made these rocks so smooth? Discuss the power of water even against rock. Fill a small glass container with water, seal it, and place it in a zipped plastic bag in the freezer. When the water freezes, guide students to conclude what happened. Explain how freezing and thawing cause roads and sidewalks to crack like rocks. Show pictures of caves and valleys that have been cut by years of flowing water. Have teams of students find cracks caused by water in the local area and share their findings.

3. *Igneous Rocks and Minerals*
    Skills: Observing; listening; reading; analyzing; evaluating
    Present igneous rocks as those formed from fire or great heat. Select a few igneous rocks that are found in the state or region or samples that contain minerals that are available for use. Give pairs of students samples of the rocks to examine, analyze, and describe. List on the board 10–12 possible uses and have the students guess at least 2 uses for each rock sample they examine. Permit students to change their guesses as you provide verbal clues. For enrichment, have students find either a sample or another example of the use of each rock studied.

4. *Studying Sedimentary Rocks*
    Skills: Observing; reading; studying; analyzing; measuring; evaluating
    Select samples of 2–3 types of sedimentary rocks for students to observe, feel, and weigh. (If possible, include a sample containing fossils.) Have pairs of students describe orally or in writing their observations. Use the descriptions for a matching game by having students read or tell their description for others to match with their samples.

5. *Rocks from Other Rocks*
    Skills: Observing; listening; reading; generalizing
    Present metamorphic rocks as ones formed from other rocks because of years of heat, pressure, and/or chemicals. Use rock samples in a manner similar to the procedures for Activities 3 and 4.

6. *Extra Practice.* • Inquire at local museums, hobby shops, or geology labs for resource people or loaner exhibits. • As different types of rocks are studied, have students develop a classification chart listing rock families, characteristics, and uses.

18. OCEANS, LAKES, AND RIVERS

DETECTION Mastery of key concepts may be difficult for students who:

- Have never studied or observed an ocean, lake, or river
- Lack fundamental knowledge about oceans, lakes, and rivers
- Have difficulty analyzing and classifying
- Experience problems generalizing
- Cannot explain the importance of bodies of water to self and society

Description. The study of bodies of water involves basic understandings of how they are formed and their value to humans, animals, and plants. Since over 70% of the earth's surface is covered with water, students should be familiar with the types, locations, compositions, and uses of the various bodies of water. Among the important concepts are the primary similarities and differences between the five major oceans, the thousands of rivers, and the many thousands of lakes. Students should be made aware of the existence of local lakes and rivers as well as local freshwater sources, such as springs, wells, and ponds. The uses of large bodies of water—recreation, travel, shipping, food sources, energy, and even water supplies—should be examined with emphasis on local needs.

Special Problems. Although many students enjoy swimming or playing in water, some also fear it. Handicapped students are sometimes not given the chances to see and experience water recreation to the extent of other youngsters. Students who seldom travel may be aware of the type(s) of water in their immediate area but few other bodies of water. Personal relevance is also less obvious to students who have never seen an ocean, lake, or river up close; it is difficult for such students to generalize about an oil spill hurting fishing or a low water level halting barges on a river. And to predict that food prices may go up because of these two problems calls not only for understanding based on experience but also some knowledge about uses of water routes for distribution of goods. Students who have difficulty analyzing, classifying, and/or generalizing may have problems mastering the content.

Instructional Implications. Because water is such an important part of life, everyone needs to have an understanding of the types, sizes, and multiple uses of different water sources. Equally important as the nature of water sources are ecological concerns; keeping water supplies safe for humans, animals, and plants should be a recurring theme throughout the learning experiences. As with the study of geographic formations, instruction should include guided observation of the water sources in the region surrounding the school as well as various bodies of water pictured in photographs and films. Local usage should be highlighted to stress personal relevance. To emphasize societal relevance, integrate study not only with ecological topics but also with social studies by carefully guiding students to conclude the sociological impact of the quality and quantity of various bodies of water.

CORRECTION Modify strategies for topical and learning needs:

1. *Important Water Words*
    Skills: Observing; listening; reading; organizing; analyzing;
        communicating; generalizing; evaluating
    Select for study a particular type of body of water. Have students cut out from
    light-blue construction paper a reasonable outline of a body of water. Ask
    them to create a labeled scene by drawing, cutting out, labeling, and then
    pasting associated items on the water. For the Pacific Ocean, for example,
    key terms might be represented by waves placed near the edges of the water.
    Other terms such as *schools, scavengers, plankton, currents,* and *mammals*
    could be labeled and included in the scene. Have students read and critique
    each scene for completeness.

2. *Locating Water Sources*
    Skills: Observing; listening; reading; studying; analyzing; synthesizing
    Use a raised relief map of the local region. Guide students to write the names
    of bodies of water and some of their characteristics on index cards. For each
    body of water, have students run yarn from a pin marking its location on the
    map to the index card off the side of the map. Have students add to the cards
    the uses of the water as they discover them.

3. *Ocean Spotlights*
    Skills: Observing; listening; analyzing; measuring; communicating
    List each of the 5 major oceans on the board and then show students where
    each is located on a raised relief map or globe. To help students remember
    what is near each ocean, discuss, repeat, and have students repeat the name
    of each ocean and the key adjacent countries, states, or cities. For some
    students, it is enough to concentrate on only the Atlantic or Pacific Ocean
    and discuss the coast and 2–3 states that border it. To enhance concepts,
    compare approximate size and depth to familiar land masses or bodies of
    water.

4. *Ocean Life*
    Skills: Observing; listening; reading; organizing; classifying
    Have students read or listen to information about 3 types of ocean life—
    benthos, nekton, and plankton—and then try matching pictures of plants
    and animals with where they live. In a file folder with 3 pockets (1 for each
    type of life), place a 1-sentence explanation and plenty of pictures showing
    each category of life.

5. *Water Uses*
    Skills: Observing; studying; classifying; generalizing; evaluating
    Begin a chart with 3 headings: Oceans, Lakes, and Rivers. As students name
    examples of each and describe their uses, write their comments on the chart.
    Assign pairs of students to research additional examples and uses to add to
    the chart. Then have students select the 3 examples that are most valuable
    to themselves and explain why.

6. *Extra Practice.* • Have students find out about the different jobs that are related to
    lakes, rivers, and oceans. • Use blank transparencies to outline ocean
    shapes and compare them to maps of land masses.

19. FOREST RESOURCES

DETECTION Mastery of key concepts may be difficult for students who:

- Have had few opportunities to observe forests
- Display limited knowledge about land ecology
- Never participated in scouting or camping experiences
- Have difficulty classifying
- Experience problems generalizing

Description. The study of forest areas includes not only trees but also other types of plant and animal life that are affected by forest lands. Of the nine types of forests common to the United States and Canada, those of regional interest should be stressed. Mention should be made of different hardwood (deciduous) and softwood (coniferous) trees that are found locally, statewide, or regionally. Also of interest are forest products and environmental issues, such as timber rights, mining, construction, disease, droughts, floods, and fires.

Special Problems.   Students who live in urban areas often have very limited real experiences with forests as do those those who seldom travel or camp out. As with many ecological issues, students' attitudes toward land ecology are often rooted in the attitudes and habits of their families. To some families, a forest is nothing more than a handy place to go and cut firewood for the winter; to others a forest is a place to hunt game. Some students view forests as a never-ending resource. Students who do not recognize the importance of land ecology may have difficulty mastering this topic. Weak classification or generalization skills also may interfere with knowledge acquisition. Forest products, although used regularly by students in the classroom (e.g., paper, pencils, books), are often not associated with their source; thus, without specific instruction, many students cannot appreciate the value of forests.

Instructional Implications.   Forestry is an area offering sources of abundant concrete experiences through products and often nearby examples. Even in urban areas, concerted efforts have been made to preserve at least some forests as parks; these are excellent areas for fieldtrips. Because forest rangers generally appeal to youngsters, they make convincing resource speakers to explain, instruct, and caution students. The study of plants and animals can be extended to include those native to forests. Study of the various types of forest products should begin with those items with which students are most familiar and which they use the most often. Paper, pencils, and desks are a good place to start. Many of the activities that are used in teaching land ecology are also appropriate for teaching about forests. If ecology previously has been taught, those concepts can be used as the foundation for understanding forests; if ecology has not been mentioned, instruction in both areas can be integrated. In either case, the problems that first nature and now humans cause for forests should be emphasized.

CORRECTION Modify strategies for topical and learning needs:

1. *Types of Wood*
   Skills: Observing; listening; reading; analyzing; classifying
   Guide students to classify trees as coniferous (softwood) or deciduous (hardwood). As different types of trees and their uses are studied (typically, there are many more types of deciduous trees than coniferous), have students complete a class listing by type. For example:

Coniferous			Deciduous		
cedar	fir	larch	ash	birch	oak
hemlock	pine	spruce	cypress	maple	poplar

   If possible, add a picture or drawing and a leaf of each tree to the listing. Discuss the major differences between the 2 types of trees and the wood from them.

2. *Deciduous Forests*
   Skills: Observing; listening; reading; studying; synthesizing
   Deciduous trees can be identified by their leaves, bark, and other features. Begin by helping students match types of leaves with the appropriate types of trees. Have students begin a leaf identification bank. Use pictures, drawings, or actual leaves on one side of a card and on the other side, include the name of the tree and 1–2 sentences about its characteristics, where it grows, and uses of its resources.

3. *Five Forest Strata*
   Skills: Observing; listening; reading; analyzing; evaluating
   Have students read or listen to information about the 5 strata of the forest: 1) canopy; 2) understory; 3) shrub layer; 4) herb layer; and 5) forest floor. Discuss how light, seasons, and waste affect events in each layer. Have students find news reports of such events, describe them, and evaluate their impact on themselves and on others.

4. *Hunting for the Forest in School*
   Skills: Observing; analyzing; classifying; communicating
   Have students compete to find the most forest products. Provide categories such as: foods; chemicals; and lumber. Extend the search outside school and reward students who find the most.

5. *Predicting Uses*
   Skills: Observing; listening; reading; analyzing; predicting; evaluating
   Provide students with this list of the primary uses of wood in the United States: plywood and veneer; lumber; fuel; and pulpwood (paper). Ask students to rank these uses in order from highest to lowest. Discuss the wood products they know about and permit them to change their rankings. Next provide a listening or reading experience about usage and have students verify or correct their answers. (Correct order: lumber, 45–50%; pulpwood, 30–35%; plywood and veneer, 9–11%; and fuel, 3–5%.

6. *Extra Practice.* • Have students use their own leaf identification banks to classify the leaves brought to school by peers. • Have students find or draw pictures of trees and label each level of the forest. • Have students gather leaves and describe differences and similarities.

20. TEMPERATURE

DETECTION Mastery of key concepts may be difficult for students who:

- Cannot read a thermometer
- Seldom stay outdoors for long periods of time
- Have difficulty analyzing and generalizing
- Cannot explain the effects of temperature on humans, animals, or plants

Description. Temperature has a greater affect on weather than does air pressure, wind, or moisture in the air. The concepts of major importance in learning about temperature are the role of the sun and its effects on the earth. Weather begins in the atmosphere above the earth. The sun is the major source of energy and as such supplies most of the energy that causes the weather on earth. Among the skills and concepts to build are measuring temperature and understanding the factors that cause the surface of the earth to be heated by the sun unevenly: colors, absorption rates of water and land, the angle of the sun's rays, and cloud cover.

Special Problems. Measurement of all types is often the neglected element of the mathematics curriculum, particularly when students are low achievers. Some students simply have not been taught measurement concepts. Students who live in rural or farming areas are usually attuned to temperature and weather because they are major topics of discussion and concern. Students who live in other areas, particularly in large cities, are sometimes not as concerned about temperature since their families spend much of their time indoors in conditioned air. Thus, a large number of students take temperature for granted. Students who come from homes where the evening news and weather is a ritual or the weather report in the newspaper is carefully studied usually have at least a rudimentary grasp of the vocabulary and a basic understanding of the importance of temperature.

Instructional Implications. As with most topics, to personalize the content, study should begin with local temperatures and the effects on the students themselves and their immediate surroundings. Activities to measure, record, and compare temperatures should be carefully structured and monitored and then frequently reviewed as each concept is presented. The study of temperature easily can be integrated with lessons in social studies and should include map and globe skills to further reinforce ideas about various temperatures and climates in different regions of the world. The sociological effects of different temperatures should also be included.

CORRECTION Modify strategies for topical and learning needs:

1. *Key Words*
    Skills: Observing; listening; reading; communicating
    As key terms are discussed, print them on the chalkboard. Use each word
    several times in sentences and then use the board to show at least 1 sentence
    with each word in context. Ask students to reread each sentence orally. Use
    3 examples to explain each term during the discussion.
2. *Reading a Thermometer*
    Skills: Observing; listening; reading; measuring; communicating
    To review reading thermometers, bring a large thermometer to class and
    place it out of direct sunlight but where it easily can be read. Explain how
    thermometers work. After students locate the present temperature, call out
    various temperature readings for students to find on the thermometer.
    Individual simulated thermometers are useful learning aids.
3. *Classroom Temperature Record*
    Skills: Observing; analyzing; measuring; communicating; evaluating
    Have students chart classroom temperatures at the beginning, middle, and
    end of the day. Have them take turns reading and recording temperatures
    for a 2-week period. Explain how to average the 3 readings for a daily average.
    Repeat this experience again during a different season and have students
    compare the differences in average temperature and in daily fluctuations to
    identify and then explain patterns.
4. *Demonstrating Temperature*
    Skills: All information acquisition, processing, and integration skills
    To demonstrate the function and effects of temperature, have students
    predict and record results as they perform activities such as these:
      • Put containers with thermometers in various places.
      • Make a thermometer and explain how the liquid behaves.
      • Make frost, icicles, ice, and/or popsicles; then place them in the sun.
5. *Determining Heat Absorption*
    Skills: Observing; listening; reading; directed experimenting; measuring;
             predicting; communicating; all integration skills
    Fill 4 small containers with potting soil, sand, gravel, and water to make 4
    samples. Ask students to predict which samples will have the highest and
    lowest temperature readings. Place a thermometer in each and put the
    samples in a warm spot. Have students note the temperature of each sample
    every 30 minutes for 2 hours; discuss differences and their causes. Next,
    place samples in the shade; have students predict which will cool fastest,
    and again check the temperatures regularly. Lead students to rank heat
    absorption rates and decide the value of that knowledge to themselves.
6. *Extra Practice.* • Have students compare daily classroom temperature averages to the
    weekly temperature estimates given in the newspaper. • After discussing
    factors that influence uneven heating of earth (e.g., light and dark surfaces,
    cloud cover, water, and shaded areas), take students for a walk outside so
    they may judge the effects of each factor on temperature and on the way it
    makes them feel.

21. PRECIPITATION

DETECTION   Mastery of key concepts may be difficult for students who:
- Have had limited experiences with many forms of precipitation
- Know little about air, temperature, and the properties of water
- Do not observe carefully
- Have difficulty analyzing and predicting
- Experience problems generalizing
- Cannot explain the value of understanding precipitation

Description. Precipitation is any form of water falling from the air to the earth. The study of precipitation includes such topics as clouds, droplets, air currents, and changing temperatures. Precipitation occurs in the form of rain, drizzle, snow, sleet, hail, and precipitation fog. Knowledge about air, temperature, and the properties of water form the foundation upon which to build the major concepts of precipitation. To understand the process of precipitation, students must synthesize and make generalizations about a number of interrelated factors.

Special Problems. Students who have never seen the various forms of precipitation firsthand may have difficulty understanding the differences between, for example, sleet, snow, and hail. Even those who have seen, heard, and touched the various forms often do not realize the differences in the development processes. Unless they are particularly observant or have studied the topic, many students and adults as well classify precipitation into two broad categories: wet, and cold and wet. Students who know little about air, temperature, or the properties of water may have problems mastering the content. Preconceived ideas about causes and types of precipitation can cause the accommodation of new concepts to be difficult. Students from families whose livelihood depends on the weather are usually more attuned to and knowledgeable about precipitation than are other students. Weak prediction, synthesis, and/or generalization skills are likely to interfere with mastery of the content.

Instructional Implications. Understanding and predicting precipitation can enhance the lives of students and their families in a number of ways: They can plan their recreational and work activities to avoid or even coincide with precipitation; they can plan to dress for the weather to avoid not only ruining good clothes but also discomfort and some illnesses; and by analyzing precipitation patterns, they can even identify the time to shop for the best quality and prices for fresh produce. Use a blow dryer on various heat settings and cold drink cans to demonstrate and review the concepts of evaporation and condensation and the interaction of air, temperature, and water. Establish the personal and societal relevance of precipitation from the standpoint of predicting precipitation and the advantages of doing so. Relevance can also be established by examining the effects of precipitation patterns on the water supplies for humans, animals, and plants, including the sociological impact on various regions and cultures.

CORRECTION Modify strategies for topical and learning needs:

1. *Forms of Precipitation*
   Skills: Observing; listening; reading; communicating
   Introduce forms of precipitation by posting the word for each on the board.
   Prompt students to describe each and write a minidefinition. For example:

   Rain: thousands of cloud droplets   *Sleet:* little bits of ice
   Drizzle: tiny water droplets   *Hail:* balls of ice
   Fog: tinier water droplets   *Snow:* thin ice crystals

   Have students use each word in a sentence orally and then write the
   sentence on the board for others to read and talk about.

2. *Forming Raindrops*
   Skills: Observing; listening; experimenting; analyzing; communicating
   As an advance organizer, briefly explain that clouds are actually made up of
   billions of tiny water droplets that are moved around by air. When warm air
   rises to meet cooler air, rain results as these tiny droplets hit each other,
   combine as bigger and heavier drops, and fall to the earth as rain. To
   illustrate the process, fill a canning jar with 2–3 inches of water; turn a
   second jar upside down and tape the open ends of the jars together with duct
   tape. Set the jar containing water into a pan of water and heat. As the water
   boils, have students describe their observations. Discuss the foggy appearance that forms around the top jar and the water droplets that form and run
   down the sides. Help students verbalize the process. Repeat the advance
   organizer and then have students retell the process.

3. *Saving Raindrops*
   Skills: Observing; experimenting; analyzing; predicting; evaluating
   To preserve and view actual raindrops, guide students to predict and verify
   as they participate in each step of this demonstration: Catch a few raindrops
   in a pan filled with flour. Shake the contents through a food strainer into a
   second pan. Pour the preserved raindrops onto black construction paper for
   analysis and evaluation.

4. *Predicting Precipitation*
   Skills: Observing; analyzing; predicting; generalizing; evaluating
   Have students describe situations when they needed to predict precipitation. Show a videotape of local weather reports and discuss what the
   forecasters look for. Then begin a daily program of study. Have students
   watch the morning weather forecast on TV, periodically observe clouds and
   temperature outside, record their observations, analyze them, and conclude
   the signs that foretell precipitation. Later, designate a student to predict
   precipitation each day; have peers evaluate the value of the signs used and
   the accuracy and value of the predictions.

5. *Extra Practice.* • Ask students to describe situations when a rainmaker might be
   needed and the people who would be most affected by a lack of rain. • Have
   students review the water cycle and retell or diagram it (see Topic 7). • Have
   students select nearby cities, look up the average amount of rainfall for each,
   and compare it to that for their area and to the national average.

22. STORMS

DETECTION Mastery of key concepts may be difficult for students who:
- Have not observed or studied certain types of storms
- Are unable to classify types of storm activity
- Appear uninformed about potential dangers of storms
- Do not understand the relationship between temperature and weather
- Display limited knowledge of how air shapes weather

Description. Storms are dramatic and most students are curious about them. Included in the study of storms are such subtopics as the different types of storm activity, the origin of storms, and the nature of the damage that may occur. The role of air and temperature in shaping weather is a prerequisite concept. Although major storm activity can be classified as thunderstorms, winter storms, tornadoes, and hurricanes, including cyclones and typhoons, the most severe storms that occur in a particular region may be variations of only one or two types. Planning for storms and safety precautions during storms are also important considerations in dealing with the potential dangers. Such planning relies upon accurate prediction of storms, a key point to emphasize.

Special Problems. Students who have not mastered the background concepts about weather are likely to have difficulty understanding storms. Many problems arise from the real experiences that students have and have not had. Without actual experience with a tornado or hurricane, for example, the strong, damaging winds and vast amounts of rainfall are difficult to conceptualize, even for adults. Families who only have been inconvenienced, not harmed, by storms may tend to ignore storm warnings, believing that concern and proper precautions are unnecessary; in such cases, students may adopt the blasé attitudes of their friends and families. Conversely, students who have experienced the turbulence and devastation of storms may overreact to the topic. Even students who have not actually experienced storms may exhibit irrational fears (based on reports of family members or friends) that cause them to resist learning about particular types of storms. The types of storms that occur most often in the local region are easier for students to understand than are the storms that never or seldom occur locally.

Instructional Implications. Appropriate safety measures prior to and during storms are key to the protection of life and property; these points should be emphasized and safety precautions directly taught for specific types of storms. The background concepts of weather should be reviewed and summarized as an introduction to storms. Although limited understanding of world storms is valuable, regional storms should be taught in depth, using the technical as well as the regional names of the storms. Use video pictures showing different types of storm activity and the inconvenience, damage, and aftermath they create, taking care to present the content calmly but realistically. Use news reports to predict and track storm systems and to supplement textbook and resource materials.

CORRECTION Modify strategies for topical and learning needs:

1. *Stormy Words*
      Skills: Observing; listening; reading; communicating
      Have students brainstorm to name as many words as they know that relate
      to storms of any type. List these on the board, read them aloud, and ask
      students to classify them according to common features. Select those that
      apply to several types of storms and are characteristic of local storms to
      begin study.
2. *Storm Watch*
      Skills: Observing; listening; reading; organizing; communicating
      Set aside an area on a bulletin board or a poster and have students post short
      news reports or their own retellings of TV and radio descriptions to predict
      and track storm activity.
3. *Storm Drills*
      Skills: Observing; analyzing; synthesizing; generalizing; evaluating
      Conduct precautionary drills for the types of storms that occur locally. To
      begin the simulation, describe the local conditions that signal the approach
      of a storm. Ask students to describe the dangers and inconveniences,
      analyze their school building to identify the most and least hazardous
      locations, list the supplies that will be needed, and devise appropriate safety
      precautions. Then have students dramatize a storm drill. Later, have them
      evaluate the effectiveness of their drill.
4. *Local Storms*
      Skills: Observing; listening; reading; communicating; generalizing
      Provide information about the types of storms that are likely to occur locally,
      how they are formed, and the damage that can result. Discuss the effects of
      such storms on property, people, and their activities. Guide students to
      analyze the resulting problems and then classify those problems using
      headings such as: *Transportation; Power; Property; Life; School; Home.*
      Compare and contrast local storms with those that occur in other regions.
      Have a student delegation contact the local police and fire departments or
      civil defense director and find out about what plans have been made for
      storm disasters in the area.
5. *Storm Precautions*
      Skills: Observing; reading; studying; communicating; synthesizing;
            generalizing; evaluating
      Guide students to develop a profile poster of pictures of several types of
      storms, major characteristics, and safety measures that should be taken if
      a warning is given. Summarize the plans for Storm Drills (Activity 3) and also
      include them on the poster. Periodically, have students add information to
      the poster and critique and revise the safety measures.
6. *Extra Practice.* • Have students record on audiotape their own descriptions of storms
      as they see them. • Have students draw their interpretation of a particular
      type of storm or its aftermath. •Have students develop a chart showing the
      time of year when certain types of storms are most likely to occur.

23. SEASONS

DETECTION   Mastery of key concepts may be difficult for students who:
- Live in areas where seasonal differences are minimal
- Spend little time outdoors
- Do not observe carefully
- Have difficulty analyzing
- Cannot explain the importance of seasons to self and society

Description. The study of the four different periods in a year—*winter, spring, summer,* and *autumn*—can be limited to the Northern Hemisphere or if appropriate expanded to include other regions as well. Attention should be directed to the factors that create seasons: Position of the earth in relation to the sun; rotation; tilt of the axis of the earth; summer and winter solstice; and vernal equinox. The depth and breadth of the study of these factors depends upon the ages and abilities of the students. In addition to examining the origin of the seasons, the seasonal influences on humans, animals, and plants are important subtopics.

Special Problems. Understanding seasons and their implications is not a particularly difficult topic for students who live in regions where seasonal changes result in dramatic differences; in such areas, observant students are typically very aware of the seasons and the ways in which their lives are affected. Students who live in regions where seasonal differences are minimal may not readily see the relevance of this topic. Those who do not spend much time outdoors also may display little interest. Very sheltered youngsters whose families dictate what to wear and what to do may not be as aware of seasonal changes as are students who are allowed more independence. Some of the concepts may be difficult for students to accept because they conflict with preconceived notions. For example, many people believe that summer occurs when the sun is closer to the earth, when in actuality the sun is farther from the Northern Hemisphere but its more direct rays cause the higher temperatures.

Instructional Implications. Understanding that life on the earth has developed around general climates and changing seasons is not readily apparent to some students. Begin by studying the seasons as they affect the section of the country where the students live before moving to key surrounding and remote areas. Place the study of temperature, precipitation, and storms in the context of the current season, guide students to make predictions for upcoming seasons, and then structure their observational experiences to verify their predictions as each season arrives. Highlight seasonal differences as a part of the study of animals and plants since both are affected by changing seasons. Stress the relationships between the seasons and certain illnesses, types of recreation, food and water supplies, and ecological concerns both here and in the study of the related topics. Emphasize the beauty and novelty of the seasons. Pair study with astronomy and also with lessons in social studies to interweave the relationships of climate and social structures.

CORRECTION Modify strategies for topical and learning needs:

1. *Seasonal Relationships*
   Skills: Observing; analyzing; classifying; communicating
   List each of the 4 seasons on the board. Have students name words they can relate directly to each season as it occurs in the local area. Use these words to begin the study of the seasons. For some regions, a partial listing might look like this:

Summer	*Autumn*	*Winter*	*Spring*
hot	leaves	cold	green
humid	windy	snow	flowers
swimming	Halloween	ice	baseball

2. *Why Seasons Change*
   Skills: Observing; listening; reading; experimenting; communicating; synthesizing
   To illustrate how seasons change, use a small globe as the earth and a flashlight for the sun. Demonstrate the tilt of the earth and have a student slowly rotate the globe and move the earth around the sun. Be sure to maintain the tilt of the earth as you explain how the earth's rotation causes the sun's light to strike the earth differently at different points during a year. Have students draw their own versions of the 4 positions of the earth as it moves around the sun over the period of a year. Have them label the seasons as they apply to the Northern Hemisphere and then add to their drawings terms that describe the seasons in their region.

3. *Seasonal Differences*
   Skills: Observing; listening; reading; analyzing; classifying; communicating; evaluating
   Ask students to locate photographs taken during a particular season, summer, for example. If possible, they should bring pictures of themselves and their families during a summer activity; or they can use pictures from magazines. Have students interpret events in each picture, describe how the picture would differ according to each season, emphasizing weather and health, and decide which season is best for the pictured activity and why.

4. *Seasonal Stake-out*
   Skills: Observing; listening; studying; organizing; communicating; synthesizing; generalizing
   Have either individual students or student teams adopt a specific plot of the schoolgrounds outside. Guide them to check their plot regularly for changes, record the changes, and compare with peers. Options for recording change include oral and written descriptions, photographs, sketches, charts, and audio and videotapes.

5. *Extra Practice.* • Organize debate teams to identify the favorite season. • Have students name specific foods or clothing that are typically associated with a specific season. • Have pairs of students compare the seasons in other countries with the seasons in their area. • Have pairs of students develop seasonal calendars, listing events such as games, trips, holidays, and other important events categorized by each of 4 seasons.

24. WEATHER PREDICTION

DETECTION Mastery of key concepts may be difficult for students who:

- Seldom observe or listen to information about the weather
- Are unfamiliar with sophisticated forecasting methods
- Have not mastered weather-related topics
- Have difficulty predicting and generalizing
- Cannot explain the value of weather forecasts to self and society

Description. Predicting or forecasting the weather has become a major industry involving the use of satellites, radar, and other sophisticated instruments to forecast weather conditions days and even years in advance. Important concepts include understanding weather forecasting as it originated and has evolved into a scientific field of study, as well as the prerequisite concepts of temperature, precipitation, storms, and seasons. Interesting subtopics, such as unusual weather facts, meteorologists, and the National Weather Service, also are appropriate content for the study of this topic.

Special Problems. As people grow older, they seem to pay more attention to weather conditions; many students are neither aware of nor concerned about weather predictions. Without a basic understanding of the interactions of air, temperature, and water, students are limited to accepting others' forecasts as mystical fact. Students who have difficulty mastering the related concepts of weather—temperature, precipitation, storms, and seasons—often experience similar problems mastering this topic. Those who spend little time outdoors or whose family's livelihood is not unaffected by weather may view the topic as unimportant. Students who live in urban areas or regions not subject to frequent or violent storms may be less attuned to weather than are students who live in other areas. Even students who are interested in forecasting may find the intricacies of interpreting weather maps and radar-enhanced pictures confusing. Students who exhibit generally weak predicting and generalizing skills are likely to experience difficulty.

Instructional Implications. Weather forecasts are a current topic that can be studied daily and locally. A number of instructional materials are readily accessible to teachers and students. When students maintain weather charts, they can be led to identify patterns to predict weather. Both the forecasts that appear in the local newspaper and those broadcast on radio and TV offer content for study. Using such forecasts, the accuracy of predictions immediately can be verified by observing actual weather events; discrepancies between predicted and actual weather can be confirmed by reading or viewing the daily weather report. By encouraging the ongoing comparisons between forecasts and the daily weather, students' knowledge of weather components can be broadened and deepened. The study of forecasting should be interwoven with the study of temperature, precipitation, storms, and seasons. To establish the relevance of weather predictions, emphasize on a daily basis the ways in which the forecasts shape the plans of students and others and the inconvenience caused by incorrect weather predictions.

CORRECTION Modify strategies for topical and learning needs:

1. *Weather Words*
    Skills: Observing; reading; studying; organizing; communicating
    Have students develop their own Weather Words directory. Include specific terms and definitions, like *fronts, pressure, heat index, wind chill,* and others. Use index cards in a box so that new words can be added alphabetically, old words can be updated, and students can access the terms when they write about weather.
2. *Weather Plans*
    Skills: Observing; listening; analyzing; predicting; evaluating
    Each morning, have a student tell the weather forecast for the day. Guide students to plan 3 things they should and should not do according to the forecast. Have them evaluate the accuracy of the forecast the next day by comparing the weather that occurred with what was predicted.
3. *Weather Comparisons*
    Skills: Observing; listening; reading; analyzing; measuring;
        communicating; evaluating
    Media obtain their weather information form different sources. Conduct telephone or letter surveys of local media to identify their source (National Weather Service or a private weather service). Guide students to compare different weather forecasts. Have student teams use information from 2 different newspapers, 2 different TV (or radio) stations, or a paper and a TV station. Over a 10–30 day period, chart each forecast and then compare the results the next day. Guide students to develop a system for evaluating and recording accuracy.
4. *The National Weather Service*
    Skills: Observing; studying; organizing; communicating; generalizing
    Have teams of 2–3 students write letters to the National Weather Service requesting information about specific instruments they use to forecast the weather. When the information arrives, have the teams summarize the purpose of a particular instrument, describe how it works, and judge its value. Then have the teams exchange reports and verbally report on another team's instrument. If possible, include pictures or have a weather specialist display actual sample instruments as part of the reports.
5. *Weather Trivia*
    Skills: Observing; reading; studying; organizing; communicating;
        synthesizing; generalizing
    Have students use tradebooks, almanacs, and encyclopedias to gather their own list of little known weather facts (e.g., highest temperature recorded, most rainfall in a day, foggiest location, and windiest city). Place facts on index cards to use in playing Weather Trivia.
6. *Extra Practice.* • Have students add to a chart of the occupations in which people are particularly interested in weather forecasts. • Have students listen to several broadcasts from the National Weather Service and compare them to weather reports on commercial TV. • Have students chart day-to-day weather and describe patterns helpful for prediction.

25. PLANETS

DETECTION Mastery of key concepts may be difficult for students who:

- Have never observed planets through a telescope
- Exhibit difficulty conceptualizing vast distances in space
- Have difficulty analyzing and classifying
- Do not readily generalize
- Cannot explain the importance of other planets to self and society

Description. Study of astronomy includes the nine major planets in the galaxy, satellites, distances, and several other related concepts, such as rotation, orbit, revolution, and stars. Teaching about other planets involves first reviewing the characteristics of the earth and then helping students relate very different and very distant places to the earth and sun in terms of size, function, and environment.

Special Problems. Many students have never used a telescope or visited a space museum. Their knowledge may be limited to television and movie presentations of popular heroes in primarily fictional space travels. The efforts of the National Aeronautics and Space Administration (NASA) have focused on earth orbiting and space exploration, but exploration per se has received less media attention than the manned space launches destined for nearby stars or in-space experimentation. Students have received very little scientific information through the general news media about planets except for sensationalized stories. Many of the concepts appear too remote and abstract for some students to master. Students who have difficulty analyzing, classifying, and generalizing may have problems with this topic. Although the topic is of particular interest to many students, often their focus tends to extend beyond what is actually known about other planets to the more appealing notion of life in space.

Instructional Implications. Without adequate skills, interest, and background knowledge, students may have difficulty mastering this topic because of its abstract nature. Existing schema may be limited and primarily consist of episodic details of encounters with other beings and unusual planets with fictitious names, environments, and inhabitants. To establish a more accurate knowledge base, use realistic films, tapes, actual accounts, demonstrations, models, and telescopic equipment to offer an entertaining and hands-on approach. Armed with correct facts, students can be guided to read or view science fiction critically. It is particularly important to begin with study of the earth and then relate all concepts to the earth for comparison.

CORRECTION Modify strategies for topical and learning needs:

1. *General Planetary Language*
    Skills: Observing; listening; reading; directed experimenting;
        communicating
    To introduce words and concepts that relate to the planets, have students
    dramatize ideas and definitions as they are explained. For example, have
    students act out the concepts of planets and their actions as they orbit,
    rotate, and revolve. Other students can serve as satellites for planets. Label
    students so that everyone can connect words, concepts, and actions.
2. *Information Center*
    Skills: Observing; listening; reading; studying; communicating;
        synthesizing
    Develop a planetary information center containing: 1) pictures or drawings
    of each planet in our galaxy; 2) student-authored informational reviews of
    each planet; 3) tradebooks about the planets; and 4) activities for students
    to complete that involve a knowledge about planets. A portion of the contents
    of the center should be developed by the students themselves. Encourage
    students to work in pairs at the center to both expand their own knowledge
    and to elaborate on the information at the center.
3. *Relative Distance*
    Skills: Observing listening; directed experimenting; organizing;
        measuring; communicating; synthesizing; generalizing
    Use the distance from the school to a familiar place several miles away as a
    unit of measure and to teach the conversion of miles to kilometers (divide by
    .6). Next, have students measure (in millimeters) the length of the school's
    baseball or football field, walk from one end of it to the other, and convert
    measurements to kilometers. (The exact size or distance is not important.)
    Guide students to use these 2 distances as reference points for determining
    and visualizing the size and distances of planets, orbits, and the like. Assign
    tasks such as: Find the distance from here to Mars in football fields or in
    "school-to-post-office" units. Guide student teams to make models of the
    relative distances on calculator tape and post around the wall or on the floor
    for ready reference.
4. *Planetary Survey*
    Skills: Observing; listening; reading; analyzing; communicating;
        synthesizing; generalizing
    Assist students to add to their distance models above or to develop a wall
    chart showing and describing the planets. For each planet, have them
    describe its size, distance from the sun or earth, number of satellites, and
    type of atmosphere. Provide printed resources for students to use as
    individuals or pairs to collect information on each planet. The chart can
    serve as a handy reference for discussions and comparisons.
5. *Extra Practice.* • Invite a regional consultant from NASA to discuss ongoing investi-
        gations of planets. • Have students watch selected episodes of NOVA on TV
        and report to peers. • Have student teams evaluate planets and rank them
        according to desirability for various activities.

26. STARS

DETECTION Mastery of key concepts may be difficult for students who:

- Report few guided experiences studying stars
- Do not observe carefully
- Have difficulty analyzing, classifying, and synthesizing
- Reveal little interest in learning about the stars
- Cannot explain the value of studying stars to self and society

Description. The study of stars can be very detailed or general, according to the needs
of the students. When classified by size, there are four major categories of
stars: dwarf, giant, medium-sized (such as the sun), and supergiant. The
easily observed and recognizable patterns, for example, animal shapes, of
the constellations of some of the stars in our galaxy are a good beginning
point of study. Other important concepts involve the characteristics of stars,
such as temperature, size, location, composition, and navigational significance.

Special Problems. Among the meanings of the term *star* familiar to many students are
those associated with romance, famous entertainers and athletes, astrology,
awards and ratings, as well as bright lights in the sky. The problem with
multiple meanings is that they sometimes make the astronomer's vision of
stars seem less interesting. Some students also have difficulty finding
personal relevance beyond the astrological charts. Because of their vast
distance from the earth and their abstract aura, stars are somewhat difficult
for some students to understand. Aside from casual observance from their
backyards at night, few students have had firsthand experiences viewing
stars in detail; this lack of experience renders the topic even more remote.
Students who have weak observation, classification, and synthesis skills
tend to find this topic difficult to master.

Instructional Implications. The study of stars should be related to the overall astronomy
program. Studying both planets and stars, for example, can be integrated in
lessons that deal at times with both topics. Since students cannot actually
touch stars, concerted efforts must be directed toward bringing the stars
alive and making them seem real. Thus, it is particularly important to
provide opportunities to actually view stars through powerful and sophisticated telescopes or if this is not possible to use filmed viewings or even
simulations. (Remember to inform students about the danger involved in
viewing the sun or using optical devices during the day.) Such activities
permit students to visualize and retrieve the visual image of each star as it
is studied. Identifying important constellations relies on both analysis and
imagination to first locate and then use imaginary lines to connect the stars;
in this case, placing star maps on the ceiling of the classroom before actual
viewing may be helpful. To assist students who have difficulty remembering
directions, review and practice classroom landmarks for north, south, east,
and west.

CORRECTION Modify strategies for topical and learning needs:

1. *Star Qualities*
   Skills: Observing; listening; reading; communicating; synthesizing
   Begin vocabulary development by studying the largest star in our galaxy, the
   sun. Use different pictures or student drawings of the sun and surround
   them with words such as *eclipse, medium sized, hydrogen gas,* and *light
   minutes.* As each additional star is studied, follow similar procedures,
   surrounding the picture with important terms. Guide students to take turns
   describing each picture using the key terms.

2. *Star Maps*
   Skills: Observing; listening; reading; studying; organizing; measuring;
   communicating
   Provide observation and listening experiences, beginning with the location
   of a major constellation. List its size, location, and distance from the earth.
   Then have teams of students stand and represent selected stars and their
   proportionate distances from each other and from the earth and sun,
   thereby forming a living Star Map. Later have students form maps to
   illustrate the galaxy, including both stars and planets. Conclude by having
   the students draw their Star Maps.

3. *Moon Watch*
   Skills: Observing; studying; measuring; communicating
   Over a period of 30 days, have students observe the moon and record how
   it looks (draw) at least 1 night per week. Have students use clay to make a
   model of the most recent shape they saw. Compare sightings and models to
   videotapes of close shots of the moon. Guide students to analyze the effects
   of viewing angles, "the Man in the Moon," the moon's effect on tides, and
   differences between reflected and generated light and between the moon's
   surface and the sun, other stars, the earth, and other planets.

4. *Star Search*
   Skills: Observing; listening; studying; analyzing; synthesizing;
   hypothesizing
   Identify several stars that easily can be viewed; have students locate the
   stars on a star map and also orally describe how to find them. Then make
   arrangements with a local astronomy club to help sponsor a Star Search
   night for the students. Ask club members to bring telescopes and help
   students use them. For the actual viewing, have students describe the stars
   they want to view, tell where they are located, and then seek them. It is
   important to have extra adult supervision to guide the students, prevent
   accidents, and keep students on task.

5. *Extra Practice.* • If possible, take students to a planetarium for expert explanations
   and a superior viewing situation. • Using an almanac or other sources, have
   students locate information about other stars and present a summary to
   peers. • Have students view, sketch, and describe the star closest to earth,
   Alpha Centauri. • After studying refracting and reflecting optical telescopes,
   have student teams analyze the differences and find the locations and sizes
   of the 3 largest in each category.

27. SPACE EXPLORATION

DETECTION Mastery of key concepts may be difficult for students who:

- Lack appropriate study or reading experiences about space
- Have not previously mastered the topics of planets and stars
- Have difficulty predicting, hypothesizing, and generalizing
- Cannot explain the value of space exploration to self or society

Description. Scientists and engineers work hand in hand to develop the scientific and technological means of exploring space. Space travel has resulted in detailed study of faraway planets, stars, and satellites; many scientific discoveries; and an explosion of information about astronomy. Although there are three major ways of exploring space, this section is limited to discussion of manned and unmanned spacecraft; a review of the study of space through utilization of powerful telescopic equipment, as discussed in the previous two sections, is a good way to introduce spacecraft exploration of space. Othjer important concepts include: the development of space exploration from the throw-away types of rockjets and spacecraft of the 1960s and 1970s to the reusable shuttle spacecraft of the 1980s; space shuttles as orbiters for extended trips of several years or longer; the scientific data collection capabilities of space shuttles; and problems associated with space travel.

Special Problems. Many students are interested in finding out about exploratory space flights and missions. Difficulties arise when somewhat technical explanations and unfamiliar pictures are encountered. Students who do not have a firm grasp of the prerequisite terms and concepts associated with space (e.g., *planets, stars, orbits, gravity*) and those from families who do not actively follow progress in space are likely to experience problems understanding space exploration. Some students have difficulty conceptualizing the vast distances involved and the time lapses between take-off and arrival or between transmission and receipt of data and pictures on Earth. Thus, many of the concepts seem too remote and abstract for some students to master. Students who have weak predicting, hypothesizing, and generalizing skills may have problems mastering this topic.

Instructional Implications. The study of space exploration is usually of interest to students. Background concepts, major factors in understanding this topic, should be reviewed and then retaught as needed. The use of models and demonstrations of launches and orbits can also enhance student interest. Use of color photographs and audiotapes featuring space sounds and descriptions are also useful to bring far-off places closer. Actual videotapes of space travel should be used to capture the sights and sounds of each moment as well as to track the progress of the various space flights. It is important to pause the tape periodically to direct students' attention to pertinent details and to direct their thinking by walking and talking them through the predictions, hypotheses, and generalizations that apply to each segment. This topic prepares students for the exciting one that follows, living in space.

CORRECTION Modify strategies for topical and learning needs.

1. *Exploration Lingo*
    Skills: Observing; listening; reading; comunicating
    Cut out several large rockets from white paper. As new words are introduced, print each on a strip of paper and glue it to a rocket. The words represent fuel for the rockets. Present the information about the vocabulary as fuel for students' minds because understanding the terms enables them to explore deeper and deeper into space.
2. *Early Exploration*
    Skills: Observing; listening; reading; studying; classifying;
    communicating; analyzing; evaluating
    To provide an historical perspective, present information about the first real space launch in 1957 by the Soviet Union. Discuss the effects of this achievement on worldwide priorities, concentrating on U.S. space efforts as well as education. Then present U.S. space achievements, beginning with the rocket to the moon in 1958, followed by the rockets carrying satellites through a series of missions that included *Mariner 9*, *Viking 1* and *2*, *Pioneer Venus 1* and *2*, *Mariner 10*, *Voyager 1* and *2*, and beyond. Be sure to include both successes and failures. Help students develop a timeline showing each space mission. Guide students to analyze spacecraft design, each mission's purpose, data collected, and the effects of each mission to evaluate progress in space exploration.
3. *The Moon Walk*
    Skills: Observing; listening; measuring; predicting; evaluating
    Guide student teams to view videotapes of and read about Neil Armstrong and the mission of Apollo, analyze key factors (e.g., dress, diet, gravity), and answer such questions as: Why is space travel dangerous? What is the moon like? Are we likely to plan a trip to the sun? Why?
4. *What's Out There?*
    Skills: Observing; listening; reading; studying; organizing; analyzing;
    communicating; synthesizing; generalizing
    Since 1973 and the Mariner 10 launch to Mercury, we have been receiving information about temperature, size, composition, radio signals, atmospheres, planets, satellites, and other discoveries. Have students make debriefing bulletins containing key findings from each of several missions. Have them pretend they are crew members or scientists explaining information received from the transmissions of each satellite. Have them include with each written or oral analysis a picture drawn to represent something observed on the trip. As an alternative to a picture, have students record on audiotape their oral descriptions of what was seen.
5. *Extra Practice.* • Using a display of rocket models or pictures, have student teams develop written or oral histories about each one and/or make their own drawings or clay models. • Have pairs of students write letters of inquiry to NASA, asking for information about space exploration. • Plan a Moon Day on which students reenact the first landing on the moon; have students simulate the moon walk and explain why it looks different.

REFLECTIONS

1. Both interest and relevance of earth science topics may vary according to the type of special student involved. Based on discussions in Part III, Chapter 2, and your own experiences, rank the topics in this section in terms of your evaluation of their probable interest and relevance to a 7-year-old special student and a 13-year-old special student in your local area. Explain any differences in your rankings as a function of age.

2. Most school systems publish a printed curriculum guide for elementary science. Locate the guide for the schools in your area. Compare the treatment of the topics in this section with their treatment in the curriculum guide. Decide how a few of the strategies in this section could be incorporated into the activities suggested in the guide. Then identify the activities suggested in the guide that you could adapt for special students; select one activity and make such modifications for a real or hypothetical special learner.

3. Observing, analyzing, classifying, and generalizing are particularly important facilitative skills for mastering many of the earth science topics. Review the recommendations in Chapter 3 for teaching these skills, and then plan how to teach these four skills as you teach the concepts for one of the topics in this section. Try out your lesson on a peer, and then modify your lesson for a particular special student. If possible, teach the lesson to the student.

4. Some of the concepts in this section are difficult to teach unless explanations are accompanied by actual demonstrations. Videotape an important example of earth science in action in the local community for three of the topics in this section. As you tape, explain each scene. Formulate questions to present to students as advance organizers before they view the tape. If possible, use your tape to introduce the topic to one or more special students.

5. Similar DETECTION behaviors are listed for several of the earth science topics. Review these behaviors for commonalities and differences across topics. Justify similarities and reconcile differences. Then suggest additional diagnostic behaviors that should be included.

6. When focused on a particular student with special needs, classroom observations often reveal important diagnostic and prescriptive data. Observe such a student in the classroom during an earth science lesson; compare observed behaviors with the DETECTION behaviors listed in this section and with the skills checklist in Figure 3.1. List your tentative conclusions and any additional information you need to confirm your hypotheses. If possible, repeat the observations of the same student on several occasions to compare progress.

7. For each topic, only a few CORRECTION strategies are listed. Based on your knowledge of earth science and of special children, add to or modify the strategies for the topic of your choice.

8. Experienced teachers usually develop a collection of activities that they have found to be effective. Interview a veteran elementary teacher to identify simple experiments for two earth science concepts. Modify the experiments for a real or hypothetical special learner. Later, demonstrate your experiment for peers and if possible, for a special learner.

9. A learning-center arrangement provides opportunities for independent hands-on science activities. Develop a learning center for the earth science topic that you believe to be the most important for special learners to master.

10. A number of resources are available for teaching about earth science. Compare and contrast the topical, conceptual, and skill emphasis of these publications with the discussions in Part III:

Ball, D. W. (1978). *ESS/special education teacher's guide.* St. Louis: Webster/ McGraw-Hill.

Bybee, R., Peterson, R., Bowyer, J., & Butts, D. (1984). *Teaching about science and society: Activities for elementary and junior high school.* Columbus, OH: Charles E. Merrill.

Cooper, E. K. (1965). *Science in your own back yard.* New York: Harcourt, Brace.

Fenton, C., & Fenton, M. (1970). *Riches from the earth.* New York: John Day.

Gega, P. C. (1990). *Science in elementary education.* (6th ed.). New York: Macmillan.

Gross, P. (1972). *Teaching science in an outdoor environment.* Berkeley: University of California Press.

McCormack, A. J. (1979). *Outdoor areas as learning libraries: CESI sourcebook.* Washington, DC: Council for Elementary Science, International.

Nelson, L. W., & Lorbeer, G. C. (1984). *Science activities for elementary children* (8th ed.). Dubuque, IA: Wm. C. Brown.

Russell, H. R. (1973). *Ten-minute field trips: Using the school grounds for environmental studies.* Chicago: J. G. Ferguson.

Schmidt, V. E., & Rockcastle, V. N. (1982). *Teaching science with everyday things* (2nd ed.). New York: McGraw-Hill.

PART IV

PHYSICAL SCIENCE

When compared to the topics of previous sections, the content of the physical sciences is probably the most difficult for special learners to master. This is due in part to the complexity of concepts as well as to the rapid pace at which ideas in some of the physical sciences change. With the exception of the basic laws of physics, research and innovations seem to almost continually upgrade and outdate both the knowledge base and the technology presented in science textbooks. The skills most heavily emphasized in mastering the content of physical science are predicting, measuring, analyzing, generalizing, and evaluating. The topics of Part IV, particularly the use of machines and technology, contain content that can enhance the lives of special students.

Part IV begins with discussions of energy sources, such as water, solar, wind, and nuclear power as well as nonrenewable resources and magnetism and electricity. Chapter 11 is about the use of energy and interrelates the concepts of conservation, ecology, and other topics that affect how we live. Although these topics will become increasingly important issues to students as they mature, teaching the safe use of electricity and nurturing an attitude of conservation might be appropriate goals of instruction for young students.

Chapter 12 is the most basic of the chapters in this section. Beginning with the treatment of force and work, this chapter moves to simple machines and then complex machines. The concepts of force and simple machines illustrate basic laws of physics and understanding them is important to special students in particular. Effective use of simple machines is an important real-life skill to increase one's work capacity and save time, effort, and money. Once understood, these principles can be applied to innumerable situations to accomplish a variety of tasks.

Chapter 13 focuses on technology and its effect on people and the environment. Many students are fascinated by technology and gadgets, making this chapter both attractive and timely. Perhaps the two topics most relevant to special students are information processing and biotechnology: the first because it assists, simplifies, and speeds all types of communication and the second because it provides the basis for assistive devices to compensate for many physical handicaps.

The intensity and emphasis of study of the topics in Part IV should be guided by the individual needs of special students within the curricular dictates of the school program. Detection of students' needs in content knowledge are somewhat different for each chapter since, for example, knowledge about force, work, and simple machines is more basic and static than information about technology or nuclear power. Based on directed questioning, informal interviews, rating scales, and observational assessment and knowledge of students' abilities and circumstances, content depth and skills instruction can be adjusted to fit the needs of individual students.

To the extent practical and possible, all three areas included in this section should be at least lightly covered. Within each chapter, however, it may be necessary to simplify and narrow the scope of the topics to fit the ability levels of students. A good grasp of the most relevant topics along with a cursory acquaintance with the others is more desirable than overwhelming students with a volume of rote memorization tasks. Their utility and direct application to daily events make understanding and mastery of simple machines particularly meaningful to many special learners. Unlike some science textbooks that begin with and heavily emphasize all types of machines, beyond stressing simple machines, we suggest highlighting technology. Special learners in particular can benefit from understanding and experiencing the advantages and conveniences of computers and various electronic equipment, ranging from calculators to voice synthesizers and sophisticated assistive devices. Direct instruction in the key skills should be incorporated into each activity since the skills of predicting, analyzing, generalizing, and evaluating can be applied to learning most of the physical science content.

28. NONRENEWABLE FUELS

DETECTION Mastery of key concepts may be difficult for students who:

- Have not analyzed fuel sources by type
- Do not predict or generalize easily
- Consider all energy sources to be renewable or unlimited
- Cannot explain the value of study of nonrenewable fuels

Description. The most widely used energy sources in the United States are petroleum products (oil, gas, and diesel fuel), natural gas, and coal. All these are fossil fuels, and they come from natural resources that cannot be replaced or regrown once they are used. The study of nonrenewable fuels includes the major topics of availability, location, and uses of the fossil fuels and conservation of nonrenewable fuels as well as the problems associated with both the mining and burning of these energy sources.

Special Problems. Without direct instruction, students are seldom aware of energy issues, including perhaps the extent to which humans depend on petroleum products. In addition to oil and gasoline, petroleum is used in thousands of products with which students may be familiar but not necessarily associate with petroleum. Once reminded, many students often associate coal and natural gas as sources for heating but not for powering machinery. Some students have never observed or communicated about their dependence upon nonrenewable products. Students who do not live in petroleum-producing areas are typically less attuned to petroleum products than are those who do. Predictions and generalizations about the loss of resources and how their burning affects the environment also are not common, particularly in families who are relatively unconcerned about ecology or conservation. Fossil fuels are so common that many students take their existence for granted. Some students may have difficulty understanding that burning of certain fuels also wastes energy, an important concept before studying other, less wasteful sources of energy.

Instructional Implications. Although the petroleum products themselves are familiar to students, study and concern about them is relatively foreign to many students. Thus, the first instructional task is to lay the foundation for building attitudes of concern and responsibility. A particularly practical issue is emphasizing the relationship between the price of fuels and world events. Pairing the study of fossil fuels with ecological studies reinforces the important concepts in both areas.

CORRECTION: Modify strategies for topical and learning needs:

1. *Vocabulary Fuels*
   Skills: Observing; listening; reading; classifying; communicating
   Post 1–2 pictures showing sources where each of 3 types of fossil fuels are
   found or transported (e.g., oil rigs, pipelines, tankers, mines, or coal trains).
   Then list vocabulary words as they are related to each of the 3 categories.
2. *Independent Vocabulary Review*
   Skills: Observing; listening; reading; classifying; communicating
   Develop a folder containing a card for each of the fuel vocabulary words. On
   the left side of the folder, label 4 columns with these headings: *Coal, Natural
   Gas, Petroleum,* and *Several Fuel Sources;* draw a box under each heading.
   On the right side of the folder, place an envelope containing the word cards.
   Have students work independently or in teams to pronounce each word and
   place it in the appropriate category.
3. *Why Fossil Fuels?*
   Skills: Observing; listening; reading; studying; organizing;
   communicating; synthesizing; generalizing
   Explain that fossil fuels contain energy from plants and animals that,
   through the process of heat and compacted earth, over millions of years,
   changed into coal, natural gas, and petroleum. Show samples or pictures of
   fossils and then layered drawings depicting their deposits within the earth.
   Have students handle several pieces of coal and notice the black deposits;
   discuss why coal is not a clean source of energy. Then have students critique
   pictures or videotapes of the extraction and refining of fossil fuels. Guide
   students to answer these questions: Why is burning petroleum to make
   energy not considered clean energy? Why are fossil fuels called *nonrenewable fuels?* Why would you not want to live next to a rig, mine, or refinery?
   What couldn't you have or do without fossil fuels?
4. *Surveying Local Fuel Supplies*
   Skills: Observing; listening; reading; directed experimenting; organizing;
   analyzing; communicating
   Guide students to develop a 4–8-item fuel survey. Have students use the
   survey to interview officials from local manufacturing companies, factories,
   and power companies. Then have students analyze the results and report
   back to the class. Include in the survey such questions as these:
   • What are the sources of energy you use to generate electricity or
     power your machines?
   • How is your fuel transported here?
   • Which type of fuel do you use the most? Second? Why?
   • What problems are associated with the fuels you use?
5. *Extra Practice.* • To learn about natural gas, invite a representative from a local gas
   distributor or public utility company to explain where their gas comes from
   as well as its uses and dangers. • Ask students to report on the types of
   energy sources they use to heat, cool, and cook at home, on a boat, in a tent,
   or other places and then compare sources.

29. WATER POWER

DETECTION Mastery of key concepts may be difficult for students who:

- Have never seen water used as a power source
- Do not predict or generalize easily
- Cannot describe sources of power
- Cannot explain the value of the study of water as a power source

Description. Water power has been used as a clean, renewable source of energy for many years. The energy created by large rivers, ocean tides (tidal energy), geysers, and hot springs is a valuable resource. By far the most common examples of water power is the damming of large rivers and the building of hydroelectric power plants to generate electricity. Major topics of study include the procedures for harnessing the power of water, the manipulation of the water to vary the power, the many uses of water power, and the potential effects on natural resources where such plants are built. Thus, this topic is closely associated with the study of water and land ecology.

Special Problems. Many students are unaware of their direct or indirect dependence upon water as a power source. Some do not understand how building a dam can generate electricity. The tremendous pressure that is necessary to turn giant turbines is difficult to imagine. Conceptualizing how geothermal energy is captured and converted for use is equally difficult to understand. The principles involved and their interrelationships are too complex for some students to conceptualize. Students from families who are not concerned with energy or ecology may lack some of the important background experiences, as may those who live in areas where water is not a major source of power. Students who have difficulty predicting and generalizing are likely to experience some problems mastering the content. Without expert instruction and an enthusiastic teacher, this is typically not a high-interest topic. Unmotivated students seldom master the topic quickly.

Instructional Implications. As with teaching about any type of energy, building the foundation for attitudes of concern and responsibility is an important first step. A second step is to generate enthusiasm about the wonders of water power; this involves accentuating the personal benefits of water energy to each student. Instruction can be improved if simple models or analogies are used to illustrate the force of water. Explaining the process while students view films or videotapes of water power in action makes the concepts seem more concrete. It may help some students to identify the locations where hydroelectric plants are presently in use, analyze the sites, and discuss what they have in common. Unlike nonrenewable fossil fuels, water is usually replenished regularly. However, the very use of water as a source of power carries with it dangers to the environment. Ecological problems can be discussed and more fully understood if students can see or hear about the effects on nearby land and wildlife when a large amount of water is dammed or diverted. When the study of water energy is paired with the study of water and land ecology, instruction in both areas is more meaningful.

CORRECTION Modify strategies for topical and learning needs:

1. *Word Searchers*
   Skills: Observing; reading; studying; communicating
   Have students use almanacs, old textbooks, and other sources to develop a list of key words that describes the uses of water power.

2. *Locating Water Power*
   Skills: Observing; reading; studying; analyzing; communicating; generalizing; evaluating
   Provide students with information about hydroelectric power and geothermal energy. Then use a wall map of the United States and have students place a pin on the sight of a dam, hot spring, or geyser. Attach a string to the pin and attach the other end to a card listing the facility, location, and other details about the site. Ask students which parts of the country use the most water power and why. Next, have pairs of students research the vicinity surrounding 1 of the sites to determine the impact of the water power source on the immediate area and then report to peers. Conclude by charting both the good and bad effects of utilization of water power.

3. *Early Uses of Water Energy*
   Skills: Observing; analyzing; communicating; hypothesizing; generalizing
   Show several pictures of old grain mills and have students explain how they think water power was used. Discuss where they would build such a mill if they had been around many years ago and why.

4. *River Power*
   Skills: Observing; directed experimenting; analyzing; communicating
   Have students work in pairs to find out what happens when water is dammed. First, pack a 1" layer of dirt in a 9" cake pan. To represent a river, make a trench down the middle with your finger. Tilting the pan about 25 degrees, slowly pour a stream of water beginning on the top of the pan into the trench, using a second 9" pan to catch the water. Next, use half a popsicle stick to create a dam about 2" from the top of the pan. Again slowly pour water, beginning from the top of the pan. Then ask students to describe what happened. Discuss how to prevent the overflow and the effects the excess water would have on people, plants, and animals above and below the dam.

5. *Old Faithful*
   Skills: Observing; listening; experimenting; communicating; generalizing
   Heat a whistling teapot of water and have students watch the steam as it rushes out. Hold a ruler near the steam, test it for heat, and then have students touch the ruler and feel its warmth. Compare this to the use of geothermal energy and then read information about Iceland's use of geothermal energy as a major source of energy. Guide students to compare the source of heat for their school with geothermal energy.

6. *Extra Practice.* • Have students write a group letter to the operations officer of a hydroelectric plant, asking about the history, power, and environmental effects of its operation. • Have pairs of students locate information about sites that use geothermal energy and report to peers.

30. SOLAR AND WIND POWER

DETECTION Mastery of key concepts may be difficult for students who:

- Are unfamiliar with solar or wind power
- Cannot explain the conversion of energy from one form to another
- Do not analyze, predict, or generalize easily
- Cannot explain the value of solar or wind power

Detection. Many students and teachers alike are relatively uninformed about solar and wind power. Although wind has been used to generate power for centuries, the widespread use of solar power is a recent trend. In the study of solar energy, concepts to build include its evolution as an energy source; beginning with its utilization as a source of heat and moving to its growing use as an economical means of generating electricity; as a power source for space satellites, replacing the atomic power packs with solar panels, and a means to power motor vehicles. The use of solar energy to power such familiar items as calculators and watches should also be explained. The study of wind power could begin with the historic windmills of Holland, used to pump water and often to grind grain, and move to the twentieth century windmills that are still used to pump water from the ground and also to turn generators to create electrical power. Other key topics to consider in studying solar and wind power are the procedures for harnessing and manipulating both types of energy and a comparative analysis of solar and wind power and other energy sources. In both cases, a major point to emphasize is that the actual source of power is essentially free; it is the devices to harness the power that are often costly.

Special Problems. The concept of capturing energy and using it to provide heat and/or stored energy is not difficult. However, it is not as easy to explain the process of turning light or wind into usable energy. Except in a few specific locales where solar and wind power are commonly used, the parents and even the teachers of most students are fairly unfamiliar with these types of energy; thus, many students lack fundamental background knowledge and their frame of reference tends to be narrow. Even the use of concrete classroom examples often is limited to solar-powered watches and calculators and references to sailboats and windmills. Students who have difficulty analyzing, hypothesizing, and generalizing are likely to experience problems mastering the topics; a strong conceptual base is needed for most students to apply these skills.

Instructional Implications. The teacher's task is to thoroughly master the content before presenting it to students. Although wind power may be easier to demonstrate in class than solar power, familiar solar-powered items should be displayed and explained. As both types of energy are studied, they should be continually analyzed and compared with each other and with energy alternatives, with emphasis on cost, impact on the environment, and value to the students and society.

CORRECTION Modify strategies for topical and learning needs:

1. *Vocabulary Sun Test*
    Skills: Observing; listening; experimenting; analyzing; communicating
    To emphasize important terms and the major concepts, mount key terms associated with solar and wind energy on 4 pieces of construction paper, 2 white and 2 dark colors, varying the order of words on each list. As each term is presented, have a student locate it on a list, read it, and explain it; repeat the process, reading from the remaining 3 lists. Post 1 white- and 1 dark-paper list on a window or somewhere that receives direct sunlight several hours a day. Post the remaining 2 lists directly in the path of an air vent. After 5 days, have students compare all 4 lists and describe and explain the differences in color and appearance.
2. *Collecting Solar Energy*
    Skills: Observing; listening; experimenting; analyzing; communicating
    After discussing solar collectors and reflectors, demonstrate the capture of energy. Fold 2 4" x 4" pieces of construction paper (1 white, 1 black) and a 4" x 4" piece of aluminum foil to form miniature puptents. Place equal pieces of chocolate candy under each tent and move all directly in the sun. Ask students to predict which piece of candy will melt first and justify their predictions. After a few minutes, have students observe the results. Discuss results, pointing out that some paper caught more energy from the sun and melted the candy rapidly. Ask: Which of these colors would work best for a surface on a solar collector? Why? Have students view pictures or examples of actual solar collectors to verify answers.
3. *Collecting and Using Wind Power*
    Skills: Observing; analyzing; predicting; generalizing; evaluating
    Use sand with a blow dryer to illustrate the strength of wind and familiar real examples to present the power of wind (sailboats, hats on windy days, etc.). Guide student teams to predict the problems of using wind as the main source of energy, to evaluate the feasibility of a windmill on the schoolgrounds, and to identify 5 locations best for building windmills.
4. *Comparing Energy Sources*
    Skills: Observing; listening; reading; organizing; analyzing; communicating; synthesizing; evaluating
    Guide students to construct an analysis sheet listing sources of energy on the top and important characteristics in a column on the left. Have student pairs compare the fossil fuels to solar and wind power. Provide reference sources so such concerns as cost can be located. Have students use the completed charts to evaluate the merits of each type of energy.
5. *Extra Practice.* • Have students contact a local public utility to find out how much and for what purposes solar or wind energy is in use locally and report on 1 project to peers. • Invite local energy experts to explain the use of solar and wind power. • Have student pairs study the use of solar and wind power in other countries and report to peers. • Have teams of students write a jingle or 30-second radio commercial to convince others to use or not use a particular form of energy.

31. NUCLEAR POWER

DETECTION Mastery of key concepts may be difficult for students who:
- Cannot describe sources of power
- Do not predict, generalize, or evaluate easily
- Have never analyzed strengths and weaknesses of nuclear power
- Cannot explain the value of nuclear power to self and society

Description. *Nuclear power* is produced through nuclear fission when atoms are split and energy is released. Utilization of nuclear energy as a source of electric power is a relatively recent development that has been received by the public with mixed emotions. A number of major concepts must be developed in order to understand nuclear power: the vast amounts of energy produced by small amounts of uranium (less than one pound of uranium produces the same amount of energy produced by burning 40-50 train carloads of coal) and the characteristics of the uranium itself; the process by which nuclear energy is harnessed and channeled from the fission in a nuclear reactor's core, releasing enough heat to change water to the steam that turns turbines to produce electricity; the ecological advantages of utilizing nuclear energy (no smoke and limited destruction of land by mining); and the high cost of constructing nuclear plants. The potential dangers associated with producing nuclear power should also be addressed, including: 1) the possibility of the cooling system failing, the reactor core overheating, a meltdown resulting, and the release of large amounts of radioactive materials into the surrounding area through the water, land, and atmosphere and 2) the hazards involved in removing, transporting, and storing the dangerous nuclear waste from the production process. The dangers associated with the production of nuclear power are equally as important as the topic itself.

Special Problems. Many people do not understand the splitting of atoms, chain reactions, uranium nuclei, reactors, and radioactive waste; the topic involves important but difficult concepts. Students from families opposed to the use of nuclear energy may have relatively closed minds to the subject. Those who live in areas that are close to nuclear power plants, particularly people who have witnessed nuclear accidents, often have preconceived ideas that are difficult to change. The effects of radiation on people and the environment are sometimes viewed as emotionally laden and unpleasant topics to be avoided. Teachers who are opposed to the use of nuclear power may transmit their biases to students.

Instructional Strategies. Demonstration models are difficult to provide for the study of nuclear energy. Videotapes that include diagrams, flowcharts, and simulations are invaluable teaching aids for demonstrating the fission process; when using such tapes, it is important to emphasize the built-in safeguards and appropriate precautions for preventing accidents. For relevant examples of the positive use of nuclear power, explain its medical applications. Both the positive and negative aspects of nuclear energy should be highlighted and then analyzed and compared to alternative energy sources.

CORRECTION Modify strategies for topical and learning needs:

1. *Nuclear Power in Context*
   Skills: Observing; reading; analyzing; classifying; communicating
   Post on a bulletin board key terms associated with nuclear power. Supply 3–4 newspaper or magazine stories in which students can locate articles about nuclear energy. Use a highlighter pen to call attention to key words students find in the articles and stories. Read or have a student read each term in context and discuss its meaning.
2. *Understanding Nuclear Reactions*
   Skills: Observing; listening; communicating; generalizing; evaluating
   To help students better understand a chain reaction, set up dominoes, tennis balls, or golf balls and demonstrate how one moving object can be used to hit another and another and so on. Although tiny uranium atoms cannot be seen in the classroom, the principle is comparable: The movement produces energy, and in a nuclear reactor, heat energy is produced. If appropriate, continue the lesson including diagrams and drawings of a nuclear reactor, rods, core, and other specific reactor-related terms. Have student teams devise additional ways to illustrate the process and vote on the best demonstration.
3. *Uses of Nuclear Energy*
   Skills: Observing; listening; reading; analyzing; communicating;
          synthesizing; generalizing; evaluating
   Provide resources for teams of students to listen to or read to find out about what the words on this list have to do with nuclear power: atomic bomb, U.S.S. Enterprise, radiation therapy, bone scan, Three-Mile Island, and Grand Gulf. Have team members analyze the use of nuclear energy in their chosen or assigned topic, citing the advantages and disadvantages, and then report to peers. Have peers decide upon alternative sources of energy and then evaluate each application of nuclear energy.
4. *Problems with Nuclear Energy*
   Skills: Observing; listening; reading; analyzing; predicting;
          communicating; generalizing; evaluating
   Present 2 vignettes of nuclear power plants: 1 positive and 1 negative. Discuss the benefits of the plants, the problems that have occurred, the effects of radiation, storage of nuclear waste, and how the location of nuclear plants is determined. Then form 2 teams to debate this issue: A nuclear power plant is proposed to be built in your community at no additional expense to consumers; the action you should take is . . .
5. *Extra Practice.* • Have students write to the Nuclear Regulatory Agency to inquire about safety and their role in regulating the industry; if appropriate, have students use the articles in Activity 2 above to: 1) rewrite sentences using the key vocabulary; 2) work in pairs and read a sentence containing key words and then explain what is meant; and/or 3) take 2 or more of the sentences with key words and combine these into a single sentence.

32. MAGNETISM AND ELECTRICITY

DETECTION Mastery of key concepts may be difficult for students who:

- Do not conceptualize magnetism as energy
- Take electrical power for granted
- Do not analyze, predict, or synthesize easily
- Have difficulty hypothesizing and generalizing
- Cannot explain the value of magnetism and electricity

Description. Magnetism is a high-interest topic that allows for hands-on demonstrations and directed experimentation. In addition to magnetic attraction, the principle of electromagnetism can be illustrated as it is used in huge hydroelectric plants. Magnetism and electricity are interrelated topics; magnetic force and fields are fundamental concepts that lay part of the foundation for understanding electricity. Other important concepts include generation of electricity by heat, light, and chemicals; the products of electricity (motion, heat, light, and chemical activity); and how electric current is transported. From a consumer point of view, instruction should focus on how electricity is and should be used safely.

Special Problems. Unlike the other topics in this section, electricity is an obvious and integral part of students' daily lives; however, even though they experience the results, they may lack fundamental background knowledge. By the time they enter school, many youngsters take electricty for granted, conceptualizing the process as one that occurs because the switch or cord is manipulated. Many adults share this ignorance about electricty and magnetism. As parents, they do not provide adequate explanations to young, questioning children. Magnets, familiar to students as the holders to display their pictures on refrigerator doors, are seldom associated with energy without directed experimentation and instruction. While students can readily observe the attracting and repelling properties and uses of magnets, in the creation of electricity, their function and that of heat, light, and chemicals is less obvious, more abstract, and thus difficult. Students who have problems with analysis, prediction, synthesis, hypothesis, and generalizing are likely to experience problems mastering the topics.

Instructional Implications. For special students, safe and informed use of electricity is a critical issue to stress. A rudimentary knowledge of the basic principles of electricity enables students to understand why, for example, defective cords, plugs, and switches and exposed wires and powerlines should be avoided or hands should be dry when connecting electricity. Such concepts may be more useful than a very technical understanding of magnetism and electricity. Understanding the production and use of electricity may be more interesting when its origin is explained from multiple sources, such as in previous Topics 28–31. Careful teacher supervision is essential when students are learning and experimenting with this topic to avoid injuries or even damage to watches and computers from magnetic force.

CORRECTION Modify strategies for topical and learning needs:

1. *Magnetic Meanings*
   Skills: Observing; listening; organizing; communicating; generalizing
   When presenting terminology for energy-related concepts, print words on 3"
   x 5" cards and glue a small magnet on the back of the card. Use something
   metal such as the side of a file cabinet, and display vocabulary words. When
   appropriate, use 2–3 major headings or key words and have subheadings or
   meanings on cards so students can place the proper card under the best
   headings such as *circuit, current, battery,* and *generator.*

2. *Magnetic Attractions*
   Skills: Observing; directed experimenting; analyzing; classifying;
   predicting; communicating; evaluating
   Place an assortment of metal and nonmetal objects on a table. Have student
   teams predict which items will be attracted to the magnet. Place these items
   in 2 different groups. Have students use a small magnet with each object to
   test predictions. Guide analysis of common properties of objects, uses of
   magnets, magnetizing other objects, and how to identify the other objects in
   the room that may or may not be attracted to a magnet.

3. *Transporting Electrical Current*
   Skills: Observing; listening; directed experimentation; communicating
   Display an assortment of wire and cords, such as string, electric wire, rope,
   extension cord, belt, and other similar materials. Guide students to identify
   the ones that can carry electric current and what they have in common.
   Working only in adult-supervised groups of 2–3, have students conduct a
   school tour and locate at least 2 lines carrying electric current. Have each
   group orally share descriptions, locations, functions served, and sketches of
   each line they find.

4. *Using Electrical Energy*
   Skills: Observing; analyzing; communicating; predicting; synthesizing;
   generalizing; evaluating
   Assign to student teams various information acquisition tasks that are
   about electricity and also involve the use of some form of electricity (e.g., read
   this page, watch or listen to this tape, or complete this computer activity).
   The next day, reassign the same tasks but to different teams. This time,
   simulate a power failure in the classroom; turn off or do not permit the use
   of electricity. Have teams describe their alternative ways to achieve their
   tasks, how electricity would have helped, and then rank the 10 most
   important uses of electricity to themselves. Have teams compare and
   critique lists and develop rules for safe use. Have students repeat the process
   at home and then compare and discuss listings.

5. *Extra Practice.* • Have student teams describe what happens when they first hold a
   compass near a magnet and then remove the magnet. • Guide teams to
   demonstrate and discuss how chemical energy in a dry cell and 2 wires can
   be used to light a bulb. • Help students develop a safety checklist for
   electrical use in their homes; with adult supervision, ask for volunteers to
   use the list and report what they found.

33. CONSERVATION OF ENERGY

DETECTION   Mastery of key concepts may be difficult for students who:
- Reveal limited knowledge about energy conservation
- Exhibit wasteful habits
- Have difficulty analyzing, predicting, generalizing, and evaluating
- Cannot explain the value of energy conservation to self and society

Description. Because of a reduction in oil supplies in the 1970s, limiting the consumption of petroleum and electricity arose as a major priority. The study of conservation of energy includes such topics as the reasons for energy shortages; fluctuations in the prices of fuels; the use of wind, solar, and nuclear power as alternatives to petroleum-based power; experimental fuels, such as those made from grain or from garbage; the reasons for energy conservation; methods of conservation; and the responsibility of individuals for energy conservation. Prerequisite concepts entail a fundamental knowledge about the major sources of fuels and their advantages and disadvantages. Also involved is a basic understanding of cause and effect as applied to individual and group actions related to energy supplies.

Special Problems. Conservation is as much an attitude as a body of knowledge. Positive attitudes result in taking care of property, being careful and tending to safety needs, and an overall disdain for waste. Such attitudes and the resulting values and practices generally begin and are reinforced in the home. Unless developed at home, such tendencies are difficult to explain and transfer into daily behaviors. Insufficient information is another source of problems; many families are not well informed about the need or methods to conserve. In some cases, conservation is an economic issue, with the motivation to conserve positively correlated with the price of energy. The length of time between cause and eventual effect renders the topic somewhat distant. Students who have difficulty analyzing, predicting, generalizing, and evaluating may experience problems mastering this topic.

Instructional Implications. Energy conservation is a family affair. The major thrust of an instructional program is establishing the foundation upon which to build appropriate attitudes and then concepts. Students must continually see positive models in teachers as well as family. Furthermore, the modeled behavior should be accompanied by verbal explanations such as: I'm turning down the heat since no one will be here over the weekend. Attempts should be made to keep parents informed about the students' study and when possible to actively involve parents in a total program of energy conservation. If students regularly write and take home brief notes explaining what they have done to conserve energy and why, some parents are likely to volunteer to participate. Many students enjoy learning about and implementing ideas to save energy, particularly when projects are personally relevant. The object is to develop an attitude of responsible consumerism. The economic issues should be explored in conjunction with lessons in social studies. Pairing this topic with ecological studies reinforces study in both areas.

CORRECTION Modify strategies for topical and learning needs:

1. *Target Behaviors*
      Skills: Observing; listening; analyzing; predicting; communicating;
            evaluating
      Help students develop two lists: entitle one list User and the other Actions.
      Ask students to think of all the things they do to use energy. Then discuss
      how they can use less energy. A list might begin like this:

User	Actions
light switch	turn off lights when not in use
refrigerator	don't leave door open
doors	close doors quietly behind you
television	turn off when not being watched

2. *Using Energy*
      Skills: Observing; listening; studying; predicting; communicating
      Name or show pictures of pairs of objects that use energy. Have student
      teams decide which of each pair uses the most energy and why.
3. *Making Good Judgments*
      Skills: Observing; analyzing; classifying; communicating; evaluating
      Give students a list of 4–8 different energy sources (e.g., solar, wind, garbage,
      petroleum products, etc.). Have them work in pairs to divide the list
      according to these categories: renewable/nonrenewable; clean/dirty; effi-
      cient/inefficient; safe/potentially unsafe. Have students explain and defend
      their choices and describe 3 ways to conserve each resource.
4. *Consequences of Wasting Energy*
      Skills: Observing; studying; predicting; communicating; generalizing
      Have student teams predict what life could be like in 100–500 years with no
      oil or coal. Ask questions such as these: What types of activities would be
      most affected? Which energy sources do you think will still be around? Why?
      What could happen to the land if mining, forestry, and plant development
      are not carefully monitored?
5. *Chart Reading*
      Skills: Observing; reading; studying; analyzing; measuring; communicating
      Display a chart showing the amount of electricity (kilowatt hours) a group
      of common appliances use. Have pairs of students read the chart and answer
      4–8 questions such as these: 1) Which appliance uses the most energy? The
      least? 2) Which uses more energy—a clothes dryer or an electric stove? A
      washing machine or a microwave oven? 3) At 22 cents per kilowatt hour, how
      much could you save by cutting the yearly use by 50%? 5) What can you
      personally do to conserve energy in your home?
6. *Extra Practice.* • Continuing the Target Behaviors list, have students list things they
      could do away from home to save energy. • Have students name and list
      activities in which they use personal energy (e.g., running, walking), and
      then rank their activities from the most to least energy consumed. • Have
      students visit a local department store to compare the energy consumption
      of similar products. • Have students develop their own ads for saving energy
      in homes and automobiles.

CHAPTER 12 /
USING MACHINES

34. FORCE AND WORK

DETECTION Mastery of key concepts may be difficult for students who:

- Have never considered the role of force in machines
- Do not observe carefully
- Exhibit specific problems connecting cause with effect
- Have difficulty analyzing, predicting, and generalizing
- Cannot explain the value of force and machines to self and society

Description. Force involves pushing or pulling an object to cause movement. Work results only if movement is obtained. Thus, pushing or pulling a building that does not move means no work is being done. The study of force and work includes such concepts as the role of force in machines; the combined use of the principles of pulling, lifting, and pushing as force to create motion; differences between mass and weight; and the basic precepts of work, which begin with a scientific definition of work and involve using types of force, such as pulling and pushing, gravity, and the control of friction and motion. Together, force and work represent the conceptual foundation for understanding both how machines function and how to utilize their power.

Special Problems. Some students take the relationship between force and work for granted. For this topic, understanding the existence of a law, or the effect, is much easier than understanding the cause. Gravity or gravitational pull can be easily demonstrated in countless ways; fully understanding its cause is more difficult. Students who have not used simple machines to help around the house typically have less foundational knowledge on which to build. The ability to analyze and predict are particularly important to conceptualizing the relationship between cause and effect; students who have weak analysis and prediction skills may have difficulty mastering the content. Although strong hypothesis and evaluation skills are desirable, they may not be essential if generalization skills can be built.

Instructional Implications. The important point here is to strive for basic understandings. For some students, prerequisite facts will just have to be demonstrated and then accepted as fact, as in the case of gravity. Measurement is an integral part of understanding force and may have to be taught directly with each demonstration. Multiple examples of force in action can help to bridge the gap between cause and effect and should be used generously, beginning with the types of force that are likely to be the most helpful to students in their everyday lives. With each example, students should be encouraged to predict the results and then explain them.

CORRECTION Modify strategies for topical and learning needs:

1. *Demonstration Words*
   Skills: Observing; studying; analyzing; classifying; communicating
   To expand students' understanding of the concepts of force, push, pull, lift,
   gravity, motion, friction, and work, provide 1–2 picture examples with the
   word identifying each printed below the picture. Then ask students to draw
   or locate pictures in magazines to illustrate the concepts expressed in each
   example given. Have students print the correct words for the concepts being
   represented on the backs of their pictures.

2. *Work and Force*
   Skills: Observing; listening; analyzing; predicting; communicating
   Explain that work is happening only if force is being used and motion is
   occurring. A person sitting quietly listening to a recording is not doing work.
   Display several pictures of people working and not working. Ask students to
   select those pictures where work is occurring, explain how they know, and
   describe an easier way to complete the task in each case.

3. *Using Force*
   Skills: Observing; listening; experimenting; analyzing; predicting
   Explain that moving things requires force. Demonstrate force by showing
   several simple actions in the class. To help develop a concept of the feel of
   force, fill 2 empty milk cartons, the first with rocks and the second with paper
   or cloth. Have students use a pencil to push each container about 10–12
   inches. Ask: Which was harder to move? Why? Which required the most
   force to move? Why? Have students think of their own examples to contrast
   varied amounts of force. Close by pointing to objects in the classroom and
   having students predict which ones will require the most force to move and
   defend their predictions.

4. *Understanding Gravity and Friction*
   Skills: Observation; listening; prediction; communication
   Explain and discuss *gravity* as a force that causes things to pull together and
   therefore causes force to be used to move things. Demonstrate the pull of
   gravity by throwing a ball into the air or letting water run down a surface.
   Show a videotape of a space flight that demonstrates the results of decreased
   gravitational pull. Have each student find a certain number of illustrations
   of gravity to share with peers. To demonstrate friction and lubrication, have
   students rub 2 fingers together, first without and then coated with oil, and
   describe the differences. Discuss the need to reduce friction, as on squeaky
   doors, and have each student find 2 examples. To illustrate dependence on
   friction, have students try opening an empty jar while their hands are
   covered with soap. Mention examples, such as special shoes and snow tires,
   emphasizing the safety factors, and have students suggest 2 more examples
   each.

5. *Extra Practice.* • Using the pictures for Demonstration Words, have student teams
   take turns showing a picture and demonstrating the concept(s). • Ask
   students to investigate, describe, and then share information about jobs
   involving force and motion.

35. SIMPLE MACHINES

DETECTION Mastery of key concepts may be difficult for students who:

- Cannot classify different types of simple machines
- Exhibit difficulty analyzing, predicting, and generalizing
- Seldom use simple machines and tools
- Cannot explain the value of simple machines to self and society

Description. *Simple machines* are so called because they have few or no moving parts. Everyday, students use different types of simple machines to perform work that they otherwise would be incapable of or that would be much more difficult to achieve. The six major simple machines to be studied include the inclined plane, screw and wedge (both derivations of inclined planes), lever, pulley, and wheel and axle. Key concepts involve their primary and secondary uses, their capabilities, the basic principles of physics underlying the function of each, and common examples of each. Perhaps the main point to be made is that the use of simple machines enables people to do work using less force. The various combinations of these six forms of simple machines to produce very complicated equipment are discussed in Complex Machines, Topic 36.

Special Problems. Many students and adults alike use simple machines without understanding the principles that govern their efficiency. Students who regularly use tools to help around the house generally have a better appreciation of the capabilities than do students without similar experiences. Some students simply grasp the basic laws of physics easier and quicker than others, even without direct instruction or experiences. Other students lack basic knowledge because they require but have not been provided with guided demonstrations of the mechanics of each simple machine. Weak analysis, prediction, and generalization skills are apt to interfere with mastery of the topic. Strong evaluation skills or guided and prompted evaluation activities are often required to help students recognize the value of these basic and essential tools.

Instructional Implications. Students need to realize the full value of understanding and using these simple machines. Among the advantages of such knowledge that should be emphasized are these: Students can push, pull, lift, move, and accomplish work much easier; they can increase and enhance their personal capabilities to work; everyday problems can be solved more readily; since several simple machines together form the core of complicated machines, they can better understand complex machines; and finally, when traditional tools are not available, they will know how to use common objects as simple machines. In short, understanding simple machines simplifies students' lives and makes them more self-sufficient. Verbally guided demonstrations are particularly important elements of an instructional program. Provide a variety of such activities and then expand them to include real-life examples that illustrate the principles, capabilities, applications, and value of each type of simple machine.

CORRECTION Modify strategies for topical and learning needs:

1. *Identification Cards*
    Skills: Observing; listening; classifying; communicating
    Have students collect pictures of objects and people doing things that involve
    work and everyday tools. Have teams of students compete to match their
    pictures with word cards that label the simple machines depicted.

2. *Using Simple Machines*
    Skills: Observing; analyzing; predicting; all integration skills
    Demonstrate or guide students to demonstrate the use of an obvious
    example of each simple machine. Prompt students to infer the function of
    each machine, verbalize the principles while demonstrating again, and then
    have students repeat verbalizations and find and demonstrate more ex-
    amples:

    Inclined Planes. Ask students why sliding down a slide is fun. Have
    students compare their efforts to move 5 books from floor to desk, first by
    simply picking up the books and then by using a board as an inclined plane
    to slide the books up to the desk. Guide students to conclude that inclined
    planes are used to move objects to higher or lower places with minimal effort.
    Repeat procedures with verbalizations. Have students use rulers as inclined
    planes and then find and demonstrate more examples.

    Levers. Ask how students are capable of lifting classmates in the air on
    a seesaw. Move the fulcrum point of the seesaw on the playground and have
    students experience the differences in their capabilities. Guide students to
    conclude that levers, such as the seesaw, increase lifting power and that the
    farther the lever is from the fulcrum, the greater the power. Repeat with
    verbalizations. Have students show more examples.

    Screws. Verbally guide a student to squeeze juice from an orange using
    a hand juicer. Guide students to conclude that screws are curved inclined
    planes and that they increase force. Repeat procedures with verbalizations
    and have students find their own examples.

    Wedges. Place the wedge of a screwdriver on a piece of scrap wood and
    tap the handle with a small book. Guide students to conclude that the wood
    split because the wedge increased the force of the blow. Repeat with verbali-
    zations; have students find more examples *outside* the classroom.

    Pulleys. Have students take turns raising and then lowering the school's
    flag on the flagpole. Guide them to conclude that pulleys are used to raise
    and lower objects. Explain that pulleys are used to move objects many times
    the weight of the pulley puller. Repeat the flag procedure with verbalizations,
    and have students locate more examples.

    Wheels and Axles. Have students move a wagonful of heavy books from
    one side to the other. Guide them to conclude that the wheels and axles
    decrease friction and the force needed to move objects.

Extra Practice. • Have student teams select and defend their choices of the best simple
    machine to help accomplish these tasks: load a 3-wheeler onto a pickup
    truck; lift a 3-wheeler to change a tire; make apple juice; split a log; move up
    5 steps in a wheelchair; move a load of rocks 2 blocks; put a steeple on a
    church. • Have teams make and use levers.

36. COMPLEX MACHINES

DETECTION Mastery of key concepts may be difficult for students who:
- Do not understand simple machines
- Seldom use tools or machines
- Have difficulty analyzing, predicting, and generalizing
- Display disinterest in machines
- Cannot explain the value of machines to self and society

Description. Complex machines are made up of combinations of many of the six simple machines discussed as Topic 35. Since complex machines are used in the mass production of most products, this topic can encompass all facets of industrial technology or be narrowed to focus on the contributions of complex machines to students' everyday lives. To many students, the bicycle is the most relevant of the complex machines and a good starting point for analysis. Regardless of the scope of study, several key concepts of complex machines are typically included: uses; component simple machines; capabilities; basic laws of physics involved; products; costs and effects on product costs; and the ways in which machines make work more productive.

Special Problems. Students who have not mastered the concepts involved in simple machines are not likely to understand the principles at work in complex machines. Some students may have problems seeing 2–3 simple machines in a single device. Simple and complex machines that perform similar functions but with different efficiency—a spoon as a simple machine versus an electric mixer as a complex machine, a shovel as a simple machine versus a gas-powered snowblower, or a backhoe as a complex machine—also are difficult for some students to connect. Analyzing a complex machine and relating it back to a simpler machine requires identifying unique features and understanding relationships and patterns as well as making generalizations, tasks that are problematic for some students. As with simple machines, some students simply grasp the basic laws of physics easier and quicker than others, even without direct instruction or experiences; poor performance may result when students need guided demonstrations of the mechanics of machines but are not provided them. And finally, teachers who are uninformed or uninterested in complex machines sometimes impart their attitudes to their students.

Instructional Implications. When teaching about complex machines, a two-step approach is suggested: 1) Highlight the products of simple machines and then regress to the machine process; and 2) guide students to analyze the machines to identify the simple machines involved. Begin with products that students value, such as those that satisfy their wants and needs or that minimize their own labor, and then analyze the machines that produce them. When identifying the component simple machines, review the basic principles governing each before attempting to demonstrate their interactions. Both approaches require carefully guided analysis and verbally reinforced demonstrations and should conclude with emphasis on recognition of the value of the machines to the students and to society.

CORRECTION Modify strategies for topical and learning needs:

1. *School Machines*
   Skills: Observing; listening; organizing; analyzing; communicating; evaluating

   After leading students on a tour of the school to locate machines in use (include the office, kitchen, and gym), list each machine by name on the chalkboard. Have teams of students select a machine and work together to identify the simple machines that comprise it and the product it makes. Permit reexamination of machines for students to critique its value. Have teams exchange analyses to edit and refine the analysis of their peers.

2. *Making the Complex Simple*
   Skills: Observing; analyzing; classifying; communicating; generalizing; evaluating

   Bring a bicycle to class for students to analyze as a group. Begin with the product of the machine, transportation, and then examine how the bike provides it. Prompt students to locate, explain, and demonstrate the action of the component simple machines—wheel and axle, pulley, lever, and working screw—and then demonstrate their interactions as students verbalize them. Finally, have students critique the value of the machine. Have each student follow a similar procedure to analyze at least 2 other machines at school or at home to share with peers.

3. *Machines and You*
   Skills: Observing; listening; organizing; analyzing; measuring; communicating; evaluating

   Have students keep a record of the machines they use during a 1–2 hour period for several days. Then guide them as they work in pairs to determine the amount of time and effort saved, their dependence on the machines, and the value of the machines and report to peers.

4. *Improvements in Machines*
   Skills: Observing; listening; studying; analyzing; measuring; communicating; generalizing; evaluating

   Comparisons of old and new toys, cars, and household goods can be an interesting activity for students. Display pictures of or actual outdated items themselves, such as a nonelectric egg beater, coffee grinder, or can opener or an old bonnet-type hair dryer. Have students decide how the old items were used, how much time and effort were required, the quality of the product that resulted, and how the items have since been improved. Have students list the characteristics that make each newer item better than the old machine (e.g., weight, speed, ease of use, size, and so on). Conclude by having students summarize their evaluations.

5. *Extra Practice.* • If students have access to very old tools or machines, arrange for select items to be shared with the class for analysis. • Have students look through the manuals for different cars, tools, and appliances and report on proper care and maintenance. • Ask student pairs to locate 2 machines that require lubrication to reduce friction. • Have student teams build their own complex machine to solve a problem.

37. INFORMATION PROCESSING

DETECTION Mastery of key concepts may be difficult for students who:

- Have had little experience with computers
- Avoid using high-tech products
- Take technology for granted
- Cannot explain the value of information processing to self and society

Description. Information processing includes two major areas: computer technology and electronic communications. As an application of science, computers have affected nearly everyone's life in the United States and throughout much of the world. Even though complex, the study of computers can help students develop a basic understanding about one of the major technological advances that affects most other technologies. In addition to a basic knowledge of the workings and capabilities of computers, important concepts to build are the elements of electronic communication systems— sound and speech, codes, print, and graphics; the many ways in which these elements are used; the types of information that can be processed, transmitted, and stored; the time and effort required; the resulting changes in communication; and the costs involved. Also important to emphasize are the constant and rapid advances in processing; the translation of advances into innovations in telephones, recordings, radios, televisions; the evolution of satellites, fiber optics, facsimiles, and electronic banking; and the effects these advances have and will have on students' lives now and in the future.

Special Problems. Most students are not fully aware of the available types of computer technology and electronic communication. Although personal computers have become rather commonplace in the classroom and numerous families now own personal computers, in many cases, the software in use and the lack of telecommunication connections severely limit the learning that can occur. Not many schools or families can afford to upgrade equipment or programs to keep pace with new developments. Some people fear and avoid opportunities to learn about electronic information processing.

Instructional Implications. Properly approached, this topic interests most students; it may be critical for special students who require assistance communicating. Provide ample activities for students to use computers and actually experience firsthand electronic communications. Contrast the old and new by examining what was done before computers, modems, or copy machines, including quality and size changes that have resulted because of steady improvements in televisions, music players, and cameras.

CORRECTION Modify strategies for topical and learning needs:

1. *Computer and Communications Terminology*
> *Skills:* Observing; listening; reading; organizing; communicating; generalizing

> Vocabulary can be divided into 2 major types: technical (or operational), and application related. Use a computer-printed handout listing key words for each lesson. If appropriate, have students use a computer to enter words and generate sentences and examples to develop their own computer catalog showing terms, pictures, and descriptions of uses for computers. Each category could begin by including such terms as these:

Applications		*Technical*	
communications	games	bit	boot
graphics	publishing	disk	load
word processing		modem	software

2. *Computer Friendly*
> *Skills:* Observing; listening; reading; communicating; generalizing; evaluating

> Expose students to computer applications by having them use a variety of software for educational games, instructional programs, and word processing. Have pairs of students take turns using the computer to teach each other and then work together to evaluate the program they used, following class-established criteria.

3. *Information Exchange*
> *Skills:* Reading; communicating; generalizing; evaluating

> Connect pairs of computers by modem and have student partners make an interactive journal entry each day or take turns writing lines to tell a story. If classroom computers can access information services by modem, give student pairs missions to accomplish. In either case, conclude each activity by having students evaluate the information exchange and suggest ideas for additional information exchanges.

4. *Technology Survey*
> *Skills:* Observing; listening; reading; analyzing; predicting; communicating; generalizing; evaluating

> Guide students to develop a list of computer and electronic communication uses, listing the use and then an alternative way of performing the job. Have them add to the list after starting them off with entries like these:

> *Airline reservations:* Books, paper files, clerks, and telephones
> *Traffic lights:* Police officers on each corner, signs
> *Banking machines:* Tellers but only during bank hours

> Extend the activity by having student teams research the cost of both methods and evaluate the use of technology in each case.

5. *Extra Practice.* • Demonstrate computer input devices, such as voice, mouse, touch screen, optical scanner, and modem, and have students use and evaluate each. • Have student teams investigate early models of radios, TVs, telephones, or cameras; compare and contrast them with present models; and report to peers.

38. PHYSICAL TECHNOLOGY

DETECTION Mastery of key concepts may be difficult for students who:

- Do not observe carefully
- Are not aware of physical technology in their everyday life
- Have difficulty analyzing, predicting, and generalizing
- Cannot explain the value of physical technology to self and society

Description. Physical technology is evident in numerous fields: in the construction of houses, roads, and buildings; throughout the manufacturing industry in such forms as mass production, assembly lines, and robotics; in the area of transportation, which involves land, air, and water vehicles; and finally in energy and power, ranging from steam engines and electric motors to solar and nuclear power. This is a very broad topic with subtopics and even subdivisions worthy of lengthy and in-depth study if time and students' needs, ages, and abilities justify it. Since energy and power are discussed elsewhere (see Topics 28–33), this section focuses on construction, manufacturing, and transportation. Among the concepts to build in each area are the types of technology involved, uses, advantages as well as disadvantages, alternatives and their feasibility and appeal, and trends.

Special Problems. As with new developments in communication, physical technology is advancing so rapidly that it is difficult even for those professionals directly involved to stay current. Thus, teachers often present outdated information. Some students are raised in homes or experience multiple problems that overshadow the contributions of technological advances in most any field. Students who do not observe carefully may take for granted or not notice the influence of physical technology on their everyday activities. Students who have difficulty analyzing, predicting, and generalizing also may have difficulty mastering the content. This may not be a high-priority topic for many low-achieving students; the depth and breadth of the various interrelated topics render this area of study challenging for even the highest achievers.

Instructional Implications. Physical technology is one of the easiest areas to illustrate since numerous examples are available in most parts of the United States and in other industrialized nations as well. Automated car washes, modern trucks and airplanes, electric- or gasoline-powered tools, factories that utilize robotics, and computer-designed and -controlled buildings are commonplace in these places. However, because the topic is so expansive, both subtopics and the examples themselves should be selected according to their availability and relevance to the particular students. Familiarity with either process or product or both are key elements in personalizing instruction in this broad area. Since textbooks are not likely to record the latest developments, teachers must monitor the news for much of the content but present it as tentative because it too will soon be outdated. Observation and analysis are particularly important skills to nurture if students are to recognize the role of physical technology in their lives.

CORRECTION Modify strategies for topical and learning needs:

1. *Word Maps*
   Skills: Observing; listening; analyzing; communicating
   As each of the 3 areas, construction, manufacturing, and transportation, is studied, present the vocabulary using a mapping format. Discuss key words and list them on a chalkboard in an organized fashion. For example:

   Nonvehicle Transportation System

conveyors	elevators	escalators	pipelines
parts	people	people	gas
assembly		goods	oil

2. *Changes in Construction*
   Skills: Observing; listening; analyzing; classifying; communicating
   Decide which of 4 building categories is to be studied: commercial, industrial, institutional, or residential. Begin by showing several pictures of such buildings that are 20–50 years old. Guide students to compare these with what they see now, classifying differences in type of materials used, appearance, size, and accommodations (air conditioning, heat, baths, etc.).

3. *Planning for Technology*
   Skills: Observing; studying; analyzing; communicating; evaluating
   Select a local construction project, such as a new factory or a road or a bridge, that is just getting underway in the local community. Have student teams use newspaper stories, independent research, telephone interviews, and video or personal visits to the site to develop a sequential history of the project. Have the teams report on the use of physical technology in the construction process and equipment to critique the value of the technology and report to peers. Develop a series of pictures depicting the site before, during, and after completion to accompany the reports and to highlight the time and planning required. Later, have students evaluate the impact of the new project on them and their community.

4. *Planning a Trip*
   Skills: Observing; listening; reading; studying; analyzing; predicting; communicating; generalizing; evaluating
   Have pairs of students plan a short holiday trip for the teacher. Have them select the best mode of transportation and route according to cost, time involved, schedules, comfort, and convenience by comparing the alternatives. Then have students analyze and evaluate the role of physical technology in the selection process. Later, have peers compare and vote on the best plan, and then repeat the process for a longer trip.

5. *Extra Practice.* • Have students rank the 5 technological conveniences they prize most and then least. • Ask students to suggest products that could be made through the use of robotics. • Invite local people to explain the role of technology in their jobs. • After planning a trip, have students describe how the trip would have differed if planned 50 years earlier. • Assign pairs of students to develop an information pack about physical technology changes, contrasting the old with the new.

39. BIOTECHNOLOGY

DETECTION Mastery of key concepts may be difficult for students who:

- Have not personally encountered obvious examples of biotechnology
- Are not technologically literate
- Have difficulty analyzing, predicting, and evaluating
- Cannot explain the value of biotechnology to self and society

Description. Biotechnology is a relatively new field that focuses on improving the quality of life. Two of the major areas affected by biotechnology are: 1) the production and preservation of plants and animals for food, clothing, and other products and 2) the advances in health care and assistive devices involving limbs, organs, mechanical and electronic aids, and diagnostic tools. Genetic engineering, a highly controversial issue that has received considerable publicity, is one of the most visible biotechnical advances. However, among the most relevant subtopics to students are the advances in agriculture and medicine and health care. In addition to the general nature of the advances, key concepts in each field include the developmental processes, purposes, efficiency, and impact on animal, plant, and human lives.

Special Problems. As with most technology, new biotechnological developments are occurring so rapidly that they are difficult to follow. Unless teachers are specifically interested and directly involved, they are not likely to be familiar enough with advances in the procedures, equipment, or learning aids of recent years to teach about them. Sometimes physically and medically handicapped students are more aware of medical advances than the general public. The same holds for students from families associated with medicine or agriculture. Students who live close to the origin or production of such advances are more likely to be familiar with them through local publicity than are those students who live elsewhere. Students who have difficulty analyzing, predicting, and evaluating may find mastery of the content troublesome, as may students whose families are strongly opposed to biotechnology.

Instructional Implications. Since much of the instructional information for biotechnical systems is not available in textbooks, the instructional content will have to be gleaned from outside resources, such as news reports, agricultural and medical newsletters, professional journals, and institutional and corporate updates. This topic interests students, perhaps because personal relevance is easy to establish and understand. However, since the content is quickly outdated, this interest should be channeled toward long-term study of advances to identify and evaluate the ones most likely to improve the quality of each student's life. As advances are studied, their impact on society also should be evaluated. Permit and encourage students who are physically and medically handicapped and those who come from families directly connected with a component field to explore the topic in depth.

CORRECTION Modify strategies for topical and learning needs:

1. *Product-Associated Vocabulary*

   Skills: Observing; listening; reading; classifying; communicating;
   evaluating

   Limit new terms to those most directly connected to the topic. For example,
   blast freezing, curing, heating irradiation and ultrasonic vibration, and
   spray drying are major means of preserving food. When presenting concepts,
   show 2–3 examples of foods that have been preserved using each method;
   post each term with pictures of products. Have students add examples and
   pictures and evaluate the importance of each term.

2. *Water Farming*

   Skills: Observing; listening; reading; analyzing; predicting;
   communicating; all integration skills

   Display a tomato and ask how students can tell where it was grown. Explain
   that aquaculture involves growing plants in water instead of soil. Guide
   students to compare growing methods in class by growing 2–3 plants in
   water and 2–3 similar plants in soil. Prompt them to develop their hypotheses and then observe and record growth and care daily. At the end of 3 weeks,
   have students analyze their results to determine which method is best. Have
   student teams identify situations and locations in which aquaculture or
   traditional agriculture would be most appropriate.

3. *Modern Miracles*

   Skills: Observing; listening; reading; organizing; communicating;
   synthesizing; generalizing; evaluating

   From the vast array of technical advances, present those of most interest to
   students, such as machines that read, pacemakers, cochlear implants, or
   artificial limbs, skin, and blood that function almost better than the
   originals. Have student teams study, analyze, evaluate, and illustrate an
   invention and present a Modern Miracles Update to peers.

4. *Healthy Bodies*

   Skills: Observing; listening; reading; analyzing; measuring; predicting;
   communicating; synthesizing

   Health care advances are not limited to high-tech machines or complicated
   equipment. Changes have occurred in footwear, exercise equipment, recommended diets, and rehabilitation treatments. One or 2 times each month,
   feature a lesson about a health-improvement technique. Have students
   participate by deciding how much the use or loss of these products (or
   behaviors) would change their lives. Combine record keeping and self-
   monitoring when possible to help students become aware of their own
   responsibilities and participation in self-improvement efforts.

5. *Extra Practice.* • Help students write or record profiles of important physically or
   medically handicapped persons, including the assistive devices they use
   and their achievements. • Have student teams identify 3–5 improvements
   in the fields of agriculture or medicine that have occurred since 1960. • Have
   pairs of students study and predict how genetic engineering could affect
   what they eat in 10 years.

40. PROBLEMS AND REWARDS OF TECHNOLOGY

DETECTION Mastery of key concepts may be difficult for students who:
- Are not aware of many examples of technology
- Seldom directly and deliberately utilize technology
- Have difficulty analyzing, predicting, generalizing, and evaluating
- Cannot explain the value of technology

Description. Technology directly affects the lives of most people in industrialized nations. Change created by technological advances will continue to bring with it both positive and negative consequences. Some of the positive results are highlighted with the discussions of information processing, physical technology, and biotechnology in Topics 37–39. However, to present realistic and balanced content to students, these rewards must be weighed against the problems that result from the use of such technologies. Also to be considered in analyzing the impact of technology are future projections for advances and the concomitant advantages and disadvantages. Present and future rewards primarily consist of improvements in the quality of life. Among the existing and potential problems accompanying the rapid growth of technology are issues such as these: the depletion of natural resources through air, water, and soil pollution; contamination from nuclear accidents and wastes; damage and injury from accidents of all types as new inventions are tested and used; and cultural changes that are created by bigger, newer buildings, better communications, and changes in living habits. Finally, ethical considerations are also involved since life-sustaining and life-generating capabilities are being explored.

Special Problems. Mastery of this topic depends in part on the teacher's and learners' philosophies; those who view a glass as half full are likely to learn more about the advantages of advances, while those who view the glass as half empty may understand more about the disadvantages. Some students are more receptive to the new and novel, while others are suspicious of the unknown. Students who have difficulty analyzing, predicting, and generalizing may experience some problems understanding the whole picture. Students who have difficulty evaluating most likely will encounter serious problems weighing the rewards against the problems of technology. Such evaluation requires not only sophisticated thinking skills but also a comprehensive understanding of technology as well as its interactions with important physical, social, and psychological factors.

Instructional Implications. Because technology impinges upon almost every field, instruction should be integrated with other studies whenever possible. Students should be guided to analyze the positive and negative consequences of each example. Since personal and societal values are at the heart of such judgments, handle the evaluation of both rewards and problems as a values clarification exercise, stressing that there are no right and wrong opinions. A particularly important element of each lesson is emphasis on the long-term consequences of each advance.

CORRECTION Modify strategies for topical and learning needs:

1. *Integration of Technological Vocabulary*
    Skills: Observing; listening; reading; analyzing; measuring; communicating
    When appropriate topics are studied in different subjects, such as social studies, present and discuss the terms that represent technological advances. For example, the study of communications provides a natural avenue to introduce such terms as touch-tone, direct dial, automatic dialing, speed dialing, and call waiting. Guide students to use analysis and measurement skills to accurately compare and contrast old and new versions of each term.

2. *Technological Problems*
    Skills: Observing; listening; reading; analyzing; communicating; evaluating
    Present problem events that are appropriate for the specific students. The nuclear accidents at Chernobyl and Three-Mile Island, the chemical disaster in India, and the explosion of the Challenger Space Shuttle are examples of accidents that involve technological advances. Prompt students to analyze the cause of each problem, the effects, and the likelihood of recurrence. Then have them analyze the positive features of the technology involved and critique the short-term and long-term values. Follow similar procedures with topics such as automobile safety or robotics in factories.

3. *Problem/Solution Situations*
    Skills: Observing; listening; reading; analyzing; predicting; communicating; generalizing; evaluating
    Have teams of students debate each side of a controversial technological issue. Either suggest topics (e.g., life extension, transplants, or genetic engineering in humans) or state several problem situations on index cards (e.g., A manufacturing plant can triple production and cut its costs by 50% by using robots on the assembly line, but 80 employees will lose their jobs.). Permit students to select the issues to debate and guide them to gather information and formulate their arguments. Later, have students suggest topics and situations for debate.

4. *Technology Display*
    Skills: Observing; reading; organizing; communicating; analyzing; generalizing; evaluating
    Display such items as an old calculator, telephone, camera, radio, or 8-track tape player. Ask students to get parental assistance and bring items to display that represent improvements in function and design and label each device with their names, the name of the device, improvements over previous models, and 1–3 problems. Have peers evaluate each device.

5. *Extra Practice.* • Have students list examples of technology in their homes, cite the advantages, and then have peers suggest potential problems. • Have students relate problems they have experienced using technology, describe the advantages of using the technology, and then critique it. • Ask student teams to describe and evaluate electronic or mechanical items that they someday hope to use or own.

REFLECTIONS

1. The field of physical science is both broad and complex. Review the introduction to Part IV and then the individual topics that are included in this section. Rank the topics from most to least relevant for young special learners (ages 5–9) and then for older special learners (ages 10–16). Which topics do you suggest deleting? Why? Which additional topics would you recommend including? Why?

2. Special learners may require several directed experiences with simple machines before mastering the concepts. Review the examples in Topic 35 and then suggest at least two additional experiences for each of the six machines.

3. The advances in technology are occurring too quickly to be recorded in most elementary science textbooks. Suggest at least three sources that are readily available to teachers for updating their knowledge of technology. Which one is most likely to provide the most current information?

4. Some teachers adhere closely to the topics and activities of the science textbooks. Review the second- and fourth-grade levels of the elementary science basal texts in use in your area. Locate the physical science topics in those books. Choose a physical science topic and plan how to teach it to a special student. Then, practice teaching your lesson to a peer; next, teach the lesson to a special student.

5. The skills checklist in Figure 3.1 can be used to assess students' skills in any area of science. Use this checklist to identify the extent to which students are able to apply each of the listed skills during physical science lessons. Then, focus on a single special learner to determine the skills which he or she uses proficiently and the ones that appear to be specific weaknesses.

6. Instructional activities often must be adjusted according to the ages and abilities of the students. Identify five CORRECTION strategies in this section that you believe would be best for teaching a 7-year-old student about technology. Which ones would be most appropriate for teaching the same topic to a 13-year-old? Defend your choices.

7. For brevity, only a few CORRECTION strategies are listed for each topic. Based on your knowledge of physical science and of special children, add to or modify the strategies for the topic of your choice. Then, restructure your strategies for a particular special student, following the principles in Chapter 3 and including direct instruction in the important science skills.

8. Carefully structured questions about a topic help special learners focus on the most important concepts and guide their thinking. Construct such a set of questions about one of the physical science topics; plan to use the questions as an advance organizer to introduce the topic to a special learner and as a test of mastery after the topic is studied.

9. Predicting, analyzing, generalizing, and evaluating are the key skills involved in mastering many of the topics in this section. Review the recommendations in Chapter 3 for teaching these skills, and then plan how to teach them along with instruction in the concepts for one of the topics in this section. Plan a lesson for a particular special learner and practice teaching it to a peer; then teach the lesson to the special learner.

10. A number of resources are available for teaching about physical science. Compare and contrast the topical, conceptual, and skill emphasis of these publications with the discussions in Part IV:

Abruscato, J. (1986). *Children, computers, and science teaching: Butterflies and bytes.* Englewood Cliffs, NJ: Prentice-Hall.

Ball, D. W. (1978). *ESS/special education teacher's guide.* St. Louis: Webster/McGraw-Hill.

Buffer, J. J., & Scott, M. L. (1987). *Special needs guide.* Reston, VA: International Technology Education Association.

Bybee, R., Peterson, R., Bowyer, J., & Butts, D. (1984). *Teaching about science and society: Activities for elementary and junior high school.* Columbus, OH: Charles E. Merrill.

Bybee, R. (Ed.). (1985). *Science technology society.* Washington, DC: National Science Teachers Association.

Gega, P. C. (1990). *Science in elementary education.* (6th ed.). New York: Macmillan.

Geisert, P. G., & Futrell, M. M. (1990). *Teachers, computers, and curriculum: Microcomputers in the classroom.* Boston: Allyn and Bacon.

International Technology Education Association. (1987). *Resources in technology* (Vol. III). Reston, VA: Author.

Maley, D. (1987). *Research and experimentation in technology education.* Reston, VA: International Technology Education Association.

Nelson, L. W., & Lorbeer, G. C. (1984). *Science activities for elementary children* (8th ed.). Dubuque IA: Wm. C. Brown.

Schmidt, V. E., & Rockcastle, V. N. (1982). *Teaching science with everyday things* (2nd ed.). New York: McGraw-Hill.

Spetgang, T., and Wells, M. (1982). *The children's solar energy book.* New York: Sterling.

Zubrowski, B. (1986). *Wheels that work.* New York: William Morrow.

Index

A

academically gifted students, 22
accidents, 97, 98, 99
active involvement, 38
activity-based instruction, 19, 31, 33, 35, 89
air, 72–75, 106. *See also* pollution
  problems with, 72, 73
  quality of, 92
  vocabulary for, 73
analysis, 7, 27, 42, 56, 68, 71, 164, 168
  organizational charts for, 42
animals, 56–59, 101, 121, 122, 130, 166
  care of, 58
  chart behavior of, 56
  classification of, 56, 57
  concepts of, 56
  friends and foes, 58
  homes for, 57
  names of, 57
  vocabulary for, 57
antibodies, 108, 109
articulation difficulties, 21
astronomy, 3, 130, 134–139
attention deficit disorders, 19
attention difficulties, 19, 40
attitude, 14
auditory distractions, 40

B

bacteria, 101
behavior-disordered students, 16
biotechnology, 166–167
blindness. *See* visually impaired
blood, *See* circulation
body odors, 80, 82
bones, 61
boredom, 22
Breakfast Club, 86

C

caffeine, 95
chart, 41, 44, 74, 83, 97, 155
  of growth, 52
checklists, 29, 37

circulation, 63
classification, 7, 11, 43.
  See also students
classroom observation, 30
clay models, 117
cleanliness, 82
communicable diseases, 103
communication terminology, 163
communication, 8
complex machines, 160–161
  identification of, 161
  personal interaction, 161
computers, 162–163
  applications of, 163
  terminology for, 163
concepts. *See* science concepts
conservation of energy, 154–155
constellation, 136, 137
construction, 165
content, of science, 2, 3, 36, 60, 84, 116
cross-categorical handicapped students, 15
cultural differences, 14
culturally different students, 11–12
cycles
  of air, 77
  of food, 78
  of land, 78
  of water, 78

D

deductive reasoning, 9
demonstration, 18, 72
diet, 84–87, 88
  control of illness, 106
direct testing. *See* testing
directed experimentation, 6, 18, 41, 68, 77, 78
diseases. *See* illness
drinking, consequences of, 93
drugs
  advertising of, 92
  alcohol as, 93
  alternatives to, 95
  as medicine, 92, 95

availability of, 92
prevalence of, 92
psychoactive, 92–95
therapy for, 106

E
earth science, 3, 114–139
eating disorders, 84. *See also* diet
ecological studies, 144
ecology, 3, 64–67, 118. *See also* land
   improving, 81
   issues in, 122
   problems in, 146
ecosystems, 76
educational recreation, 96
electric current, 153
electricity, 146, 148, 152, 155
   safe use, 153
electronic communication systems, 162
emergencies, 99
energy
   alternatives to, 144–145, 147, 148
   capturing, 148, 149
   comparing, 149
   conservation of, 154–155
   economic issues, 154
   electrical, 153
   sources of, 144, 145, 147, 148, 153, 155
   supplies, 154
   using, 155
   vocabulary for, 145
   water as, 147
environment
   awareness of, 76
   problems in, 77
ethical precautions, 9
evaluation, 9, 13, 46
exercise, 88–91
   vocabulary for, 89
experiencing, 20, 24, 122
experimentation, 16, 22, 33, 64, 71, 72

F
facts, application of, 14
farming, 64, 167
feedback, 36
financial aid for medical services, 104
fine-motor incoordination, 20
fitness, exercise, 88–91

food. *See also* diet
   analysis of, 86, 101
   categories of, 85
   chains of, 78
   commercials for, 86
force, 156–157
   relationship to work, 156, 157
forecasting, 132–133. *See also* prediction
forests, 122–123
   products from, 123
   strata, 123
fossil fuels, 144, 145, 146
friction, 157
fuels, sources of, 145, 154

G
generalization, 46, 168
   process, 12, 13
   to space exploration, 138
geographic formations. *See* land formations
geography, 116
geothermal energy, 146, 147
gifted students. *See* academically gifted students
globe, 119
gravity, 156, 157
gross-motor incoordination, 20
guest speakers, 81, 94

H
handicap, 18
handicapped students, 15, 26, 32, 88, 166
hands-on activities, 52, 60
   hands-on approach, 33
   health and safety topics, 20
health care advances, 167
health, 82, 84–87, 96, 110, 167
   and food, 85
   and hygiene habits, 60
   and nutrition, 3
   and water, 68
   growth and development, 86
   vocabulary for, 81
   safety, 60
health, applicability to lifelong practices, 60
hearing loss, 17
hearing-impaired students, 17
heart, 63

heat absorption, 125
human body, 60–63
    identification of bones, 61
    muscle power, 61
    vocabulary for, 61
hygiene, 108
    personal, 80–83
    rules of, 111
hygienic habits. *See* health and nutrition
hypotheses, 8, 9, 45, 138
hypothesize, 81

I
illicit drug use, 92
illness
    causes of, 100–103, 130
    communicable diseases, 101–103
    noncommunicable diseases, 103
    prevention of, 102, 108–111
    symptoms of, 104
    treatment of, 104–107
    understanding of, 3, 100–111
    vocabulary for, 101, 109
immunization, 108, 110
impulsiveness, 19
independent experimentation, 45
individualization, 31
inductive reasoning, 9
industrial technology, 160
infections, 33
informal interviews, 34
informal tests, 26
information acquisition skills, 4, 14, 18,
    19, 28, 39, 42, 44, 84
information processing skills, 4, 6, 14, 19,
    26, 28, 39, 41, 84, 162–163
information processing, electronic,
    162–163. *See also* technology
informational sources, 166
instruction, basic principles of, 31
instructional plan, 16, 24
instructional program for behavior-
    disordered, 16
integration of information, 12, 14
integration skills, 4, 8, 9, 13, 22, 29, 35,
    39, 44, 45, 68
interaction of living things with environ-
    ment, 76
interactive learning, *see* activity-based
    format

interdependence cycles, 77
    of humans and animals, 56, 76, 77
    of life forms, 76–79
interpreting results, 43
intervention strategies, 26
interviews, 27, 28, 81
    of students, 24, 27
    of teachers, 27
investigation, 77

J
journal, for exercise, 91

L
labels, on food, 86
lakes, 118
land, 64–67
    abuse, 64
    changing appearance, 65
    cycle, 78
    ecology, 122, 146
    formations in, 116–117
    misuse of, 67
    prediction of future, 65
    preservation of, 64, 66
    vocabulary for, 65
language arts, 18
language disabilities, 18
language fluency, 12
language, 18
    limited, for hearing-impaired, 17
    manipulation of, 18
language-disabled students, 12, 18
learning groups, 31
learning habits, 6
lesson length, 21
life science, 3, 50–113
listening, 5, 26, 27, 40, 41
    assistance in, 40
    exercises, 40
living things, 3, 33, 76
    vocabulary of, 77
local storms, 129
low self-esteem, 92

M
machines, 33, 158–161, 164–165
    complex, 160–161
    improvements in, 161
    simple, 158–159

value of, 161
magnetism, and electricity, 152–153
magnets, 152–153
magnifying glass, 102
manipulative models, 60
map, 117, 121, 137
mastery of skills, 24
mathematics, 86
measurement, 7, 18, 41, 43, 52, 68
    information, 7
    instruments, 7
    of prior knowledge, 34
    of work and force, 156
    techniques of, 7
medical quackery, 104, 107
medical specialties, 105
medical treatment, 104
    facilities, 105
medically handicapped student, 20
medicinal drugs, 95, 106
mental health, 111
mental professionals, 107
mentally retarded students, 19
meteorologist, 132
microorganisms, 101, 103, 104, 109
    spread of, 101
microscope, 69, 102
minerals, 119
moisture, retention in land, 65
moon, 137
moonwalk, 139
motor coordination, 21
multiple choice, 12, 18
muscles, 61
music, 90

N
nails, 83
National Aeronautics and Space Admini-
    stration (NASA), 134
National Weather Service, 132, 133
noise pollution, 77
noncommunicable diseases, 103
nonrenewable fuels, 144–145
nuclear power, 150–151
    power plants, 150
    problems with, 151
    process of, 151
    uses of, 151
    vocabulary for, 151

nutrition. See diet

O
observation, 4, 5, 18, 26, 39, 40, 41, 52,
    56, 64, 68, 72, 164
    of students in the classroom, 24
oceans, 118, 119
    life in, 119
oral
    expression, 17
    interview, 30
    presentations, 41
organization skills, 7, 41
organizational chart, 44
organs, 63

P
parental involvement, 37, 76
participatory experiences. See activity-
    based format
performance in science, 26
performance information, 26
personal hygiene, 80–83. See also hygiene
perspiration, 82
physical activity. See exercise
physical fitness program, 88
physical science, 142–169
physical technology, 164–165
physical therapy, 106
physically or medically handicapped
    students, 20, 60
plan ahead, 97
planetarium, 137
planets, 134–135
    vocabulary for, 135
planning
    and implementing science lessons, 36
    instruction, 24, 34
    lessons, 34
    process, 38
plants, 52–55, 121, 130, 166
    as food, 53, 54
    as medicine, 54
    concepts and content of, 52
    dangerous, 55
    dependency on, 55
    families, 53
    names of, 53
    vocabulary for, 53

pollutants, in air, 73, 72
pollution, 72, 73, 74
positive attitudes, 154
poverty, 80
practical application, 3
  skills of, 2
  specialty of, 2
practical scientific knowledge, 13
precautions for storms, 129
precipitation, 126–127, 130
  analyzing, 126
  forms of, 126, 127
  process of, 126
  predicting, 126, 127
prediction, 7, 27, 43, 44, 45, 56, 64, 68,
  74, 123, 127, 168. *See also* forecasting
  for seasons, 130
  for storms, 128
  for weather, 132–133
presentation, of scientific information, 3
President's Council on Physical Fitness, 89
problematic information acquisition skills,
  14
problems, 26
process skills, 31
  measurement of, 27
processing information, 12
processing skills, 44
psychoactive drugs, 92–95. *See also* drugs

R
radiation therapy, 107
radiation, 150
raised relief map, 117, 119
reading, 26
reading, 26, 27, 39, 40, 42
  assistance in, 40-41
real-life concepts, 32
recreation, and safety, 96–99
  vocabulary for, 97
recycling, 67, 77
reinforcement of knowledge, 13, 37
relevance, 38, 56, 76, 96, 118
religious beliefs, in medicine, 104, 107
review activities, 35
rivers, 118, 120–121
rocks, 118–119
  changes to, 119
  families of, 118
  history of formation, 118

roleplay, 94
rote memorization, 14
rural areas, 52, 56, 64, 124

S
safety, 9, 35, 96–99, 128, 152
  at home, 99
  in class, 97
  in sports, 99
  in storms, 128
  measures and precautions, 128
  rules for, 97
  vocabulary for, 97
scale, concept of, 117
science concepts, 2, 4, 34, 35
  and skills, 35
  directed experimentation, 4
  listening, 5, 6
  mastery of, 31
  needs of special learners, 11, 24–27
  observation, 4, 5
  positive attitude development, 6
  program
    modification of, 15, 22
    structure of content and format, 36
  reading, 5, 6
  study, 6
science fiction, 134
scientific advances, 37
  sources of, 38
scientific knowledge
  application of, 9, 10
  evaluation of, 9
scientific principes
  understanding of, 9
scientific program
  categories of, 3
  content of program, 2, 3
  relevancy, 3, 12
  topic selection, 3, 16
  use of concrete objects as examples, 12
seasons, 130–131
seeds, 54
self-concept, 15, 56
self-monitoring, 36, 42
sense of self, 60
senses, 62
simple machines, 158–159
  identification of, 158, 160
  personal relevance, 158

using, 158
skill competencies, 26, 39
skin, 81, 82
slow learning rate, 12
slow-learning students, 13
smoking, problems with, 81
social interaction, 31
    acceptance by peers, 80
social studies, 86
socially offensive habits, 83
society
    impact of, 166
    relevance to, 64, 72, 76, 116, 118
sociological impact, 116
soil, 65, 66
solar energy, 148–149
space
    exploration, 134, 138–139
    launch, 139
    museum, 134
    predictions for, 138
special education students, 15
special learners, 24–47, 60, 96, 104
special needs in science, checklist, 28
speech-disordered students, 21
standardized test scores, 26
stars, 136–137
    characteristics of, 136
    vocabulary for, 137
steam, 147
stimulus/response format, 21
storms, 128–129, 130
supervision, 36
student. See individual listing
study skills, 6, 26, 41
stuttering, 21
subtopics, 14
    and activities, 17
surgery, 106
synthesis, 44
    of available data, 24

T
teacher
    and peer modeling, 17
    enthusiasm of, 38
    limits of, 13, 22
teacher-disabled students, 13
teaching science, basic principles, 31
technology, 33, 162–169

advances in, 167
improvements in, 169
planning for, 165
problems with, 168–169
rewards of, 168–169
vocabulary for, 169
teeth, 83
telescope, 134, 136
temperature, 124–125, 126, 130
    chart, 125
    function and effects of, 125
    measuring, 124, 125
testing, 25–26
    direct, 25
    formal, 25
    informal, 26
tests, 25–26
    instruments for standardized, 26
    nonstandardized, 26
    review of, 36
    scores, 26
    timed, 26
    textbook, 26
therapy, 106–107
thermometer, 124, 125
thinking process, 46
tides, 137
time-lapse productions, 52
timeline, 139
topics, 31, 33, 34, 38
    application of, 32
    selection of, 3, 18
    relevance of, 32, 35, 56
touch, 82
tracking storms, 129
transportation safety, 98
transportation systems, nonvehicle, 165
treatment, of illness, 105
trees, 122

U
underachievement, 14, 22
underachieving students, 14
understanding of content, 27, 40
urban, 52, 56, 64

V
vaccine, 110
verbalization, 41
virus, 101

vision, 21
visual cues, 17. *See also* hearing impaired.
visualizing consequences, 64
visually impaired students, 21
vocabulary, 2, 5, 12, 34, 35, 40, 60, 68,
    77, 97, 153, 169

W
waste recycling, 67
wasting energy, 147, 155
water, 68–71, 146–147
    analysis of, 69
    availability of, 68
    bodies of, 118
    conservation of, 70
    pollutants, 71
    power, 146–147
    problems with, 68

purifying, 69, 70
routes, 118
sources of, 69, 118
taste test, 69
uses of pure water, 70
uses of, 70, 119
vocabulary for, 69, 119, 147
water cycle, 69, 78
weather, 33, 124–133
    prediction of, 124–133
    vocabulary for, 133
wind power, 148–149
wind, history of, 148
wood, 123
work, 156–157
    and force, 156
    vocabulary for, 157
writing, 42

ABOUT THE AUTHORS

THOMAS A. RAKES has more than two decades of experience as an educator, researcher, author, and consultant. He holds an Ed.D. from the University of Tennessee and is presently Professor of Education and Chairman of the Department of Curriculum and Instruction at Memphis State University. In addition to the graduate and undergraduate courses he teaches in research, content methods, language arts, and assessment, his experiences have included directing a university diagnostic center and teaching at the middle school, secondary, and adult education levels. A prolific writer, he is the author of more than 80 professional articles in several areas of diagnostic/ prescriptive instruction. He is co-author of *Language Arts: Detecting and Correcting Special Needs* (1989), *Reading: Detecting and Correcting Special Needs* (1989), and *Assessing and Programming Basic Curriculum Skills* (1987), all published by Allyn and Bacon, two reading diagnosis texts, and a series of worktexts. Dr. Rakes has presented papers at numerous national and state conferences and has been a consultant for school districts, colleges, and businesses in 44 states. He is on the advisory board for a major basal reading series and has been on the editorial board for several professional journals.

JOYCE S. CHOATE is Consulting Editor for the *Allyn and Bacon Detecting and Correcting Series.* She holds an Ed.D. from Memphis State University and is presently Professor of Curriculum and Instruction at Northeast Louisiana University. Her teaching experiences have ranged from the preschool to the graduate levels in both regular and special education; she has also been an educational diagnostician and reading specialist. In addition to editing the books in this series, she is co-author of *Language Arts: Detecting and Correcting Special Needs* (1989), *Reading: Detecting and Correcting Special Needs* (1989), and *Assessing and Programming Basic Curriculum Skills* (1987), and texts about prescriptive teaching, reading diagnosis, and gifted education. Dr. Choate has presented numerous papers on assessment and prescriptive teaching at state and national conferences. She is presently Publications Chair of the Council for Educational Diagnostic Services (and formerly President), an associate editor of *Diagnostique*, and a field editor of *Teaching Exceptional Children.*

READER'S REACTION

Dear Reader:

No one knows better than you the special needs of your students or the exact nature of your classroom problems. Your analysis of the extent to which this book meets *your* special needs will help us to revise this book and assist us to develop other books in the *Detecting and Correcting* series.

Please take a few minutes to respond to the questionnaire on the next page. If you would like to receive a reply to your comments or additional information about the series, indicate this preference in your answer to the last question. Mail the completed form to:

> Joyce S. Choate, Consulting Editor
> *Detecting and Correcting* Series
> c/o Allyn and Bacon
> 160 Gould Street
> Needham Heights, Massachusetts 02194

Thank you for sharing your special needs and professional concerns.

Sincerely,

Joyce S. Choate

Joyce S. Choate

READER'S REACTIONS TO
SCIENCE AND HEALTH: DETECTING AND CORRECTING SPECIAL NEEDS

Name: _____   Position: _____

Address: _____   _____

_____   Date: _____

1. How have you used this book?

   ___College Text   ___Inservice Training   ___Teaching Resource

   Describe:_____

2. For which purpose(s) do you recommend its use?

3. What do you view as the major strengths of the book?

4. What are its major weaknesses?

5. How could the book be improved?

6. What additional topics should be included in this book?

7. In addition to the topics currently included in the *Detecting and Correcting* series—basic mathematics, classroom behavior, instructional management, language arts, reading, science and health, social studies, and speech and language—what other topics would you recommend?

8. Would you like to receive:

   _____a reply to your comments?

   _____additional information about this series?

Additional Comments:

THANK YOU FOR SHARING YOUR SPECIAL NEEDS AND PROFESSIONAL CONCERNS

1798   4191